An Unforgiving Sport

An Unforgiving Sport

An Inside Look at Another Year in Boxing

Thomas Hauser

The University of Arkansas Press
Fayetteville
2009

ISBN-10: 1–55728–910–7
ISBN-13: 978–1-55728–910–0

13   12   11   10   09   5   4   3   2   1

⊗ The paper used in this publication meets the minimum requirements of the
American National Standard for Permanence of Paper for Printed Library
Materials Z39.48–1984.

Library of Congress Cataloging-in-Publication Data

Hauser, Thomas.
  An unforgiving sport / Thomas Hauser.
      p. cm.
  Includes bibliographical references.
    ISBN-13: 978-1-55728-910-0 (pbk. : alk. paper)
    ISBN-10: 1-55728-910-7
    1. Boxing. 2. Boxers (Sports) I. Title.
    GV1133.H3448 2009
      796.83--dc22

                                                              2009018537

For Nick, Reece, Brooke, And Will

Contents

Round 4: Issues and Answers

Author's Note

An Unforgiving Sport contains the articles about professional boxing that I authored in 2008. The articles I wrote about the sweet science prior to that date have been published in *Muhammad Ali & Company; A Beautiful Sickness; A Year at the Fights; The View From Ringside; Chaos, Corruption, Courage, and Glory; The Lost Legacy of Muhammad Ali; I Don't Believe It, But It's True; The Greatest Sport of All,* and *The Boxing Scene.*

Special thanks are due to Secondsout.com and ESPN.com, under whose aegis most of the articles in this book first appeared.

Round 1
Fights and Fighters

In the beginning, there was John L. Sullivan.

John L. Sullivan Revisited

October 15, 2008, will mark the 150th anniversary of the birth of John L. Sullivan.

In recent decades, Sullivan has faded from memory. To many, he's now more myth than reality, a sporting Paul Bunyan. In a way, that's fitting because, in his era, Sullivan was a near-mythic figure as large as Babe Ruth, Joe Louis, and Muhammad Ali were in their prime. He was America's first mass-culture hero and the most idolized athlete who had lived up until his time.

Good writing about Sullivan is hard to find. His autobiography (like much of the contemporaneous writing about him) is unreliable. The best book on the subject is *John L. Sullivan and His America* by Michael Isenberg (University of Illinois Press, 1988). Isenberg mined the mother lode of Sullivan material and crafted a work that's superb in explaining the fighter as a social phenomenon and placing him in the context of his times. Twenty years after publication, it's still the standard against which Sullivan scholarship is judged.

More recently, Adam Pollack has contributed *John L. Sullivan* (McFarland and Company, 2004); an exhaustive review of contemporaneous newspapers, magazines, and other primary sources as they relate to Sullivan's fights. Various ring histories, most notably *The Manly Art* by Elliott J. Gorn (Cornell University Press, 1986) also contribute to the archival heritage. Reading their work, an outline emerges.

The Irish potato famine of the 1840s led to a flood of immigration to the United States. One of those arriving in America was a young man named Mike Sullivan, who settled in Boston circa 1850. In 1856, he married Catherine Kelly, whose family had also come to Boston from Ireland.

Mike Sullivan was a small man, 5-feet-2-inches tall. His wife was considerably taller and weighed 180 pounds. On October 15, 1858, in the Roxbury district of Boston, she gave birth to a son, John Lawrence Sullivan.

The Irish, in the mid-eighteenth century, were largely scorned in America. They were manual laborers and household domestics, shackled by ethnic prejudices and anti-Catholic sentiment. Mike Sullivan was a day laborer, who dug trenches, laid bricks, and took whatever other work was available to him.

John Lawrence's formal education ended when he was fifteen. Thereafter, he drifted from job to job as a plumber's apprentice, tinsmith's apprentice, and mason. He was physically strong and had his mother's size, weighing close to two hundred pounds by the time he was seventeen. More significantly, he was athletically gifted and, from time to time, played baseball in local semi-professional games.

Prizefighting was introduced in the American colonies by British sailors during the Revolutionary War. But it never took hold and, by the time Sullivan was of fighting age, it was banned in all thirty-eight states. More significantly, the law was largely upheld, particularly in urban areas. Thus, boxing was a vagabond sport. Word of a forthcoming bout would pass quietly from mouth to mouth, after which the combatants and spectators would travel on short notice to the designated site.

The London Prize Ring Rules were the standard for prizefighting in America. Those rules provided that:

> (1) A fight would take place on turf in a 24-foot-square enclosure.
> (2) A mark would be drawn in the center of the enclosure as the "scratch line." Areas large enough to hold a fighter and two seconds for activity between rounds were enclosed by other marks in the turf in opposite corners.
> (3) A fight consisted of an undetermined number of rounds. A round ended when a combatant was down on at least one knee.
> (4) Once a combatant was down, his seconds had thirty seconds to revive him. "Time" was then called and the combatant had eight seconds more to come to scratch or lose the fight.
> (5) Eye-gouging, hair-pulling, head-butting, blows below the waist, kicking, falling without receiving a legitimate blow, and striking a combatant when he was down were grounds for disqualification at the referee's discretion.
>   Beyond that, the rules were pretty much "anything goes" (including wrestling and throwing an opponent to the ground).

Growing up, Sullivan had been involved in fights in the schoolyard and at work. In 1878 (at age twenty), he took things to a higher level. At a local entertainment show at the Dudley Street Opera House, he was challenged by a man named Jack Scannell, who'd heard that John had a bit of a reputation. Sullivan and Scannell went onto the stage. Each man shed his coat and rolled up his sleeves.

In a matter of seconds, Sullivan obliterated his foe. Thereafter, he began to spend time around the prizefight crowd and made the decision to prepare himself to fight for money. Isenberg writes, "He already had accumulated a history of arguments and disputes ending in challenges to fight. He could see a grim future in the model of his father. A choice between fame in the ring and sweating through twelve-hour days in dank ditches was not hard to make. And above all, boxing gave him what plumbing, tinsmithing, and masonry never could—a sense of importance and self-esteem. Once he heard the cheers, once he had a sense of his ability to dominate other men, he never looked back."

But as Isenberg notes, "Sullivan could not have been attracted to pugilism because it offered him a living. No one could see that this chosen walk of life would produce anything more than facial scars, scrambled brains, and trouble with the law. No one in American history—no one— had ever made a living as a prizefighter. Some of them owned or worked in saloons. Others moved from odd job to odd job. Nor did the calling afford a chance to rise in the world. The social stigma against prizefighting ran broadly and deeply through American life. Prizefighting was against the law, and prizefighters were considered the dregs of society."

The one glimmer of respectability that attached to boxing related to a new code of conduct for matches. In 1866, Henry Sholto Douglas (the eighth Marquis of Queensberry) had authored what were known as the Queensberry Rules. These rules provided that:

> (1) Fights would be contested in three-minute rounds with a minute rest in between each round.
> (2) A man who was knocked down had ten seconds to rise unassisted by his handlers or be declared the loser by knockout.
> (3) Wrestling, grappling, and throwing were forbidden.
> (4) A fight could be contested as a fight to the finish or for a predetermined number of rounds.
> (5) The combatants would wear gloves.

At the time Sullivan turned to fighting, gloved "exhibitions of skill" were permitted in some states as long as they didn't turn too unfriendly.

Often, the police were stationed at ringside and intervened if they believed that the fighters were throwing punches "with intent to injure." But sometimes (particularly when financial inducements were offered to the authorities) actual fights under Queensberry Rules were allowed to proceed until, in the judgment of the police, one of the fighters was badly hurt and in danger of being more seriously incapacitated.

Various record books and scholarly studies are at odds regarding Sullivan's ring record. The discrepancies come from the discovery of previously unknown matches and inconsistencies as to whether certain bouts are recorded as prizefights or exhibitions.

What's clear is that Sullivan preferred to ply his trade with gloves. He wore them in all but three of his recorded fights and fought all but five of his fights under Queensberry Rules. By early 1880, he'd established a following with a series of exhibitions in Boston and New York. Then, on April 6, 1880, in Boston, he had what Isenberg calls his first "fight"—an event publicly styled as an "exhibition" against American heavyweight champion Joe Goss (who was preparing for a May 30 bout against challenger Paddy Ryan).

In front of 1,800 spectators, Sullivan knocked Goss down and battered him for three rounds. On June 28, also in Boston, he knocked out an experienced fighter named George Rooke. On December 24, he journeyed to Cincinnati and, fighting under the London Rules for the first time (albeit with skintight gloves), disposed of John Donaldson in ten rounds.

The following spring, Sullivan won his "break-out" fight. On May 16, 1881, fighting on a barge that had been towed up-river and anchored off Yonkers to avoid New York law enforcement authorities, he vanquished John Flood in eight rounds. That conquest, conducted under the London Rules with skintight gloves, paid him a purse of $750.

Two months later, under the auspices of Billy Madden (his first manager), Sullivan began a tour of the northeast and midwest, during which he sparred with all comers and offered fifty dollars to anyone who could last four rounds with him under Queensberry rules.

Boxing in Sullivan's day was crude and unskilled compared to what came later. Regardless, those foolish enough to challenge him on the tour (for the most part, they were novices) were quickly disposed of. Sullivan had sloping shoulders, massive forearms, and enormous fists. He was blessed with size, strength, and agility. In Pollack's words, he was "a vicious slugger with huge power and very good speed. He knew how to land his punches and land them well. He had an underrated ability to avoid being hit and absorbed the blows he did receive very well."

Contemporary descriptions of Sullivan's fighting refer to his "bull-like rushes" and "sledge-hammer right hand." He was "quick as a cat . . . a whirlwind of activity . . . What he lacks in science is fully made up by his tremendous strength and hitting power coupled with a quickness of action not often found in big men . . . So rapidly are his blows delivered that parrying them is an impossibility."

Sullivan's 1881 tour gave him a reputation outside of Boston. But more importantly, it established him as the next logical challenger to Paddy Ryan (who had defeated Joe Goss subsequent to Sullivan boxing an "exhibition" against the American heavyweight champion).

The term "champion" was loosely applied in those days. As Isenberg explains, "Champions were made and unmade in the press as often as in the ring. Essentially, a 'champion' was he who won a noteworthy fight and kept winning, particularly over those who had styled themselves similarly." Indeed, Ryan had only one serious victory to his credit (his May 30, 1880, triumph over Goss).

But Ryan had a powerful backer. In 1876, an Irish-born American named Richard Kyle Fox had assumed editorial control of the *National Police Gazette* and, focusing on crime and sex, established it as a journal for the masses. Then Fox discovered boxing and styled the *Gazette* as "the leading prize ring authority in America," lifting its circulation to 400,000.

Fox and Sullivan didn't like each other. They'd met for the first time in New York in spring 1881. Sullivan considered Fox a pompous bore, and Fox resented the fighter's refusal to act in an appropriately obsequious manner to gain favorable coverage in the *Gazette*.

In May 1881, Paddy Ryan authorized Fox to serve as his emissary in arranging a title defense pursuant to the London Rules and said that he'd fight anyone for the winner's share of the purse plus a $5,000 side bet ($2,500 per side). Fox put up Ryan's $2,500 share. Sullivan found backers for his end.

Ryan's partisans took heart in the fact that their man had won the title by defeating Joe Goss in a bare-knuckle contest that lasted 87 rounds contested over 84 minutes. Sullivan, by contrast, had never participated in a bare-knuckle fight, and the longer of his two matches under the London rules had lasted only ten rounds. Thus, the challenger's stamina and the strength of his hands were in doubt.

What Ryan's backers failed to consider was that Sullivan, even then, was probably the greatest fighting man who had ever lived.

The match was made for February 7, 1882. Because prizefighting was illegal throughout the United States, it was to be contested at a site "within one hundred miles of New Orleans."

At 5:00 A.M. on February 7, Ryan, Sullivan, and more than a thousand fight enthusiasts boarded a special train that had twelve passenger cars. Three hours later, they arrived in Mississippi City. A ring was pitched. Ryan is believed to have weighed 192 pounds. Sullivan had trained down to 182 pounds and was in the best condition of his life, having readied for a long grueling fight.

The battle began shortly after noon. Thirty seconds later, Ryan lay on the ground, felled by a series of blows to the ribs followed by a vicious right hand to the jaw. At the end of nine rounds, his handlers threw in the sponge. Less than eleven minutes of fighting had elapsed. Bob Farrell (a ring veteran who helped prepare Sullivan for the bout) said afterward, "I never saw such work as Sullivan did. He went at Ryan as you would chop a log of wood and broke him all up from the start."

Ryan acknowledged, "I never faced a man who could begin to hit as hard. I don't believe there is another man like him in the country. He spars as well as the general run of pugilists, and he can hit hard enough to break down any man's guard. Any man that Sullivan can hit, he can whip."

The *New Orleans Times-Democrat* reported, "Sullivan cared nothing for Ryan's blows, and his own hitting is so tremendous that it seems beyond the power of a man to recover from the shock of one of his hands let out from the shoulder. His style of fighting differs from that of any pugilist that has entered the ring of late. He is a skillful wrestler and a good in-fighter, quick to dodge and always on the alert for any opening that an opponent may leave. He is a rusher, and it is this quality and his tremendous hitting powers that make him a great pugilist. Against his sledge-hammer fists, the naked arms of a man are but poor defense."

After the fight, the *National Police Gazette* gave Sullivan his due. Richard Kyle Fox had previously labeled the match as being for "the championship of the world" (the first time that designation had been used). "As much as any other single event," Elliott Gorn writes, "the fight fostered the development of modern sports coverage. The *National Police Gazette* presses rolled for days with an eight-page illustrated special. All of the major dailies sent reporters, stimulating and fulfilling the demand for news."

Still, after Sullivan's conquest, there was little to distinguish him from his predecessors. A series of exhibitions and fights against unskilled opponents followed.

Then things began to change. Sullivan discovered that, trading on his notoriety, he could make money outside of boxing. He was paid five hundred dollars a day to tour with a variety-show. Next, on May 28, 1883, he pitched in a semi-professional baseball game at the Polo Grounds in New York. Four thousand spectators attended. Sullivan gave up fifteen runs and committed four errors in a 20-to-15 triumph. His 50 percent share of the gates receipts amounted to $1,585.90.

As a man of newly acquired means, Sullivan also became more attractive to women. One of them whom he began spending time with was Annie Bates Bailey.

Sullivan was on familiar terms with more than a few prostitutes. Annie had a reputation as "a loose woman." She was a year older than he was and, like his mother, a tall woman who weighed in the neighborhood of 180 pounds. After Sullivan won the championship, she traveled with him as his "wife" for about a year. On May 1, 1883, they were married.

Meanwhile, in due course, Sullivan was called upon to resume the business of serious fighting. Prior to his beating Ryan, there had never been a recognized "gloved" champion. Sullivan created that role.

"They said that I was only a glove-fighter and that I was afraid of the bare knuckles," Sullivan had said after winning the championship. "For that reason, I consented to fight Ryan as I did. Now anyone who wants to tackle me will have to do it in my fashion."

On March 23, 1882 (six weeks after defeating Ryan), Sullivan issued a public challenge, declaring, "I am willing to fight any man in this country in four weeks from signing articles for five thousand dollars a side; or any man for the same amount at two months from signing; I to use gloves and he, if he pleases, to fight with bare knuckles. I will not fight again with bare knuckles as I do not wish to put myself in a position amenable to the law. My money is always ready, so I want these fellows to put up or shut up. John L. Sullivan."

On May 14, 1883, pursuant to that challenge, Sullivan fought Charlie Mitchell of England (his most credible opponent since winning the championship). Their bout at Madison Square Garden was labeled an "exhibition" to stay within New York law. But the ten thousand spectators who attended understood that it would be something more. Mitchell knocked Sullivan down in the first round; the first time that John L. had ever been floored. But the champion rose and battered his opponent around the ring until the fight was stopped by the police in the third round. Sullivan's share of the gate was roughly $12,000. An August 6, 1883, third-round knockout of Australia's Herbert Slade, also at Madison Square Garden, was equally profitable.

Sullivan was now gathering increasing attention. "Other boxers begin by sparring," Irish-born novelist John Boyle O'Reilly (then editor of a Boston newspaper called the *Pilot*) wrote. "Sullivan begins by fighting, and he never ceases to fight."

To that, Sullivan added, "When I started boxing, I felt within myself that I could knock out any man living. I go in to win from the very first second. And I never stop until I have won."

But greater heights lay ahead. On September 18, 1883, Sullivan announced a venture of unprecedented proportions. He intended to embark upon an eight-month national tour, during which he would visit every region of America.

Sullivan was accompanied on his Grand Tour by heavyweight boxers Herbert Slade, Jem Mace, and Steve Taylor, and also by two lightweights (Pete McCoy and Mike Gillespie). Frank Moran (a friend of Sullivan's) served as the master of ceremonies. Al Smith (Sullivan's new manager) was the advance man. Jack Menzinger handled the finances. Annie Bates Bailey Sullivan was the final member of the group.

The tour wouldn't have been possible without recent advances in communications (most notably, the telegraph) and rail travel. It lasted from September 28, 1883, through May 23, 1884. Sullivan visited twenty-six of the thirty-eight states, five territories, the District of Columbia, and British Columbia.

Every major American city west of New York was on the tour. So were dozens of small communities, whose residents had never seen a boxing exhibition let alone come face-to-face with a person of renown. Sullivan made 195 appearances in 136 cities and towns over the course of 238 days. No one, not even a presidential candidate, had undertaken such an ambitious tour before.

Each stop on the Grand Tour centered around forty-five minutes of gloved sparring by the fighters. Rounds were three minutes long. Sullivan explained the concept to his audience as follows: "We are giving exhibitions of what can be done in the art of boxing. Two of these gentlemen fought me in New York and I done them up, but they are my friends now and I am their friend. Though we hit hard, we suffer no injury. We do no fighting, but it would be terrible punishment if a novice had to take it. We are simply giving these exhibitions that the people may see something of the art of boxing."

Sullivan was warmly received in virtually every locale he visited. Isenberg recounts a typical welcome: "At the railroad station, official greeters including the community's leading men. At the hotel, punctilious service. In the streets, crowds of men and boys eager to get a look at the Boston marvel. Audiences were composed of a mix of the better sort and riff-raff. Occasionally, some women attended."

Sullivan had the look of a champion. He was the first famous person that most of the onlookers had ever seen. And there was one more enticement to come see the show.

To heighten interest in the tour, Sullivan agreed to fight any man at any stop and pay $250 to anyone who lasted four rounds with him under Queensberry Rules. "John L." Isenberg writes, "was literally challenging all of America to fight."

No one accepted the offer. Thus, the prize money was raised to $500. The first taker was a man named James McCoy, who challenged Sullivan in McKeesport, Pennsylvania, and lasted twenty seconds with him. By the end of 1883, only four men had been willing to step into the ring with the champion; each of them a novice who lasted a matter of seconds. Thus, the bounty was increased to $1,000. The first taker was a transplanted Texan named Fred Robinson, who challenged Sullivan in Butte, Montana, and was knocked down fifteen times over the course of two rounds.

Sometimes, challenges were halted by the local police. But as a rule, if a challenger got in the ring and the bell rang, the battle (such as it was) didn't last long enough for the police to intervene.

In Oregon, on February 1, 1884, Sullivan faced a challenger named Sylvester Le Gouriff; a giant of a man who weighed more than three hundred pounds. Before the bout, Sullivan surveyed his foe and proclaimed, "The bigger he is, the harder he'll fall." Twenty seconds after the bell for round one rang, Le Gouriff was unconscious. "I break wood and fences with my fists," he told Sullivan afterward. "You break stone."

Five days later, Sullivan was in Seattle, where more than two thousand spectators saw a strong well-conditioned man named James Lang vie for the thousand-dollar prize. As reported in the *Seattle Daily Post-Intelligencer,* "It took a little less than seven seconds to make Mr. Lang aware of the fact that he had business elsewhere. In that time, he was knocked from side to side as if he were a child, battered to the floor, and forced to quit. It was simply impossible to withstand the rain of blows and the force with which they were delivered."

Other descriptions of Sullivan's ring prowess were equally chilling:

> • "For a big man, he is a marvel for activity and precision in delivering a blow. He swings the right across about as quick as most men can shove out the left hand. He will pound a man about, regardless of size, the same as he would handle a sandbag or punching ball. No man can stand up to his hurricane work."
>
> • "Sullivan is a marvel of strength, skill, and agility. If there is another man on earth who is equal, certain it is that that man has never been publicly known. The force with which he delivers a blow is simply appalling to ordinary people. There is nothing comparable to it, unless it be those guns holding several charges, which are discharged one after another. He is wonderfully agile, and his motions resemble those of a tiger in the act of springing on its prey. No ordinary man has any chance at all before him, and it is idle, foolish, to talk otherwise."
>
> • "He is such a prodigy in the fistic world that there seems to be no rule, whether physical or mental, that can apply to him. He is a phenomenon. It is his nature to fight. He is as lithe as a panther and his rush is like an avalanche."
>
> • "Even in imagination, the ancients never conceived such a hitter as Sullivan. No man that ever lived can evade Sullivan if he is well and strong. He is the quickest big man that ever fought in the ring. When he gets an opponent in the ring, that is the end of that man's chances."

On March 6, 1884, in San Francisco, Sullivan faced his first serious challenger on the Grand Tour; a professional prizefighter named George Robinson, who had defeated Herbert Slade a year earlier. Twelve thousand spectators watched the contest. Robinson survived, but only through cowardice. The *San Francisco Chronicle* reported that he fell to the canvas to avoid blows sixty-six times in four rounds.

Meanwhile, in addition to making money, Sullivan was using the tour as a pedestal upon which to preach the gospel of his profession. "Why is it that people raise such a cry against boxers?" he asked during an interview in Minnesota. "Aristocratic gentlemen in Europe, and sometimes in this country, go out with a couple of friends and try to kill each other with swords or revolvers at twenty paces. Why don't they settle the question with their fists? There would be no loss of life and it would be equally effective in determining who is the better man."

"I claim to have worked a revolution in the public sentiment by substituting gloves for the naked fists," Sullivan proclaimed. "Fist-fighting [bare-knuckle] days are over for me. I have introduced the new rules of the fight into this country, and I intend to stand by them. It will ere long not be considered a disgrace to be a boxer. It will not be long before the best people in the country will attend boxing contests."

For eight months, America embraced its champion as it had never embraced a common man before. "No matter where I go," Sullivan told a reporter, "there is a multitude of people who seem to know me and consider it an honor to shake my hand. I am gazed at by everybody, and at first this overawed me. But I have gotten used to it. It is an innocent request to satisfy, and I don't mind them a bit."

But there was a problem. A big one.

Sullivan was a drunkard. He had grown up in a drinking environment and, by his early twenties, was an alcoholic.

After Sullivan defeated Paddy Ryan to become champion, the public became aware of his drinking. John L. acknowledged that he was "no temperance man" but claimed to "never carry drinking to excess."

The number of brawls that he was involved in and the number of public appearances that he showed up for "under the weather" indicated otherwise.

Often, Sullivan would drink himself into a stupor in a saloon and boast, "I can lick any son-of-a-bitch in the house." He had a hair-trigger and frequently pulled it when he was drunk.

On the Grand Tour, Sullivan's drinking was a problem from the start. He denied it. "I don't drink much," he told a reporter for the *National Police Gazette.* "Say, five or six glasses of ale a day and a bottle for dinner if I feel like it."

That would have been too much, and it understated the matter. As the tour progressed, the champion's drinking spiraled out of control. With increasing frequency, when he performed before the public, he was drunk. Only one exhibition is known to have been cancelled because of it. But as Isenberg notes, "This meant that audiences throughout the country were often treated to a shambling drunk rather than a muscular advocate of the manly art crisply showing his stuff."

In later years, Sullivan claimed to have fought fifty-nine challengers during the Grand Tour. More likely, the number was twelve. Estimates of his earnings vary. The champion said he made a profit of $145,000 ($3,187,000 in today's dollars) after the deduction of $42,000 in expenses from gross receipts of $187,000. Isenberg places the profit at between $80,000 and $90,000. Regardless, no professional athlete (indeed, no common man) had earned anything close to that amount of money before. And more significantly, more than 100,000 Americans had seen Sullivan in the flesh.

Other than presidents and a few military heroes, John L. Sullivan had become the most famous person in the United States.

★   ★   ★

Throughout American history prior to Sullivan's ascent, most recreational activity had a practical side. Horse racing was the nation's most popular spectator sport, but hunting and fishing were far more prevalent.

In Sullivan's time, games that were games began to spread. They were sport for its own sake and for the entertainment of others. Casual play was augmented by professionalism in baseball, football, and other sporting endeavors. A class of professional athletes rose to prominence within organized business structures. At the same time, a national popular culture fueled by advances in transportation, communication, and journalism emerged. Sullivan was at the vortex of all of these trends.

"His name, his face, and his deeds were now known throughout the land," Isenberg writes. "He was constantly before the public in newspapers and magazines. The lithograph and the photograph produced images that heretofore had been private or the property of a limited circle and spread Sullivan's likeness far and wide. The flood of likenesses rapidly saturated the masculine world, no saloon being complete without the champion on display. Every avenue of communication tieing together the popular culture brought his name before the public. The sporting press and respectable metropolitan dailies carried his exploits into practically every literate home in America. Crowds would wait hours just to glimpse him or, even better, shake his hand. He was instant history, a living epic, a public symbol like none had seen before."

"Sullivan's popularity," Isenberg continues, "transcended class barriers and raised him to a level reached by no previous sporting figure. His most rabid following was among his fellow Irish-Americans. But to identify John L.'s following with immigrants and working-class men only is to ignore his standing among many American males regardless of background. He was arguably the most popular man in the United States."

Sullivan reveled in the spotlight. Virtually nothing about his life was private. No public figure (let alone, a member of a looked-down-upon ethnic and religious minority) had been the subject of such constant attention. Other than those occasions on which the attention was called to his drinking, he seemed to like it.

But the drinking remained a problem. "And lest his public be disposed to forget," Isenberg writes, "John L. was disposed to provide a flagrant new lapse every few months or so. His public career was a veritable parade of drunken escapades, most of them fully reported by the nation's press. Loud boisterous behavior was the least of it. In practically every city in the Union, he drank, quarreled, came to blows, and often ended up standing sheepishly before a magistrate and paying a fine. He did it all so publicly. When he was drunk, people saw it. He was one of the greatest exemplars of unrestrained vice the nation had to offer. John L. Sullivan had become big business, a celebrity, and a public disgrace all rolled into one."

As a counterbalance to his drinking, Sullivan had redeeming personal qualities. When sober, he was usually polite and considerate toward others. He was honest and generous. Much of his money was poorly spent on jewelry and expensive clothes (he was a flashy dresser, frequently in poor taste). Too often when drinking, he paid the night's tab for everyone in the saloon. He lived lavishly and "loaned" money to friends who had no intention of paying it back. But he also supported his parents, bought them a nice house, gave generously to other family members, and donated large sums to charity.

In April 1884, Sullivan's wife bore him a son. But their marriage was in shambles. Rumors were spreading that he beat Annie when he was drunk. Several months after John Jr was born, she moved back to Rhode Island (from whence she'd come). In February 1885, she sued for divorce, accusing her husband of cruel and abusive treatment and "gross and confirmed habits of intoxication."

Sullivan contested the divorce, and the case was dismissed. The marriage remained intact as a matter of law for another twenty-three years. But as a union of two hearts, it was over.

Meanwhile, although it hardly seemed possible, Sullivan's drinking worsened. He was involved in numerous street-fights and saloon brawls and, at one point, was criminally charged with kicking a carriage horse three times in the underribs and striking the horse with his fist.

The first major ring appearance scheduled for Sullivan after his Grand Tour was a "sparring session" to be conducted under Queensberry Rules at Madison Square Garden on June 30, 1884. The opponent was Charlie Mitchell, who had knocked Sullivan down before succumbing in three rounds in their previous encounter. Five thousand fans paid between two and twenty-five dollars each for the show. Sullivan arrived three hours late, staggered to the ring dressed in a black suit, and told the crowd, "Gentlemen; I am sick and will not be able to box." It was clear that he was drunk; a fact that was reported in newspapers across the country.

Al Smith quit as Sullivan's manager after the Mitchell fiasco. Thereafter, the champion followed a pattern of "Fight an unskilled foe. Binge. Fight an unskilled foe. Binge." But despite his drinking, when he entered the ring, he won.

"Sullivan frightens his man every time," an article in the *Pittsburgh Dispatch* declared. "They all lose their nerve the moment they face him."

Biographer R. F. Dibble explained what it was like to face the champion: "The rival, looking across the ring, would see a burley menacing figure. The iron muscles bulged and swelled. Black coarse hair bristled all over the huge head. The deep thick hairy chest and sloping shoulders betokened a man of extraordinary strength. The broad face, the square pile-driver jaw, and the ominous droop at the corners of the mouth blended into a terrifying grin. There he sat, his clenched fists resting on his knees, his stony gray eyes glancing toward his opponent. Time would be called. Sullivan would rise slowly and advance, slapping his left hand against his thigh."

Joe Choynski (a leading heavyweight of his day, who later knocked out a young Jack Johnson and fought Bob Fitzsimmons, Marvin Hart, and James Jeffries to draws) said of Sullivan, "His right arm comes across like a flash of lightning with a jerk. And if he misses, he's so quick you can't get your head out of range before it's back ready for another shot at your jaw."

"I can tell pretty well when my man is giving in," Sullivan proclaimed. "I watch his eyes, and I know at once when the punishment is beginning to tell on him."

But Sullivan was also firm in saying, "There is more intelligence required in this business than outsiders give us credit for. A man fights with his head almost as much as he does with his fists. He must know where to send his blows so they may do the most good. He must economize his strength and not score a hit just for the sake of scoring it. Learn to strike straight and clean. Swinging blows nearly always leave an opening for your opponent. It is always well to do your leading with the left, reserving your right for a good opening. Always watch your opponent. As soon as you see him about to lead, shoot your left into his face. The force of his coming towards you will increase your blows considerably.

"I endeavor to hit my man above the heart or under the chin or behind the ear," Sullivan explained. "A man wears out pretty soon if one can keep hammering away in the region around the heart. A blow under the chin or behind the ear will knock a man out quicker than a hundred blows on the cheek or any other portion of the face. I have always considered it necessary that a young man, in order to become an accomplished boxer, should have brains as well as muscle. I never knew a thick-headed fellow yet to become skillful in the manly art."

Sullivan also took pride in the fact that he was self-taught and had learned his trade from sparring and watching other fighters. "I never took a boxing lesson in my life," he said. "No professor of sparring can ever claim me as a pupil. What I know about boxing, I picked up from hard experience and intelligent observation. I belong to no school of boxers and have copied no special master's style. I always fight according to my own judgment. If a man can't train himself, no one in the world can do it for him."

Sullivan's contemporaries understood his ring savvy. Mike Donovan, who sparred with the champion, acknowledged, "He is the cleverest big man the ring ever saw. He can stand off ten feet and fiddle in a way that disconcerts you and breaks your guard. Then he comes at you like a battering ram, you get it on the jaw, and down you go."

And the *Chicago Herald* proclaimed, "Sullivan is as clever as any man. His unquestioned ability as to being the hardest hitter has caused the overlooking of the fact that his blow is always planted where it will do the most good. The truth is that Sullivan is a careful scientific fighter."

Meanwhile, the public remained fascinated with the champion. Popular songs such as "Let Me Shake the Hand that Shook the Hand of Sullivan" abounded. For twenty weeks, he performed as "model statuary" in a venture called the Lester and Allen Minstrel Show. For five hundred dollars a week (clad as what the *National Police Gazette* called "the biggest undressed heroes of antiquity") Sullivan posed as the curtain rose and fell between him and the audience. Thus, the American public was treated to such visions as the Gladiator in Combat, the Dying Gladiator, Hercules at Rest, and Cain Killing Abel.

In 1887, Sullivan began living with a statuesque blonde named Anna Nailor, who had worked as a chorus girl in Boston under the name Ann Livingston. She was a few years older than he was, divorced, with an active romantic history. In October 1887, with Ann at his side, the champion left the United States for a tour of the United Kingdom.

Sullivan was enthusiastically received in England, Scotland, and Ireland. Although overweight and in poor condition, he sparred in fifty-one exhibitions and had one actual fight; a bare-knuckle bout under London Rules against Charlie Mitchell. After 39 rounds in the rain during which Mitchell fought almost entirely defensively, the contest was declared a draw.

The anecdotal highlight of Sullivan's European tour came on December 9, when he was introduced to Edward, Prince of Wales. There followed twenty minutes of conversation between the son of Irish immigrants and the man who, upon the death Queen Victoria in 1901, would succeed to the throne. Sullivan is said to have closed the conversation by telling the prince, "If you ever come to Boston, be sure and look me up. I'll see that you're treated right."

The champion arrived home in Boston on April 24, 1888. One witness to his return said that he weighed 280 pounds. Shortly thereafter, refusing to tolerate his drinking and abusive behavior, Ann Livingston left him.

In June and July 1888, Sullivan appeared in a show called the John B. Doris and Gray Circus that saw him spar briefly and ride a pony. Later that summer, most likely as a result of his incessant drinking, his liver and stomach lining became inflamed. The champion's temperature rose to a dangerously high level and a priest administered the last rites. He recovered after losing eighty pounds. And for one month, at least, he had been dry.

Meanwhile, given the decreasing frequency of Sullivan's ring combat against serious opposition, Richard Kyle Fox was seeking to anoint a new "champion of the world." His chosen vessel was a fighter from Baltimore named Jake Kilrain.

Kilrain was four months younger than Sullivan and, like the champion, Irish American. He was a stable family man and a pretty good fighter, having defeated some of the better competitors of his day. In May 1887, Fox had gone so far as to present him with a silver championship belt on behalf of the *National Police Gazette*. In response, Sullivan's financial backers and admirers in Boston presented John L. with the most celebrated sports symbol of all time.

Their gift to Sullivan was a championship belt made of 14-carat gold. It was four feet long and weighed close to thirty pounds. The belt had eight panels with scenes depicting Sullivan in addition to various Irish symbols and the flags of the United States, England, and Ireland. The panels were separated in the middle by a large shield bearing the legend "Presented to the Champion of Champions, John L. Sullivan, by the Citizens of the United States." Sullivan's name was beneath a three-carat diamond and encrusted with 256 diamonds of its own.

The belt was valued at $8,000. Sullivan famously said that it made Fox's gift to Kilrain look like a dog collar.

But Sullivan was destined to fight Kilrain. He needed the money and wanted the acclaim. On January 7, 1889, the two men entered into a contract for a fight to the finish to be held on July 8, 1889, at a site "within 200 miles of New Orleans" under the London Prize Ring Rules for a side bet of $10,000.

There were doubts about Sullivan's fitness to fight Kilrain. Fox observed, "Sullivan has been drinking hard for several years and undermined his constitution to an alarming extent. No man can expect to drink almost continuously and not injure his health. I tell you; John L. Sullivan is not the man he once was."

To ready Sullivan for the fight, the champion's backers turned to a conditioner named William Muldoon. Isenberg recounts, "Muldoon liked Sullivan, was saddened by his chronic dissipation, and viewed him as an ideal test for his theories of physical fitness. For the first and only time in his life, Sullivan was training thoroughly under the guidance of a man who understood the rudiments of physical culture."

They worked together pursuant to an agreement under which Muldoon paid all of the training expenses. If Sullivan lost, the trainer would receive no compensation. If Sullivan won, Muldoon would be paid a share of his winnings.

Sullivan despised training. "A fellow would rather fight twelve dozen times than train once," he said. "But it has to be done."

Muldoon kept Sullivan active from dawn to dusk, chopping down trees, plowing fields, skipping rope, and eventually sparring. He built up Sullivan's legs and wind and wrestled with him to reacquaint Sullivan with the grappling and throwing allowed under the London Rules. Of equal significance, he kept Sullivan away from alcohol. When they began working together in May 1889, Sullivan weighed more than 240 pounds, much of it fat, not muscle. During the next two months, he shed thirty pounds and, more importantly, regained his strength and speed.

As Sullivan-Kilrain neared, the national press paid more attention to the fight than it had ever paid to a sporting event before. But there was a fly in the ointment. Prizefighting was illegal in Louisiana and all other states "within 200 miles of New Orleans."

On July 7, 1889, in Marion County, Mississippi (103 miles north of New Orleans), laborers began constructing a twenty-four-foot-square ring

fronted by bleachers on three sides. They worked under the supervision
of a young Mississippian named Charles Rich, who owned a sawmill surrounded by thirty thousand acres of pine forest in an area known as
Richburg. As they worked, three trains departed from New Orleans. The
first carried Sullivan, Kilrain, and their respective entourages. After the
fighters arrived in Richburg, Kilrain spent the rest of the night in Rich's
home, while Sullivan stayed with Rich's chief clerk. The other two trains,
filled with fight enthusiasts, arrived in Richburg after sunrise.

At 10:13 on the morning of July 8, 1889, John L. Sullivan and Jake
Kilrain "came to scratch" bare-knuckled for what would be the last
heavyweight championship fight ever fought under the London Prize
Ring Rules.

Sullivan weighed 215 pounds and was wearing green fighting tights
with white stockings. Kilrain, twenty pounds lighter, wore black tights and
blue stockings. The weather was muggy, the temperature close to one
hundred degrees.

Referee John Fitzpatrick (who would later be elected mayor of New
Orleans) called "time." The defining fight of John L. Sullivan's career had
begun.

Fifteen seconds into the match, Kilrain grabbed Sullivan around the
neck, leveraged him over his hip, and threw him to the ground. Sullivan
returned the favor to end round two. In round six, after three more falls,
Kilrain drew first blood with a right hand blow to the nose. But before
the challenger could survey the damage, Sullivan knocked him down with
the hardest punch of the fight thus far, leaving it to the dazed fighter's seconds to lift him up and lead him to his corner.

From that point on, Kilrain had the look of a beaten fighter. His face
grew more and more disfigured. Frequently, he fell without cause in order
to gain relief and end a round. His strategy was to survive; perhaps close
Sullivan's eyes with jabs; and failing that, hope that Sullivan wilted in the
heat.

As the temperature rose, by some accounts reaching 114 degrees,
Muldoon asked Sullivan how much longer he could stand the heat. "I can
stay here until daybreak tomorrow," Sullivan told him.

By round thirty-six, Kilrain was so tired that he had to be lifted from
his chair by his seconds at the start of each round. The outcome seemed

a foregone conclusion. Then, five seconds into the forty-fourth round, Sullivan began to vomit.

"Will you draw the fight?" Kilrain asked.

"No, you loafer," Sullivan told him.

The battle continued. In addition to the damage caused by blows, each man's upper body was blistered by the sun. Kilrain's corner began giving him large amounts of whiskey to dull the pain. He was now exhausted and barely conscious. Two hours and sixteen minutes after the battle began, he refused to come to scratch for the seventy-sixth round.

Word of Sullivan's victory was transmitted by telegraph throughout America. Some big-city newspapers recorded it on page one. Richard Kyle Fox conceded, "By this fight, Sullivan has proved that he is a first-class pugilist in every respect. He is a stayer as well as a slugger."

Sullivan, for his part, told reporters, "I knew after two or three rounds I was the sole master of the situation. If Kilrain had stood up and fought like a man, I could have whipped him in about eight rounds. He hardly fought fairly, going down, as you know he did, numbers of times without a blow." But the champion added, "Jake is a good fighter. He gave me a better fight than I ever got before. He took far more punishment than I believed he would."

Both Sullivan and Kilrain left Richburg immediately after the fight and returned to New Orleans. There, the champion was informed that a sheriff from Mississippi was searching for him with a warrant for his arrest on a charge of violating Mississippi's law against prizefighting. He boarded a train headed north, was arrested in Tennessee, and held in jail overnight. He was released the next day but arrested again on July 31; this time in New York. From there, he was escorted under guard back to Mississippi, where, on August 16, he was found guilty of prizefighting and sentenced to a year in jail.

Sullivan made bond and was released by the authorities pending appeal. In March 1880, the Mississippi Supreme Court overturned his conviction on a technicality that rendered the indictment faulty. He was re-indicted, pled guilty, and was sentenced to a five-hundred-dollar fine.

Kilrain was arrested in Baltimore in August. Charles Rich posted his bond. The fighter returned to Mississippi for trial in December, at which time he was found guilty of assault and battery, fined two hundred dollars, and sentenced to two months imprisonment. Under Mississippi's prison contract system, he was allowed to serve his sentence at the home of Charles Rich.

After defeating Kilrain, Sullivan began drinking heavily again. Later that year, he announced that he would stand as a candidate for Congress. He was a lifelong Democrat, and Boston was solidly in the Democratic column. But given his much-publicized drinking and outside-the-ring brawling, the local Democratic machine wanted no part of him. He failed to get the nomination.

In 1890, Sullivan turned to acting. On August 28, 1890, he opened in the role of a blacksmith turned pugilist in a melodrama entitled *Honest Hearts and Willing Hands*. By this time, he weighed close to three hundred pounds.

Isenberg recounts, "Sullivan performed like a wooden Indian. He tended to entangle himself in lines and was so intent on his speeches that, when the audience interrupted a sentence with applause, he doggedly retreated to the beginning and started again."

But audiences loved him. *Honest Hearts and Willing Hands* was soon on national tour.

Sullivan had no intention of fighting again. "His stomach," Isenberg notes, "was a veritable mountain of flesh, the weight of which left him winded after the slightest exertion. He was in no condition for any kind of athletic endeavor, never mind the strenuous demands of the prize ring. Yet he could not give it up. Money filtered through his wallet like water, spent in saloons, given to friends, and in all probability lavished on prostitutes. He had to keep the money coming in. And he could not walk away from the one thing that gave him purpose, sustained his ego, and nourished his existence. All else stemmed from what he achieved in the ring. The theater crowds, the civic awards, the adoring hordes of small boys, the gaping adults at every train station and hotel."

Inevitably, Sullivan would fight again.

★   ★   ★

The Marquis of Queensberry Rules that Sullivan proselytized for throughout his career didn't make boxing less violent. Gloves were worn to protect fists, not an opponent's brain. And under the new rules, a fighter could no longer gain thirty seconds of relief by falling to the ground.

But as Elliott Gorn writes, "The Queensberry Rules redrew the arbitrary border separating acceptable deviance from unpardonable vice. They sanitized prizefighting just enough to make it a legal spectator sport and changed the social composition of the crowd and the environment in which fights were held. The ring continued to call forth images of primitive brutality, of lower-class and ethnic peoples venting their violent passions. But gloves and new rules appeared to curb the animality sufficiently to allow a titillating sense of danger inside safe and civilized boundaries."

Nowhere was this change more evident than in New Orleans. In 1890, the New Orleans City Council voted to allow fights that were contested under Queensberry Rules as long as those fights were not held on a Sunday, no liquor was served, and the promoter contributed fifty dollars to charity. One year later, the New Orleans Olympic Club (one of several athletic associations in the city) mounted a successful court challenge to Louisiana's statute against prizefighting insofar as it related to gloved fights.

The New Orleans athletic associations spearheaded the modernization of boxing. Fighters were divided into six weight classes. Club employees were trained as referees and empowered to stop fights if a combatant was hurt and unable to properly defend himself. Of greater significance from a commercial point of view, the clubs built indoor arenas and began to contract for fights under a system in which they chose the fighters and supervised every aspect of a promotion. On September 7, 1892, John L. Sullivan put his imprimatur on this new world.

By 1892, more than two years had passed since Sullivan had entered the ring against Jake Kilrain. Criticism of his reluctance to fight was mounting. And he needed money. Hence, in early March, he issued a public challenge that read in part, "This country has been overrun by a lot of foreign fighters and also American aspirants for fistic fame and championship honors, who have endeavored to seek notoriety and American dollars by challenging me to fight. I hereby challenge any and all of the bluffers to fight me either the last week in August or the first week in September at the Olympic Club, New Orleans, Louisiana, for a purse of $25,000 and an outside bet of $10,000, the winner of the fight to take the

entire purse. The Marquis of Queensberry Rules must govern this contest, as I want fighting, not foot racing."

One of the fighters whom Sullivan mentioned by name in his challenge was James Corbett.

A native of San Francisco, Corbett, like Sullivan, was the son of Irish
immigrants. He was not a particularly strong puncher. But he was fast,
quick, and a skilled counter-puncher with exceptional stamina. At age fifteen, Corbett had been let into Mechanics' Pavilion in San Francisco free
of charge by a compliant ticket-taker and seen Sullivan in the ring during the champion's Grand Tour. Two years later, when Sullivan returned
to San Francisco to fight Paddy Ryan for the last time, Corbett attended
the fight.

In 1891, Sullivan and Corbett were formally introduced. The champion was in Chicago, performing in *Honest Hearts and Willing Hands*.
Corbett, by then, was twenty-four years old and a fighter of some renown.
After Sullivan's performance, the two men went drinking together, with
Sullivan doing most of the drinking. They met again in June of that year
and "sparred" together at a benefit in San Francisco. But Sullivan insisted
that they wear formal dinner attire for the occasion to negate any hint of
competition.

After reading Sullivan's public challenge, Corbett and his manager
(William Brady) traveled to New York and raised the money for the
$10,000 side bet. On March 15, 1892, a contract was signed. Sullivan-
Corbett would be fought at the New Orleans Olympic Club on September 7, 1892, as a fight to the finish under Queensberry Rules. The
fighters would wear five-ounce gloves. The Olympic Club put up the
$25,000 purse. With each man posting a $10,000 side bet, the winner
would receive $45,000, the largest sum in the history of prizefighting.

Sullivan was a 3-to-1 favorite in the early betting. He was John L.
Sullivan. Those who thought that his hedonistic lifestyle would destroy
him had learned their lesson when he defeated Jake Kilrain. Kilrain,
who'd lost to both men, predicted a Sullivan victory.

But Sullivan had been inactive as a fighter, binge-drinking, and
overeating for three years. He was just shy of his thirty-fourth birthday,
whereas Corbett was twenty-six. Moreover, Corbett had begun serious
training for the fight in early June at a fit 190 pounds. Sullivan didn't go

into training until July. When he did, he weighed more than 240 pounds. His workouts were light, and there was no conditioner to oversee his training.

Future heavyweight champion Bob Fitzsimmons voiced the concern of many when he observed, "From what I have heard of Sullivan, he will not do his work like a man who is going to meet a good and clever boxer. It may be that Sullivan will underestimate Corbett. If he does that and will not train, he will be beaten, for Corbett is a remarkably clever man and can hit a hard blow."

Corbett, for his part, paid tribute to the champion, acknowledging, "The man I am going up against is the best that has ever lived. I don't know as I will win. But I will be in the ring on September 7 and, if I am defeated, will go the way of many other good men."

However, that bit of humility was offset by the declaration, "I think that I can defeat him. I always thought that I could. Ever since we boxed a friendly bout together in San Francisco, I have had my mind made up that I could whip him. No man who has lived the life that Sullivan has lived can beat me in a fight to the finish."

As the fight neared, New Orleans was consumed by Sullivan versus Corbett. Thousands of boxing enthusiasts, hustlers, prostitutes, and legitimate entrepreneurs descended upon the city. The Olympic Club built a new arena, replete with electric lights, that could hold ten thousand spectators.

The bout was more eagerly anticipated than any sporting event ever up until that time. Word of its outcome would be transmitted instantaneously by telegraph across the nation. In New York, two beacons were mounted on top of the Pulitzer Building. A red one would be lit if Sullivan triumphed; white if Corbett prevailed.

A flood of "smart money" on fight day dropped the odds to almost even. Sullivan entered the ring at 212 pounds; Corbett weighed 187.

The bout began shortly after 9:00 P.M. At the start, Sullivan stormed across the ring in his usual manner, slapping his left hand against his thigh. For the first few rounds, Corbett evaded the champion's blows. In round five, he landed a solid left that brought blood gushing from Sullivan's nose.

From that point on, the challenger beat up the champion. "Sullivan is big and strong," Corbett said afterward. "But I knew that he could not hit me. I kept my right in reserve and cut him down with my left. When I saw I had him safe, I ended it as soon as possible. I won by whipping him, not by keeping away."

By round seven, Corbett was landing hard blows to the body. Sullivan found it increasingly difficult to even lift his arms as the challenger danced around him, raining down blows. By round fourteen, Corbett was landing virtually at will. The champion kept coming forward. It was the only way he knew how to fight. Now and then, when Corbett landed a telling blow, Sullivan acknowledged, "That's a good one, Jim." But he was powerless to retaliate in any meaningful way.

The end came in round twenty-one. Isenberg describes the scene: "The iron constitution and raw energy that had served John L. Sullivan so long and so well could do no more. The tree-trunk legs were barely holding him up. His arms ached, hanging straight down at his sides. He could barely see through puffed-up eyelids. Dazed, he hardly knew what was happening around him. But he would not fall. Wavering, he stood helplessly in his corner as Corbett advanced, at last determined to go for the kill. Corbett feinted, then slammed home a right to the jaw. Sullivan dropped to his knees; then incredibly, slowly raised himself to his feet. There he stood, completely defenseless, waiting for the inevitable."

An account in the *New York Sun* tells what happened next: "The blood from Sullivan's face flowed in torrents and made a crimson river across the broad chest. His eyes were glassy. It was a mournful act when the young Californian shot his right across the jaw and Sullivan fell like an ox."

John L. Sullivan, champion of champions, had lost.

Sullivan was barely conscious as his handlers carried him to his corner. There, they sought to revive him by placing ammonia beneath his nose and pressing ice against the back of his neck and head.

The crowd was cheering wildly for the new champion. Years later, Corbett would write in his autobiography, "I was actually disgusted with the crowd, and it left a lasting impression on me. It struck me as sad to see all those thousands who had given him such a wonderful ovation when he entered the ring turning it to me now that he was down and out. I realized that some day they would turn from me when I should be in Sullivan's shoes, lying there on the floor."

Then, still dazed, Sullivan rose from his stool and lurched toward the ropes. Holding onto a ring post to steady his body, the now-ex-champion held up his right hand and cried out to the crowd. "Gentlemen, gentlemen." The crowd grew silent. "All I have to say," Sullivan continued in a wavering voice, "is that I came into the ring once too often. And if I had to get licked, I'm glad I was licked by an American. I remain your warm and personal friend, John L. Sullivan."

Later that night, having gathered his senses more fully, the defeated champion acknowledged, "He hit me whenever he wanted to. I tried in every way to hit him, but I couldn't. I am gone now. I can't fight anymore, and that settles it. I could, at that fellow's age, have licked any one of them in the world, but that time has passed." Then, on a more defiant note, Sullivan added, "Let him go through what I have. Let him knock them all out for twelve years and then see if he can do any better than I did."

Sullivan-Corbett marked the first transfer of the gloved heavyweight championship of the world. There was a new king. But Sullivan had reigned for ten years. He was still famous. And in defeat, he refused to leave the public stage.

For the next fifteen years, the former champion continued to make money by going on theatrical and vaudeville tours. "The monologue was his bread and butter," Isenberg recounts. "John L. would walk slowly from the wings to center stage, where he would plant both feet and not budge for the remainder of his routine. Clad in full dress suit, he would slip his left hand into a trouser pocket and use the once-lethal right for gestures. And off he would ramble. Drunk or sober, he was seldom a disappointment for the confirmed fan. And on his good nights, he could be positively enchanting."

Unfortunately, many nights were bad. After Sullivan was beaten by Corbett, boxing was no longer in the back of his mind, which meant that there were no constraints whatsoever on his drinking. A series of embarrassing incidents followed.

In 1893, Sullivan was indicted for assault and battery after beating up a one-armed man on a train. Settlement of the resulting civil suit and legal fees (civil and criminal) cost him $1,200. In 1894, he was arrested after assaulting a carriage driver. In 1896, he was arrested and fined after beating up a streetcar conductor and assaulting a police officer. That same year, in a drunken stupor, he fell off a moving train while trying to urinate onto the tracks. He was knocked unconscious and suffered an eight-inch gash on the back of his head.

There were frequent hospitalizations for drinking-related ailments. Along the way, pressed for cash, Sullivan pawned his championship belt. Decades later, the diamonds having been removed, the belt was melted down and sold for its gold content.

In 1902, at a matinee performance of his monologue in Detroit, Sullivan staggered out in front of the audience dead drunk, almost fell through the backdrop, and resisted efforts to forcibly remove him from the stage. After a struggle, he was taken back to his hotel, went out on another drinking binge, and wound up in jail for eight hours.

And so it went.

On March 1, 1905, Sullivan was on tour in Grand Rapids, Michigan. Several recent theatrical appearances had been cancelled because drinking had rendered him unfit to appear onstage. Badly in need of money, he agreed to step into the ring against a young fighter from Texas named Jim McCormick.

Sullivan was forty-six years old. He weighed 273 pounds and had not fought competitively in more than twelve years. He knocked McCormick unconscious in the second round.

Four days later, Sullivan was in Terre Haute, Indiana. The previous night, his theatrical performance had once again been cut short because heavy drinking rendered his monologue unintelligible. After being led back to his hotel, he'd slept until noon.

It was March 5, 1905. Sullivan walked into the hotel bar, ordered a glass of champagne, poured his drink into a spittoon, and declared, "If I ever take another drink as long as I live, I hope to God I choke."

Perhaps the victory over McCormack had released the demons within him. Maybe he'd simply had enough. He never drank in public again and his antisocial behavior came to an end.

Meanwhile, backed by religious reform groups, the temperance movement was gathering strength nationwide. Sullivan personally opposed the prohibition of alcoholic beverages, believing that drinking was better addressed as a matter of education and conscience. He also cast a jaundiced eye at "reformers," noting, "In all my years of wild spending, I never heard of nobody refusing to take the money of John L. Of all the money I gave for churches, schools, and other charities, I can't remember a single cent being flopped back to me because it was earned by biffing some chap on the jaw."

Nonetheless, after going dry, Sullivan became a sought-after lecturer and powerful symbol for advocates of prohibition. "If I had not quit drinking when I did," he told his audiences, "there would be somewhere in a Boston suburb a modest tombstone with the inscription on it, 'Sacred to the memory of John L. Sullivan.' There is only one way to get the best of John Barleycorn, and that is to run away from him. There are men who say about liquor that they can take it or leave it. But those are the ones who always take it. And in the end, it gets them. I say to the young men of the United States, 'Leave liquor alone.'"

Sullivan's transformation earned him praise in high circles. Theodore Roosevelt (then president of the United States) observed, "John's best fight was made after he lost to Corbett. I mean his whipping John Barleycorn. That was a real victory, and I'm proud of him for having made it. Since then, he has been the most effective temperance lecturer I have known of. He has been effective because he could appeal to classes of men and boys others could never hope to reach."

Thereafter, Roosevelt and Sullivan established a friendship of sorts, and Roosevelt told biographer John Leary, "Old John L. has been a greater power for good in this country than many a higher respectable person who would scorn to meet him on terms of equality. I know that his former profession is not a very exalted one. But he has profited by his travels and he is better informed on most matters than most men who have had no better opportunity in school work than he had. He was a good fighter and clean. He never threw a fight. In his way, he did his best to uphold American supremacy. He has been my friend many years, and I am proud to be his."

After Sullivan renounced liquor, he began spending time with a woman named Katherine Harkins, six years younger than he was, who he'd known since childhood. In 1908, he sued Annie Bates Bailey Sullivan (who was still living in Rhode Island) for divorce. At the hearing, he told the judge, "When a man ain't lived with a woman for twenty-five years, he don't want to call her his wife. I've always fought shy of divorce courts on account of my religion. But there's a time when the torture is too strong. I don't want that woman to have my bones."

The divorce was granted. The only child of their marriage, John Jr, had died of diphtheria twenty-three years earlier.

Sullivan and Harkins were married on February 7, 1910, and moved to a small house twenty miles south of Boston. The following year, he retired from the stage. They lived together in contentment until 1916, when "Kate" died of cancer.

During the last few years of his life, Sullivan suffered from cirrhosis of the liver and was almost totally deaf in his left ear. His weight fluctuated between 270 and 320 pounds. At a 1917 banquet held in his honor in Boston, the Great John L. told the admiring crowd, "If the good Lord shall call me right now, I may say that I have seen it all. I know the game of life from A to Z, from soda to hock." On February 1, 1918, he suffered a heart attack and died.

Evaluating Sullivan through the haze of history is a complex task.

Late in life, James Corbett declared, "It is very hard to tell, as you gaze down the list at all the defeated champions of the past, which was supreme. And all argument as to their respective merits is foolish and futile."

Be that as it may; Sullivan was likely the best fighter ever under any rules of boxing up until his time. He was an honest fighter with enormous physical gifts. Shortly before his thirty-fourth birthday, his body a shell of what it once was, he remained standing into the twenty-first round against James Corbett (who was in his prime). That alone showed extraordinary courage and heart.

Sullivan made fighting under the Marquis of Queensberry Rules acceptable to the fight crowd. That led to the acceptance of boxing among the higher classes of society and under the law. By his insistence on adhering to the new rules, he modernized boxing. And by his persona, he popularized it.

The most significant blot on Sullivan's ring record was his refusal to fight a black opponent. "I will not fight a negro," he said on more than one occasion. "I never have and never shall."

The best defense of that stance (and it's a poor justification) is that a man must be judged by the standards of his time. Sullivan had been born

into a world in which slavery was the bulwark of the economy in a substantial portion of the United States. Throughout his life, separation of the
races was law in much of the land. In drawing a color line, he was reflecting values he'd been taught as a child and saw all around him.

That said; more than anyone else, Sullivan created modern boxing.
Without him, the sport would have evolved in an entirely different way.
Before Sullivan, there were title claimants. He founded a line of kings
who were universally recognized heavyweight champions of the world.
He brought new value to the championship and paved the way for a
more businesslike approach to the sport. He gave boxing a new foundation to build on.

As for Sullivan the person, Elliott Gorn sums up, saying, "He was a
hero and a brute, a bon vivant and a drunk, a lover of life and a reckless
barbarian. He cut through all restraints, acted rather than contemplated,
and paid little regard to the morality or immorality of his behavior. He
was totally self-indulgent, even in acts of generosity, totally a hedonist."

But his most endearing personal quality, the one that made him
loved, should not be forgotten. Sullivan, it was said at the peak of his
reign, "modestly accepts plain citizens as equals and friends."

American novelist Theodore Dreiser (then a young newspaperman)
met Sullivan shortly after the fighter's ring career ended. Later, Dreiser
recalled, "John L. Sullivan, raw, red-faced, big-fisted, broad-shouldered,
drunken, with gaudy waistcoat and tie, and rings and pins set with enormous diamonds and rubies. Surrounded by sports and politicians of the
most rubicund and degraded character. Cigar boxes, champagne buckets,
decanters, beer bottles, overcoats, collars and shirts littered the floor. And
lolling back in the midst of it all in ease and splendor, his very great self.
What an impression he made!"

Otis Grant was knocked out by Roy Jones in ten rounds in 1998. "Roy was so good," Grant said in 2008. "I wish he was out of the game by now. He was too great a fighter to go out the way he's going out. But I guess that's the way most great fighters go."

Jones–Trinidad and the Long Road To Where?

On May 15, 2004, one moment of violence turned Roy Jones's world upside down. Antonio Tarver landed a single perfectly-timed punch in the second round, and the cloak of invincibility that had led boxing's reigning "pound-for-pound" king to be mentioned in the same breath as Sugar Ray Robinson was gone.

Jones was somber in his dressing room after the fight. "One shot," he said, sitting on a chair, looking straight ahead. "I know exactly what happened. I threw a right hand and tried to come back with the left. He read it and fired his gun first. I just got caught." Roy took a breath and let it out slowly. "Nothing like this ever happened to me before. In your heart, you always know it can, even though you hope it never will. I guess God wanted me to go through this at least one time."

The door to the dressing room opened, and Felix Trinidad (who'd been at ringside) entered. Jones rose, and the two men embraced. "I'm sorry," Trinidad said in heavily-accented English. "You are a great fighter."

There's a fraternity among great fighters. Jones and Trinidad were great. For much of the past two decades, they were on the short list of boxing's biggest stars and participated in some of their sport's most significant fights.

There was a time when Jones was so good that his ring encounters seemed like performance art. At his best, he reduced fighters like Bernard Hopkins and James Toney, to props. "Roy Jones would have been great in any era," Jake LaMotta acknowledged after Roy dismantled John Ruiz to become the first former middleweight champion in more than a century to capture a piece of the heavyweight crown.

Trinidad had his own moments of glory, toppling Pernell Whitaker, Oscar De La Hoya, and Fernando Vargas. Jones was a craftsman known for his virtuoso performances. "Tito," by contrast, was a joyous warrior, whose fights were memorable for the roaring crowds that poured forth their adulation each time their Puerto Rican countryman fought.

But fighters get old young. It's hard to remember a boxer who fell as far as fast in the public mind as Jones did after his 2004 loss to Tarver. Trinidad had his own fall from grace, getting beaten up by Bernard Hopkins in 2001 and being thoroughly outclassed by Winky Wright four years later. Still, both men are legends and, more to the point, successful brand names. There was money to be made in having them fight each other.

Boxing is a business where people ask you to put your money where their mouth is, and Don King is a master of the art. For Trinidad-Jones, first he prevailed upon Madison Square Garden president James Dolan to buy the live gate for $8,500,000. The deal was made over the objection of Joel Fisher (MSG's senior vice president for sports properties and the Garden's point man for boxing), who is said to have calculated that, if the fight was properly marketed, the right purchase price would be no more than $6,500,000.

Then King signed Trinidad for a reported $15,000,000. That number was hard to believe. But reliable sources close to the promoter are firm in saying that Trinidad's contract called for him to receive a check for $7,000,000 on fight night and an additional $8,000,000 on or before February 9th.

That left Jones to be taken care of. "It takes a lot of convincing for me to do anything," Roy has said. But King played to Jones's ego and the fighter's current business advisers, signing him to a contract that called for a small guarantee against a percentage of pay-per-view revenue. "We're partners," King said of his relationship with Roy. But one of the partners had his financial bases covered better than the other.

"I never saw the contract," says Fred Levin (the Pensacola attorney who represented Jones from the fighter's first pro bout through the glory years). "I do know that Roy felt he needed this fight from an image standpoint. It was important to him to have a big fight against a name opponent in Madison Square Garden on HBO Pay-Per-View. He was aware of the financial risks involved and took the gamble."

"I came here to win," Jones said at the final pre-fight press conference; "not to count the pay-per-view."

Six years ago, Roy Jones versus Felix Trinidad would have defined an
era. King genuinely believed that it would still be a blockbuster fight.
Both of the combatants are future Hall of Famers. Trinidad has a fervent
following, and Jones still inspires respect among his peers. By way of
example, at the New York State Athletic Commission rules meeting one
day before the fight, Andrew Golota approached Roy and asked if he
could have his picture taken with him.

But Jones-Trinidad never caught on as an event. The pieces of the
puzzle were there: Roy Jones, Felix Trinidad, Don King, HBO, and
Madison Square Garden. But they didn't fit.

The first problem the promotion faced was that tickets were over-
priced. After James Dolan bought the live gate for $8,500,000, he hired
outside consultants, who scaled the house with front-row seats costing
$15,000. Second row cost $12,500; third row, $10,000; fourth row, $7,500.
"Regular" ringside seats were priced at $5,000. The cheapest seat in the
house was $100. That created a negative buzz and led people to examine
the fight more closely.

Was Jones-Trinidad worth the money? Roy had won two fights
(against Anthony Hanshaw and Prince Bada Ajamu) and lost three during
the preceding fifty months. Trinidad had won only twice (with two losses)
since May 2001, and his most recent victory had been in 2004 against
Ricardo Mayorga. Taken together, Roy and Tito were 4-and-5 in their last
nine outings with three "KOs by."

Thus, Jones-Trinidad was derided by some as a match-up between
fading legends. One observer likened it to the Army-Navy football game;
a once-great spectacle that no longer commands the attention of the
sports world. And to make matters worse, the New York media was giving short shrift to the fight.

The only mention of Jones-Trinidad in the *New York Times* sports section during fight week was a short article on page six of Saturday's paper.
That put Madison Square Garden's first big fight of the year on a par with
rowing, harness racing, and darts; each of which were also the subject of
one article. The fact that the Giants would be playing Green Bay in the
NFC championship game the following evening was a further blow to

the promotion. The *Times* had seventeen articles about the National Football League in the three days leading up to the fight.

King did his best to put a positive spin on things, calling Jones-Trinidad a fight for The People's Championship. "Roy Jones is Superman," the promoter told the media. "And Tito Trinidad is a one-of-a-kind icon. Little old ladies in Puerto Rico were coming up to him on the street with tears rolling down their cheeks, saying, 'Tito, come back.' Old men were pleading with him, 'Tito, represent us.'" That was followed by King advising his listeners, "People who are old and biased are trying to kill this fight, but I'm going over their heads and appealing to the masses. This fight is capturing the imagination of the people. This is a fight for me and you."

But as fight week progressed, King seemed like the Little Dutch Boy trying to keep a sea of negativity from overwhelming a fragile dike. The Jones camp was troubled by increasingly pessimistic financial reports (remember, Don and Roy were "partners"). And King was moved to declare, "The people who would destroy boxing make money seem more important than the pride and glory of the event. The pride and glory and dignity that come with competing well and winning are more important than any amount of money."

King also had to keep James Dolan happy. Thus (for one week, at least), the Garden president replaced George Bush as the primary object of the promoter's public adoration.

The final pre-fight press conference for Jones-Trinidad began when King strode to the podium at Madison Square Garden and proclaimed, "Jim Dolan is a risk taker. The greatest deeds and discoveries of all-time could not have happened without risk; so this is a time to pay tribute to Jim Dolan. I honor and pay homage to Jim Dolan."

A thirty-three-minute monologue followed before King introduced the first speaker other than himself. The proceedings evolved from there with the promoter talking about family values, pride, love, desire, Cyrano de Bergerac, Hannah Montana, loyalty, manhood, dignity, respect, charity, honor, opportunity, spirituality, the Talmud, glory, God, the Alamo, 9/11, and swimming to freedom through shark-infested waters. He also mentioned Jones-Trinidad from time to time.

The bottom line was, the bottom line didn't look good. Bob Raissman wrote in the *New York Daily News,* "King is a master salesman. He's going to have to be a magician to sell tickets for this fight."

Finally, one day before the bout, Madison Square Garden took the desperate step of adjusting ticket prices downward and issued a statement that read, "We've explored various ticket-pricing options across all price categories for this fight and sales have been brisk. We've adjusted some prices in certain locations and are thrilled that boxing fans are so excited about this upcoming event."

But the damage had been done. On fight night, the announced attendance was 12,162. However, New York State Athletic Commission records indicate that the paid attendance was only 9,962 with gross gate receipts of $4,069,236. In other words (after the cost of opening the arena, a $50,000 ticket tax, and other expenses), MSG lost close to $5,000,000 on the promotion.

Meanwhile, there was a fight to be fought on January 19th and Jones was a 3-to-1 favorite. Each fighter had celebrated a birthday earlier in the month. Roy had turned thirty-nine; Felix was thirty-five.

"A lot of people think I don't have it anymore," Jones acknowledged at the final pre-fight press conference. "I hear what they're saying."

But Trinidad had fought only once in the preceding thirty-nine months (against Winky Wright) and looked bad doing it. He's markedly slower than Roy. And the youthful exuberance that was once his trademark isn't so youthful anymore.

In the days leading up to the fight, Jones declared, "Tito is one-dimensional, and Tito has always had trouble with opponents who move and give him angles. He'll be looking to get that one big punch in. That's the only fight plan he has, but there's nothing he can do to defend himself. Trust me; he's not going to go twelve rounds with me."

Trainer Alton Merkerson (who first worked with Jones at the 1988 Olympics) concurred, adding, "Roy was very motivated during training. I saw some things in this camp that I haven't seen in three or four years. Roy put a lot of money in the bank; did all the right things. Actions speak louder than words. You'll see it in the fight as it comes up."

But two issues were cause for concern among Jones partisans.

The first issue was weight. On the surface, the 170-pound contract limit seemed to work in Roy's favor. Trinidad's best days were as a welter-weight. The only legitimate world-class fighter above 147 pounds that Tito has beaten was Fernando Vargas; and that was at 154 pounds seven years ago.

But Jones believes that his losses to Antonio Tarver and Glen Johnson were in significant part the residue of being forced to lose twenty pounds of muscle after conquering John Ruiz. He hadn't fought at 170 pounds since 1996. And when he went into training for Jones-Trinidad, he weighed 188.

"I don't like it," Roy admitted when asked about the 170-pound contract weight during a conference call to announce the match-up. "For a big fight, you have to do those things. But it's going to be very difficult."

Ultimately, Jones weighed in at 169–1/2 pounds, looking cut and fit. He was 179 on fight night. Trinidad tipped the scales at 170 pounds (one-fifth of a pound more, according to some) and appeared to be in less than top form.

But the primary concern among Jones's fans wasn't his body. It was his chin, which at times has evoked images of a trapeze artist performing high above the floor without a net. The Jones faithful remember Roy's knockout loss to Antonio Tarver and his lying unconscious on the canvas for eight minutes after being felled by Glen Johnson. They were worried by the fact that Tito can whack.

Trinidad played on that theme. "One of Roy's weaknesses," he said, "is that everyone he has boxed that punches well, he was knocked out. And I punch well."

Nor were Merkerson's words on the subject overly encouraging. "Looking at the whole picture," Roy's trainer said, "everyone has a glass jaw. Anybody who gets hit right goes. Every fighter's chin is suspect. If you fight long enough in this game, eventually you're going to go down."

On Saturday night, Jones entered his dressing room at Madison Square Garden at 9:45 P.M. He was wearing a light-blue warm-up suit. Earlier in the day, the full beard he'd grown during training camp had been trimmed.

There was a different kind of energy in the dressing room than in years past. The eager anticipation of Roy's younger days was gone. Now he's a seasoned veteran; an older man who prepares for a dangerous job that takes him down a road he has traveled many times before.

As the clock ticked, Jones rubbed extra virgin olive oil on his legs; then stood still as it was applied to his shoulders and back. Merkerson taped his hands. There was no shadow-boxing or hitting the pads. As a matter of course, Roy does nothing more strenuous than pace back and forth to warm-up for his fights.

At 10:52, the final preliminary bout (Andrew Golota versus Mike Mollo) began. Referee Arthur Mercante Jr came into the room and issued his pre-fight instructions. Jones gloved up.

"All the hard stuff is over now," Merkerson told his fighter. "It's your waltz. Have fun tonight. Watch his legs; he'll get weak quick. When you hurt him, take your time. When you hit him good up-top, go downstairs and get some more."

But Golota-Mollo wouldn't end. Roy stood almost motionless, watching the rounds unfold on a small television monitor in a corner of the room.

"We're ready to go," Merkerson said in another corner. "I haven't had a heart attack yet, but this waiting around drives me crazy. Every time Roy fights, I feel like I used to feel in the Army when I was getting my men ready to go out on patrol."

Finally, Golota-Mollo came to a close.

Jones had fought in The Theater at Madison Square Garden on three occasions but in the main arena only once (against Merqui Sosa in 1996). This was Trinidad's sixth appearance in the big room, where he has experienced some of his best moments in boxing (against Pernell Whitaker, William Joppy, and Ricardo Mayorga) and also his worst (Bernard Hopkins). The buzz this time wasn't equal to the electricity that accompanied most of Tito's past fights. In recent years, Miguel Cotto has stolen some of his thunder in the Puerto Rican community. But when he and Roy entered the ring, everyone understood; yes, they were old; and yes, they were past their prime; but they were still Roy Jones and Felix Trinidad.

It was three minutes after midnight when the bell for round one rang. Each fighter began cautiously, showing respect for the other. Jones didn't throw much in the early rounds, so Trinidad stepped things up a bit and took four of the first five stanzas, scoring largely with hooks to the body. Then Roy seemed to get his rhythm. Clearly, he was faster and stronger than Tito, whose punches were losing steam.

For those who remembered the fighters as young men on the rise with charisma and talent to burn, there was poignancy in watching them fight. Jones showed bits and pieces of greatness. But he has lost the preternatural speed and reflexes that separated him from everybody else when he was young. Once upon a time, Roy threw punches in bunches faster than anyone could count. Now it's one punch at a time and he can no longer fight "like Roy Jones" for three minutes a round.

One minute ten seconds into round seven, a sharp right to the temple dropped Trinidad for a count of eight. Thereafter, Roy stalked his foe but was more measured in his attack than he was when he was young. Meanwhile, Tito seemed to have come into battle without a Plan B. Twenty seconds before the bell ending round ten, a jab followed by a grazing right hand put him down for the second time.

Thereafter, Trinidad seemed content to simply finish the fight and collect his $15,000,000 (or whatever the amount was) without suffering further damage. This observer scored the bout 116–110 for Jones. The judges were in accord, delivering a 117–109, 116–110, 116–110 verdict in Roy's favor.

"It was like the good old days," Jones said ebulliently after the fight. "I fought like me. I lost that for a time, but the rooster is back. When I fight like this, I'm unstoppable."

Once again Roy was where he wanted to be, doing what he wanted to do. As Patrick Kehoe observed, "He may currently be without a title, but he's still Roy Jones. And that makes him president for life of his own constituency: Planet Roy."

But let's not get carried away with notions of "turning back the hands of time." No fighter whose greatness is built on a foundation of speed and reflexes is great at thirty-nine. An aging fighter can remember the past; he can't relive it. On January 19th, Jones looked good against a thirty-five-year-old middleweight who has won two fights since May 2001. The Roy Jones of six years ago, had he gone for the kill, would have knocked out the thirty-nine-year-old Roy Jones in six rounds. It would sell Roy's greatness short to say that he's as good now as he was then.

It must be hard for Jones to hear people talk about his greatness in the past tense. One wonders what goes through his mind when he watches tapes of himself in the ring when he was young and in his prime. At some point, he'll have to accept the reality that being the greatest fighter in the world is part of his past and that he isn't anymore. What does he do when his fighting days are over? Even he knows that, someday, they have to end.

But right now, Jones still needs boxing. It's who he is. It's what he does. It's the environment he lives in. It's how he defines himself. The permanent rope burns on his back from years of sparring without a shirt are a visible reminder of how deeply the sport is ingrained in his psyche. He's fighting for his self-identity. "You judge a man by how he fights back when he's down," he says.

So for the moment, let's celebrate the fact that Roy Jones prepared properly to fight Felix Trinidad and did what he had to do. In a perverse way, his diminished skills give him an opportunity to show that his most severe critics are wrong. The cynics have said that Roy lacks courage. Now that the odds aren't stacked in his favor, he can prove to the world beyond a shadow of a doubt that he has a fighting heart.

There's debate over Paulie Malignaggi's ring skills. But everyone agrees that, outside the ring, Paulie is a great "writer's fighter."

Paulie Malignaggi:
Taking Care of Business

"The truth comes out in a boxing ring," says Paulie Malignaggi. "I've seen a lot of guys who are tough on the streets come into the gym and turn their back once they get in the ring. Boxing does one of two things. It makes a coward out of you or it makes you a man."

In Malignaggi's case, boxing has made him a man. It has taken a self-described "street punk," given him self-esteem, and (through his own Herculean effort) made him one of the best junior-welterweights in the world. But on January 5th, Paulie's future was up for grabs when he defended his 140-pound IBF championship against Herman Ngoudjo in Atlantic City.

Malignaggi is a compelling personality. He's media-friendly, gracious with fans, and never says "no" to a microphone or camera. Words come out of his mouth like bursts of machine-gun fire. He wears his heart on his sleeve and craves attention. "I love big crowds," he says. "It doesn't matter whether they're cheering for me or booing. I send the ones that are booing home unhappy."

"Boxing is brain over brawn," the legendary Ray Arcel once noted. "If you can't think, you're just another bum in the park."

Malignaggi is a thinking fighter. He has won 24 of 25 pro fights and gives 100 percent every time out. "I'm never completely satisfied with what I do," he says. "I'm driven by negatives. I always expect more of myself."

The naysayers expect more too. Their primary criticism of Paulie is that he has only five knockouts in 25 fights. Adding fuel to the fire, three of those knockouts came in his first three outings, leaving Malignaggi with a .091 knockout average in his last 22 bouts.

"I'm a world champion," Paulie says in response. "My punches hurt. You never hear a fighter say 'ow' when he gets hit, but all punches hurt. I hit hard enough that guys don't walk through me. Common sense should tell you that."

In a way, Malignaggi's lack of knockout power makes his ring accomplishments all the more impressive. Often, when he goes into battle, his opponent is armed with a machete, while Paulie is carrying a pocket-knife. But as Patrick Kehoe observes, "Fans crave the big blow, the definitive ending marking the clearest statement of dominance. Champions knock guys out, turn contenders into defenseless heaps." And Paulie fights jab-by-jab, one round at a time.

The sole blemish on Malignaggi's record is a loss by decision to Miguel Cotto at Madison Square Garden on June 10, 2006. "Going into the Cotto fight," Paulie says, "I was prepared to get hit and I knew his fans would go crazy if he hurt me. But even though I was psychologically prepared, it was a very lonely feeling in the ring that night. My first mistake was I thought the ring was too small to move around the way I normally do, so I tried to smother him. That meant I was fighting inside and got cut [from a head butt] in the first round. Then I took the fight to him so I'd be ahead on the judges' scorecards if they stopped the fight because of the cut, which meant I was fighting his fight even more and got knocked down in the second round. It was a chain reaction where one bad thing led to another."

"I can't complain about the decision," Paulie continues. "Cotto won. A different move here, a break there, maybe it would have been different. I won four rounds; five on one judge's scorecard. I showed I can get off the canvas, go twelve rounds, and fight my way back into a fight when I'm hurt. But you judge a fighter based on results, and I lost. I'd spent my entire life waiting for that moment and I came up short. It was a very disappointing night for me. The loss to Cotto hurt me more than winning the title last year lifted me up. I only hope I have a chance to win in an event of that magnitude again."

Some fighters quit when they're getting beaten up. Others just try to survive. It wasn't lost on the boxing public that, against Cotto, no matter how badly Paulie was hurt, he kept trying to win.

"After the fight," Malignaggi says, "people were saying, 'Wow; Paulie has lots of courage. Paulie is better than we thought.' And I knew I didn't fight as well as I could have. It's something I'll always be obsessed with. I know I can beat Cotto. I might come out of it with more broken bones in my face, but I can beat him. Whatever else happens to me in boxing, no matter how many titles I win; if I retire without fighting Cotto again, there will always be an empty spot inside me."

Not many fighters come back from the kind of beating that Malignaggi absorbed against Cotto and are as good as they were before. "I was in the hospital with a fractured orbital bone," Paulie remembers. "I had surgery on my face. People watch a fight and, when it's over, they turn off the TV and go to bed. The next day, they're out doing whatever they want to do. My whole life changed after that fight. I spent the whole summer recuperating."

But Malignaggi came back. On February 17, 2007, he won a ten-round decision over Edner Cherry at the Hammerstein Ballroom in New York. Four months later, he got a second title opportunity and won every round against Lovemore N'dou to capture the IBF welterweight crown. That's when he learned that sometimes, even for a champion, the fight to get in the ring can be as hard as the fight in it.

Hand surgery had sidelined Paulie for all but one fight in 2005. The damage he suffered against Cotto kept him out of action for the second half of 2006. After beating N'dou, he hoped to make up for lost time. But the television dates weren't there.

"My whole career," Malignaggi says, "I'd been told, 'You have it all; the looks, the mouth, the personality, the style. Once you win a championship, you'll be big.' So I won a championship and it still didn't happen for me. Other countries support their fighters. If I was fighting in Sicily [where Paulie's parents were born], everyone in the country would be behind me. Joe Calzaghe is a hero in Wales. He's a good fighter; but if I made a title defense against someone like Will McIntyre or Tocker Pudwell, I'd be boiled alive. Ricky Hatton is a hero in England. He's a good fighter too; but he fought a bunch of handpicked opponents like Joe Hutchinson and Michael Stewart."

"I was in Times Square and saw a big billboard for *Mayweather-Hatton 24/7*," Paulie continues. "I want that to be me. I don't want to not love boxing because of the problems I have getting fights, but it's already happening a little bit. I make all these sacrifices; I'm good at what I do; I'm willing to go in tough. And I couldn't get a TV date after I won the title."

Finally, Showtime stepped up to the plate, offering promoter Lou

DiBella a $300,000 license fee for Malignaggi's mandatory title defense against Herman Ngoudjo.

Ngoudjo was a quality opponent. Born in Cameroon and now a Canadian citizen, he had 16 victories in 17 fights. His only loss was a split-decision verdict against Jose Luis Castillo in January 2006.

There was the usual pre-fight trash-talking during the build-up to Malignaggi-Ngoudjo. "I'm the best you ever fought, you stupid boxer," Paulie told Ngoudjo during a pre-fight media conference call. "You're not even close to the best I've fought. I've been in the ring with sparring partners better than you. I'm going to use your head as a pinball."

But on a more realistic note, Malignaggi acknowledged, "Ngoudjo is a hard worker and he does what he does well. I know the hunger that he has inside him. I remember what it was like when I fought for the title."

On fight night, Atlantic City was overrun by pre-teen girls in town for a concert by fifteen-year-old Miley Cyrus (a/k/a Hannah Montana). It was a telling commentary on the strength of boxing versus kiddie culture in today's economy that Cyrus had sold out the 13,000-seat Boardwalk Hall, while Paulie would be fighting in a room at Bally's that seated 1,300.

"It takes an elite fighter to test me and a great fighter to beat me," Malignaggi said shortly before the fight. "I'm a better fighter than Herman Ngoudjo. It's as simple as that."

Paulie's "dressing room" was part of a larger meeting room adjacent to the ballroom where the fight would be held. Cordoned off by a black curtain, it was eight feet wide and twenty-eight feet long. The nearest running water was in a public restroom across a nearby corridor.

Paulie entered the ring dressed in silver and black with twelve tassels on each shoe. The crowd was solidly behind him.

Most of Malignaggi's fights have a similar look. He establishes control early with his jab and reduces matters to what looks like an intense sparring session. Against Ngoudjo, Paulie won the first three rounds with his footwork, speed, and jab. The challenger moved steadily forward, trying without success to set Malignaggi up for a big right hand. He also tried to rough the champion up on the inside, but it's hard to rough up mercury that's flowing.

Then Paulie stopped using his jab effectively, which allowed Ngoudjo to close the distance between them. Thirty seconds into round four, a right to the body caught the champion off balance and put him down. Referee Allen Huggins ruled it a slip. But more significantly, Paulie suffered a cut on his left eyelid in the same round and the challenger intensified the process of tracking him down.

Rounds five and six were more of the same, with Ngoudjo landing solidly and dictating the flow of the flight. He started round seven by scoring with two big right hands and, at the forty-second mark, landed a third right that buzzed Paulie and had him holding on. A barrage of punches followed.

Malignaggi was hurt. His only defense was his heart. "I knew what was going on but it kept happening," he said afterward. "I just told myself, 'You know you're getting hit, so it could be worse. Get through it.'" He survived but was in trouble.

Then, in round eight, Paulie returned to his jab and some of the intensity went out of the challenger's attack. For the rest of the fight, Ngoudjo didn't press the action as much as he had before. Maybe he was tired. Maybe getting hit in the face again and again by Paulie's jab took its toll. Either way, Ngoudjo let Malignaggi back into the fight.

This observer scored the bout a draw. Most of the ringside media had it even or 115–113 one way or the other. The judges were more generous to Paulie, ruling in his favor by a 117–111, 116–113, 115–113 margin.

Late that night, Malignaggi sat in his hotel room at Bally's surrounded by a coterie of family and friends. The skin around his left eye was discolored and swollen. The cut on his eyelid had been glued shut.

Paulie is his own worst critic. "I had a good training camp," he said, reflecting back on the battle just won. "I was in shape, but I couldn't get up for Ngoudjo. I never got that hard mental edge, which is my own fault." He waved his arms in exasperation. "Let's face it; I fought like a fucking retard tonight. I looked like shit."

"You're still the champ," he was told.

"Yeah; but I'm not where I want to be. When I was twenty years old, I thought I was going be the next Oscar De La Hoya. I haven't thought that for a while now; but I did think that, once I won a championship, my name would be out there more than it is. This is the way I make my living. I don't want to be one of those guys who, after his career is over, people look back and say, 'He was better than we thought. Too bad he didn't make any money.' Boxing is all I have, and I'm not set financially yet. I wish I was still 21, but I'm not. I'm 27, and time runs out. I have to take advantage of being champion now."

"My top priorities used to be fame and my legacy," Paulie continued. "Now I'm more concerned with being financially secure when I stop fighting. My hand will never be the way it should be. I'm always just one punch away from something bad happening to my hand that could end everything for me. There's permanent nerve damage in my face from the Cotto fight that will be with me my entire life; and who knows what will happen next. I just hope, when this is over, that I'm not messed up and broke."

Then Paulie's face brightened a bit. "There's talk that Ricky Hatton wants to fight me," he said. "That would be another chance to become a superstar and prove that I'm best junior-welterweight in the world. Beating Hatton might even get me a rematch against Cotto. I still believe it's in me to be a superstar. I have my dreams; and no one but me knows how much I want them to come true."

So let's appreciate Paulie Malignaggi for what he is: a talented fighter who's always in shape, works hard to promote his fights, comes to win, does the best he can with what he has, and refuses to quit. If that's not faithful to the best traditions of boxing, I don't know what is.

As 2008 began, Kelly Pavlik was seeking inclusion on the short list of boxing superstars.

Pavlik–Taylor II: Courage under Fire

The crowning achievement for one fighter is often the low point for another.

In July 2005, when Jermain Taylor dethroned Bernard Hopkins, it was his greatest triumph. But for the Executioner, it was the most bitter defeat in an illustrious ring career. Two years later, boxing's wheel of fortune turned again. Kelly Pavlik seized the middleweight title by knocking out Taylor in seven rounds. This time, it was Jermain whose world was turned upside down while Pavlik enjoyed the celebration.

Pavlik is from Youngstown, Ohio; a city in the heart of the nation's rust-belt that has fallen upon hard economic times. After the fight, Youngstown and the surrounding region embraced its new hero with a fervor that America reserves for reigning sports champions.

Kelly is a hometown boy who made good. Like Youngstown, he'd been on the canvas. But he got up and won in dramatic fashion. "My style is to come out swinging and keep swinging," he says. "The thing I like most about boxing is, when the bell rings, it's straight up; me and you."

When Pavlik returned from Atlantic City after his victory over Taylor, his SUV was met at the Ohio border by a caravan of police cars and fire trucks that escorted him home. Thereafter, the perks kept coming.

Pavlik threw out the ceremonial first pitch before Game 4 of the American League Championship series between the Cleveland Indians and Boston Red Sox ("It was a good pitch; 45 miles an hour, I think"); sat beside the legendary Jim Brown after presiding over the coin toss before a Browns-Dolphins match-up ("a real thrill"); and addressed the Ohio State Buckeyes before the Ohio State–Michigan football game; ("the greatest sports event in America").

"These are teams I've rooted for my whole life," Kelly says. "So it was awesome." He was also the subject of a Congressional resolution that praised him for his commitment and continuing loyalty to the community.

But after a while, it got a bit tiring. "I'm a simple guy," Pavlik acknowledges. "I don't like flash and the limelight too much. I like to do things around the house and spend time with my daughter, and there's been a lot of times lately when I haven't had any 'me' time. People just show up at my house with ten gloves for me to sign. That's the part I don't like."

And there were other pressures. "In Youngstown," Pavlik notes, "when you're on top, you're on top. But when you let them down, you're the worst person in town. It's funny how that works. You don't want to become the bad guy in the city for failing at something. But at the same time, it's pretty neat to be that guy, to be in that situation. You have to take in what you like and enjoy all the great things from it. And the things you don't like, you've got to just block out. The main thing is, I won the world title. That's something nobody can ever take from me."

There was a blip on the radar screen in early November, when Pavlik was reported to have put his hands through a glass window in the kitchen while doing repair work. The early word was that more than a hundred stitches had been needed to close the wounds, but that number was later downgraded to fourteen. Why had Kelly been fixing the window instead of having a repairman do it?

"That's what I do," he explained. "It's my house."

Trainer Jack Loew also enjoyed the fruits of victory. The Cleveland Cavaliers asked him to give an inspirational talk to their office staff. More fighters (amateur and pro) sought him out. "I'm a lot more popular in Youngstown now than I was before," Loew observed. "And I'm getting to play at some of the finer golf courses around town."

Jermain Taylor was familiar with the drill. Two years earlier, he'd enjoyed similar adoration after lifting the crown from Bernard Hopkins. "Anywhere I go," Jermain said at the time, "restaurants, clubs, wherever; they don't charge me. Of course, when I was broke and needed it, no one gave me anything for free."

Now Taylor had an agenda that was far more pressing than free meals. "I believe in, you fight the guy that beat you," he said. "It's like, you beat me fair and square. Let's see if you can do it again."

The contracts for Taylor-Pavlik I had included a rematch clause. But because Jermain had encountered difficulty making weight for earlier fights, he'd insisted that the rematch (if there was one) be contested at 166 pounds. That meant Pavlik-Taylor II wouldn't be for the middleweight championship. But Taylor didn't care about getting the belts back. "It's all about revenge now," he said. "Kelly took something that I think is mine. When I win, I'll be walking out of there with everything he took from me. I'll be walking out with my pride."

"Win or lose, I'll still have my title when this is over," Pavlik countered. "But that's not what this is about. This is about personal pride, me and Jermain, and keeping the '0' on my record."

The fight was scheduled for February 16, 2008, at the MGM Grand in Las Vegas. That was where Taylor had beaten Bernard Hopkins to annex the middleweight crown. Throughout fight week, Kelly wore the black-red-and-white colors of Youngstown State University and mingled freely with fans. Two days before the bout, he was eating in the Studio Café (an MGM Grand coffee shop), posing for photos and signing autographs for well-wishers who came by.

Bob Arum (Pavlik's promoter) played the Youngstown angle to the hilt. Ray Mancini and Harry Arroyo (two former champions from Youngstown) were brought in to bolster the promotion. At the final pre-fight press conference, Arum proclaimed, "We're all from Youngstown." One half-expected the promoter (who'd served in the Justice Department during the Kennedy Administration) to follow with the proclamation, "Ich bin ein Youngstowner."

Taylor partisans pointed to Pavlik's flaws as the first building block in their theory that Jermain would win the rematch. "Kelly is tough," they acknowledged. "Kelly has lots of heart and throws lots of punches. If you stand in front of him, he'll beat you down. But he's less effective if you move on him and keep him turning so he can't plant his feet and punch. And Kelly is a good long-range fighter but, on the inside, his punches lack leverage. Inside, an opponent can use Kelly's long arms against him and smother his punches."

Taylor's backers also noted that Jermain had come very close to winning the first fight. Midway through round two of that encounter, he'd timed a right hand over a sloppy Pavlik jab and landed solidly. "I was hurt," Kelly acknowledged afterward. "I don't care how good your chin is. If you get hit hard behind the ear where he hit me, your equilibrium will go."

Once he was hit, Pavlik staggered backward and Taylor followed with a fifteen-punch barrage that put him down. Kelly rose at the count of two, but was on shaky legs with eighty-eight seconds left in the round. Another right hand sent him reeling backward. A lot of referees would have stopped the fight at that juncture.

Ultimately, Pavlik rallied to win. But five rounds later, when he scored his knockout, Jermain was ahead 59–54, 58–55, 58–55 on the judges' scorecards.

That led to point three in the case for Taylor. Boxing is the most demanding of all sports. A fighter who wants to be great but doesn't work hard is daydreaming, that's all. But prior to Taylor-Pavlik I, Jermain had sloughed off. Instead of doing roadwork, he'd run on a treadmill in his room. He hadn't sparred enough or otherwise paid his dues in the gym.

"I got too comfortable," Taylor admitted after the loss. "I didn't do what I was supposed to do in training camp. I lost what it took to become world champion. I took it for granted. Somewhere around the sixth or seventh round, I started getting real tired. Then I started going into survival mode, backing up to the ropes, and Kelly capitalized on it.

"I think about it all the time," Jermain continued. "Boxing is hard but it's fair. What comes into my head now is how I could have trained harder. But all the 'should haves' and 'could haves' in the world aren't going to change anything. It took me getting my butt kicked to get me back on track. This time in training camp, I got back to the way it used to be; getting up in the morning, running, working hard. I'm in tip-top shape now. Kelly knows what happened in the second round last time and that the fight should have been over. His ass was beaten and he knows it. I give him credit. He got up and did what he had to do to win. But this time, when I get him in trouble, I'll finish him off."

But the case for a Pavlik victory was just as compelling, if not stronger. Kelly is big, strong, and relentless. He keeps coming and his punches take a toll. He wears opponents down with hard thudding blows. "It's a small ring to begin with," Ray Mancini observes. "And when you've got a 6-foot-2 guy like Kelly coming at you, it gets smaller real quick."

Taylor was thought to have permanent soft-tissue damage beneath his left eye that could cause him difficulty during the fight. And Pavlik was free of a problem that had hindered him during their previous encounter. "Last time, Kelly's nose was all banged up from sparring and he had a sinus infection," Mike Pavlik (Kelly's father) confided. "There was no sense in talking about it afterward, but he could hardly breathe out of his nose. That's not a problem now."

Nor could Taylor count on getting Pavlik in trouble again in the early rounds.

"I won't sell Jermain short," Kelly promised. "He had it in him to beat Bernard Hopkins twice. But there were a lot of things I did wrong last time that I've worked to fix. Last fight, I got lazy and dropped my left hand, and Jermain took advantage of it. That won't happen again. If I keep my left hand high and don't lean in with my head, I should be able to avoid getting hit behind the ear. Jermain is expecting the second round to happen again, but he's wrong."

As for Taylor's conditioning, Pavlik observed, "Before the last fight, all we heard was, 'Jermain is eating, drinking, and sleeping boxing. He's more focused than he's ever been.' Emanuel Steward told us that he'd never had a fighter who was in better shape than Jermain. And now they're telling us something completely different. I know what kind of shape I'll be in on Saturday night. I never want to go back to the dressing room after a fight and say, 'If I had trained a little more when I was tired or pushed a little harder when it got tough during the fight, I would have won instead of lost.' If I do my job right, Jermain's shape won't matter."

The contract weight of 166 pounds also seemed to favor Pavlik. Prior to recent fights, Kelly had depleted himself in order to make weight. Most likely, it had been harder for him to make 160 pounds last September than it had been for Jermain.

"I think the Taylor people are crazy, but that's fine with us," Jack Loew said of the contract weight. "Kelly can get down to 163 with no problem, but the last three pounds are murder. We're all but chopping off body parts. This is the first time in four years that Kelly won't have to go into the sauna and run on a treadmill right before the weigh-in. 166 pounds is great for us."

In the days leading up to the fight, Pavlik looked visibly stronger than he had before Taylor-Pavlik I. His cheeks were less sunken and there was more color in his face. "It's hard for me to make 160," he acknowledged. "With the added weight, I was able to train harder and refuel my body. My energy level is sky high. I won't be drained. There will be more snap on my punches because I'll have fresh legs. I love it."

And there was one more factor at work. When Taylor turned pro, his management team hired Pat Burns to train him. Over the next five years, Burns did his job, which was getting Jermain ready to do his. Taylor won all twenty-five of his fights and defeated Bernard Hopkins twice to become the undisputed middleweight champion of the world. But Pat was at odds with Ozell Nelson (the "surrogate father" in Jermain's life, who had taught him to box as an amateur). In January 2006, Burns was forced out and replaced by Emanuel Steward.

Steward and Taylor were not a good fit. Emanuel lamented "a series of bad opponents, style-wise, that made it very difficult to teach Jermain and develop him as a fighter." Whatever the cause, Jermain's ring skills appeared to deteriorate in successive fights against Winky Wright, Kassim Ouma, and Cory Spinks. Then Pavlik knocked him out.

On October 30, 2007 (a month after his loss to Pavlik), Taylor telephoned Burns and the two men talked for the first time since Pat had been unceremoniously dismissed eighteen months earlier.

"Coach, I owe you an apology," Jermain said. "I made a mistake; I was wrong. I listened to people I shouldn't have listened to. I want to go back to the way things were between us."

"I'll work your ass off," Burns told him.

"That's not a problem. I understand now why you made me train so hard. That's what got me through against Hopkins. After the second round against Pavlik, I had nothing left. And the strategy they gave me wasn't as good as yours."

Burns told Taylor to think about it for a week to make certain that Jermain would be fully committed to their reunion. There was also the matter of Ozell Nelson, who'd been a key figure in forcing Pat out.

"I'll talk to him," Jermain said. "Either Ozell gets with the plan or he goes."

On November 10th, Jermain called Burns a second time. "Coach; I told Ozell that I want you back. He fought it for a while, but it's final. I'm going away for a few days, and then we can start."

Burns began planning to go to Little Rock to meet with Taylor and

Nelson. In his view, Jermain needed a mini-camp to work on core conditioning. Then regular training could begin.

It wasn't to be. Taylor and Burns never spoke again. Instead, on November 20th, Jermain told a handful of reporters in Little Rock that, henceforth, Nelson would train him.

"I'm going back to what made me a champion," Taylor said. "This fight [the Pavlik rematch] will bring everything out. I know Coach [Ozell Nelson] and he knows me. I feel good about it."

"Me and Jermain made the decision," Nelson added. "I just felt like it's time for me to take over. I'm the one who built Jermain. I'm the one who built the motor."

Team Pavlik was more amused than anything else by the switch. Even if Jermain were more focused in the upcoming training camp than before, there was an issue as to whether Nelson could properly direct that focus.

"Ozell is the guy who taught Jermain all the bad habits, and now he's back," Jack Loew said. "This would have been a much tougher fight for Kelly if Jermain had brought Pat Burns back."

There was an illogic to it all. Taylor was attributing the loss to Pavlik to his not having being in shape. But if he really believed that, he would have retained Steward and simply gotten in better condition the second time around. The rationale for releasing Burns that was fed to Jermain in early 2006 had been that Pat was an "amateur." But Nelson had considerably less experience than Burns in the professional ranks. And Jermain was now admitting that he'd lied to himself about his conditioning prior to the first Pavlik fight. But he'd had plenty of enablers, and some of them were still around.

In sum, the talk about Taylor going back to Nelson to recapture his past success was questionable at best. Instead of going back to the way things were when Jermain was an unpolished amateur, why not go back to the way things were when he beat Bernard Hopkins twice? There was a lot of tap-dancing around the essential truth that Pat Burns should have been there.

Champions trust in their own ring superiority as an article of faith. But success as a boxer isn't just about what a fighter does in the ring on fight night. It's about what he does and all the decisions he makes before he gets there. Under Burns's tutelage, even in the days leading up to the first Hopkins fight, Jermain had exuded an aura of quiet confidence. By contrast, at the final pre-fight press conference for Pavlik-Taylor II, he seemed plagued by self-doubt. He looked anxious and fidgeted a lot. The feeling in the Pavlik camp was that Taylor was lying to himself and didn't believe the lies.

It's scary to get in a boxing ring and fight. A fighter has to be able to absorb punishment and fire back with damage-causing blows of his own. "Going into a fight, you know you're going to get hit," Pavlik said. "I don't know how Jermain will react to the knockout. I don't know if mentally he's going to be hesitant. I don't know neurologically how he'll respond. Some guys get knocked out, come back, and are fine. Some guys get knocked out and are never the same again. Either way, I'm winning on Saturday night. Once the bell rings, it will be just a matter of time before Jermain makes that one big mistake. Even if he changes things, one good crack and he'll go back to old habits."

"I want revenge," Taylor said in response. "Kelly can be hit and Kelly can be hurt. It's gonna be a fight. I know that, and Kelly knows that too."

But there was a difference. Taylor thought he could close the show. Pavlik knew he could.

Two days before the fight, Kelly was asked if he wanted to get the fight started or get it over with. "I just want to get it started," he said. "I'm tired of the talking; I'm tired of thinking about it. I want to get in the ring and do my job."

There was a school of thought that Jermain just wanted to get the fight over with.

Pavlik arrived at the MGM Grand Garden Arena on Saturday night at 5:50 P.M. He was wearing the same Youngstown State windbreaker that he'd worn for much of the week. Now it was matched with grey-red-and-white Ohio State warm-up pants.

Larry Merchant came into the dressing room for a brief interview that would air during HBO's pay-per-view telecast. Kelly's comments were short and to the point: "The fact that Jermain wants to fight me again shows that he's a champion at heart. But so am I."

When the interview was over, HBO production coordinator Tami Cotel thanked Pavlik for his time.

"No problem. That's what I'm here for."

When a fighter gets to the championship level, his dressing room reflects his preferences. Pavlik opts for low-key and quiet. Sitting on a chair, he took out his Blackberry and began playing a video game called *BrickBreaker.*

The first televised fight of the evening began. On a nearby television monitor, Ronald Hearns could be seen beating up on an overmatched opponent named Juan Astorga, who fights out of Topeka, Kansas. As the punches landed, Mike Pavlik winced and turned to Cameron Dunkin (Kelly's manager).

"I wish we were back in Kansas, Toto."

"There's certain guys who shouldn't fight," Dunkin responded. "Astorga is so slow. I feel sorry for him."

Kelly looked up from his Blackberry and joined the conversation. "I used to feel sorry for Wile E. Coyote," he said. "Just once, I wanted to see him get his hands around that Road Runner's neck."

That led to reminiscences between father and son about cartoons that Kelly had liked in childhood. "I watched *Bugs Bunny* and *Looney Toons* all the time," Kelly recalled. "*Tom and Jerry* is still my favorite." Then he went back to playing *BrickBreaker.*

Mike and Jack Loew began talking about the time that Jack accidentally let his cat crawl into the clothes-dryer before an eight-minute cycle. The cat survived but wasn't happy about it. John Loew (Jack's son) and Michael Cox (a Youngstown cop who's Kelly's friend and third man in the corner) were engaged in quiet conversation.

At 6:50, referee Tony Weeks came in. Kelly put his Blackberry down long enough to receive the ritual pre-fight instructions. After Weeks left, Mike Pavlik rubbed his hands together. "It doesn't change," he said. "We could be fighting Penelope tonight and I'd be nervous."

Jack Loew began taping Kelly's hands. When the job was done, Kelly sat down on the floor and began doing stretching exercises. "If I tried to stretch like that, they'd have to call 911 twice," Mike noted.

Kelly finished stretching, put on his black sequined trunks, and gloved up.

On the television monitor, Christian Mijares emerged with a twelve-round decision over Jose Navarro. Fernando Montiel versus Martin Castillo began. Castillo had nothing. Mike Pavlik stared at the monitor. "This is such a brutal sport," he said.

Kelly and Jack Loew began working the pads.

Montiel stopped Castillo in four.

The padwork increased in intensity. "You're gonna catch him," Loew told his fighter. "It doesn't matter what he does. Back him up. Double jabs. Sooner or later, you'll catch him."

Cutman Miguel Diaz (who had worked Castillo's corner and would do the same for Kelly) entered and did a quick change into a Pavlik corner jacket. "Poor Castillo," Diaz said. "He had nothing tonight."

Loew rubbed Vaseline on Kelly's chest and arms.

Mike Pavlek put a small green amulet around his son's neck. "Someone gave it to Kelly before the last fight and told him the Pope had blessed it," Mike explained. "He won last time, so why not?"

Then it was time for battle.

There were hugs all around.

Mike turned to Jack Loew. "Remember to take that green thing off before the fight," he said.

The crowd was heavily pro-Pavlik. The odds were 8-to-5 in Kelly's favor, but Jermain was a live underdog. He was also in better shape and fought a more measured fight than in their previous encounter.

In the early going, Taylor looked to establish his jab and kept his right hand in reserve for defensive purposes. He also kept Pavlik turning, which made it hard for Kelly to set his feet and punch. Clearly, Jermain was the faster of the two fighters. But Pavlik appeared stronger and kept coming forward.

That was the story of the fight. There were some good exchanges. Taylor began landing right hands and Pavlik never got his double-jab working ("Jermain was countering off it quicker than last time," Kelly said afterward). Taylor also managed to stay off the ropes for most of the night, which was essential to his strategy. But Pavlik was relentless in his assault, testing Taylor's resolve and throwing punches for three minutes of every round.

In round nine, Kelly began to pour it on, but Jermain didn't submit. Not then; and not in round eleven when a brutal body shot caused him to gasp and hold on to survive. Taylor fought bravely and he fought well, but it wasn't enough.

It was a difficult fight to score despite the fact that Pavlik outlanded Taylor by a 267-to-178 margin. All three judges (and most of the media) gave rounds one, eleven, and twelve to Kelly. The other rounds were up for grabs. The judges had it 117–111, 116–112, 115–113 for Pavlik, reflecting the conventional belief that, in Nevada if you go forward, you win the fight. The consensus at ringside was that, of the three scores, 115–113 was closest to the mark.

"I'm pleased with my performance," Kelly said afterward. "This is the first time that I've gone twelve rounds [his previous longest effort had been nine rounds against Fulgencio Zuniga]. And this wasn't twelve rounds with just anybody. This was twelve rounds against Jermain Taylor."

As for what comes next; Taylor still has a future in boxing. There's ample precedent for a champion losing two fights in a row to the same opponent and coming back strong afterward. Think Bernard Hopkins (who lost twice to Jermain) and Shane Mosley (bested on consecutive occasions by both Vernon Forrest and Winky Wright).

But Jermain has to get his priorities in order; particularly when it comes to choosing a trainer. He has now lost two fights that he could have won. Did he lose with honor? Absolutely. Still, one is reminded of Johnny Ray (Billy Conn's manager), who said of his fighter after the first Louis-Conn encounter, "He was swell in defeat, but we'd rather have won."

Meanwhile, Pavlik is stronger at 168 pounds than he is at 160. But he believes he has unfinished business in the middleweight division. "It took a long time to get the belts," he says. "I don't want to give them up just yet."

Kelly's next fight is tentatively scheduled for June 7th. Lucrative potential match-ups against Arthur Abraham, Bernard Hopkins, and Joe Calzaghe lie ahead. It's also possible that Bob Arum will broker Pavlik's way onto broadcast television in an effort to increase his marketability. The on-site attendance (9,706) and pay-per-view numbers (roughly 225,000 buys) for Pavlik-Taylor II were disappointing. But Kelly is expected to become more marketable as time goes by.

"This will only last for so long, so I've got to make the most of it," Pavlik says, putting matters in perspective. "I want to make enough money to support myself and my family so we're covered whatever happens in the future. And I have other goals. I watch television sometimes and see great fighters that are legends from the past. That's something else I want to reach. It's a long road and I've got a lot more to accomplish. But so far, so good."

There are thousands of young fighters who are full of hope. Kevin Burnett is one of them.

Kevin Burnett: Prospect or Project?

Heavyweights are a different breed of fighter.

There's something about a promising young heavyweight that makes cynical boxing aficionados swoon and normally cautious investors open their wallets. As legendary matchmaker Teddy Brenner once observed, "There's boxing and there's heavyweight boxing."

Kevin Burnett, age 25, is one of seven children from a single-parent family in Georgia. He's handsome and likeable with a resonant baritone voice. He's also a professional fighter, who stands 6-feet-6-inches tall and weighs 262 pounds. Earlier this month, Burnett took another step on his journey into the unknown when he faced off against Ryan Thompson in a six-round walk-out bout after Paulie Malignaggi's successful title defense against Herman Ngoudjo in Atlantic City.

Burnett has been boxing professionally for three years and has a 10-1-1 record with six knockouts. His adviser is Craig Hamilton, who guided Michael Grant from a second-round stoppage of Stanley Wright in 1995 through a 2003 knockout loss at the hands of Dominick Guinn. During that time, Grant earned $8,000,000 in purses, highlighted by a $3,500,000 payday for fighting Lennox Lewis at Madison Square Garden. Burnett receives a monthly stipend, and all of his training expenses are paid by investors who Hamilton has brought together.

Kevin's first few years as a pro have been rocky (and that doesn't mean "Marciano"). As an amateur, he'd dislocated his right shoulder and suffered ligament damage in a fight. After two pro bouts, he underwent surgery. "I went home to recover afterward," he remembers. "I was worried about whether I'd be able to fight again and my mom fed me a lot. I was miserable, very unhappy."

By Thanksgiving Day 2005, Burnett's weight had ballooned to 338 pounds. Thereafter, he began the process of getting in shape. But in his first fight back, weighing 290 pounds, he was held to a draw by Anthony

Ottah. Then, after a victory over a novice fighter named Clifton Adams, he was knocked out by Willie Walker.

"The fight that was a draw was the toughest one I've been in," Burnett says. "I had real conditioning issues back then. I lost the first two rounds and didn't have much left. But part of being a fighter is having nothing left and finding something more to give. As for the knockout, that loss made me a better fighter. It taught me the way nothing else could have that, if I'm not going to do everything right, I shouldn't be in boxing. It made me mentally stronger. I'd love to fight both of those guys again."

But the investors were beginning to question their investment. And in the hope of turning things around, Hamilton turned to Pat Burns (the man who trained Jermain Taylor from his first pro bout through two victories over Bernard Hopkins). Burns took over the job of training Burnett and supervising his conditioning last summer.

"I asked around before I took the job," Pat recalls. "A lot of people were so-so on Kevin. Big guy, limited skills; I heard that a lot. When I first met him, he was weaker than he should have been. He had very little upper-body strength and he wasn't throwing his jab properly. But right away, I was impressed with his speed and footwork. And he seemed like a young man who was willing to work hard and eager to learn."

During the past six months, Burnett has undergone a physical transformation. His weight is down and his strength is growing; particularly in his right shoulder. "When Pat got me," Kevin says, "I couldn't do a right-handed push-up; not one. Now I can do twenty of them. And losing weight hasn't just made me a better fighter. I'm happier; I'm healthier; and I feel better about myself."

"In some ways, a coach is like a father," Kevin continues. "Growing up, I never had a father. My father came around now and then, but he was never there for me when I needed him. I had to learn a lot of things from other people that I should have learned from him. My mom was my mother and father. But Pat treats me like a father. When I go on the road, it's, 'Do you have your Triple-A card with you? Call me when you get there.' If I'm down about something, he sees it and asks what's on my mind. He gets on me sometimes, especially in the gym, but I know he cares."

"Pat doesn't just tell you; he teaches you," Kevin says, turning to boxing. "Of all the trainers I've had, he's the best teacher for me. I'm learning skills and I'm more relaxed now than I was before. I've learned to be patient in the ring. I take my time now and pick a guy apart. In my mind, I've always wanted to get in there and fight. But Pat has taught me the value of defense. He doesn't like for me to get hit at all."

"No one learns to fight overnight," Burns says of his charge. "No matter how much instinct and natural talent a fighter has, he has to be taught. But Kevin is a good student. He's very consistent and reliable. Each day when I come to the gym, Kevin has already done his thirty minutes of jumping rope so we can start right in. His best weapon is his jab. His jab hurts people. There's real pop at the end of it. Kevin's jab snaps heads back and it cuts. That's a good foundation to build on."

"And I have to say," Burns adds, "Kevin is fortunate to have Craig Hamilton and some money people behind him. That means his bills are paid and he can concentrate on boxing. A lot of fighters work eight hours a day to pay their bills before they even get to the gym."

Burnett's first two fights under Burns's tutelage were a first-round knockout of Steve Lewallen in August 2007 and unanimous six-round decision over Willie Perryman a month later. The match-up against Ryan Thompson on the undercard of Malignaggi-Ngoudjo was an opportunity for Kevin to be seen by the media and audition for future appearances on television.

Thompson is thirty-seven years old. He started boxing professionally in March 2007 and had compiled a record of 4-and-2 with four knockouts. The day before the fight, he weighed in at 263 pounds with a lot of flesh sagging around his middle. Burns thought that the opponent would be dangerous early, but all would be well if Kevin did what he was supposed to do and broke Thompson down with his jab.

Burns and Hamilton had been told that Kevin's bout would be the first of the evening and that he should be ready to fight at 6:30 sharp. They arrived at the ballroom in Bally's (where the fight would be held) at 5:00 P.M. and settled into one of a dozen small cubicles separated by black curtains that had been erected in a conference room adjacent to the ring area. Glen Johnson (who defeated both Roy Jones and Antonio Tarver in 2004) and Yoriokis Gamboa (an Olympic gold-medalist from Cuba) had been assigned cubicles on either side. Thompson was in a cubicle directly across the aisle.

Minutes after Burnett arrived, Joe Quiambao (the matchmaker for promoter Lou DiBella) came in and told Burns that the opening bout had been changed to Lovemore N'dou versus Rafael Ortiz. Burnett-Thompson was now a swing bout, which meant that it would be used to plug a gap during a yet-to-be-determined part of the card.

Burns is a stickler for detail and, on fight night, meticulously calibrates his fighter's routine. "Things like this used to be stressful for me," he acknowledged once Quiambao was gone. "But you can only control what you can control, so I've learned to take things like this in stride. This is part of boxing unless you're in the main event."

Kevin's hands were taped by 6:15. He and Burns chatted in relaxed fashion. Then, with the night open-ended, they went into the ballroom, took seats in the back row, and watched as N'Dou-Ortiz unfolded. "This could be a long night," the trainer said. "I can't make Kevin sit in a ten-foot-square cubicle for six hours."

N'dou-Ortiz went into the seventh round, when Lovemore ended matters with a body shot. Next, Glen Johnson stopped a blown-up Hugo Pineda in eight. That was followed by Chazz Witherspoon (a possible ShoBox opponent for Kevin) against Kendrick Releford. As the fight progressed, Burns and Burnett discussed what each boxer was doing right and wrong and how Kevin might exploit it should they meet. Witherspoon won a unanimous decision but didn't put fear in Burns's heart with his performance.

Now there was only time for a four-rounder before Malignaggi-Ngoudjo. Burnett-Thompson was slated for six. That meant Nicky DeMarco against Alberto Amaro got the call. After that, the ring was cleared for the main event.

As Malignaggi and Ngoudjo fought, Burns and Burnett retreated to the dressing cubicle, gloved up, and readied for battle. The championship bout went the distance followed by the usual post-fight interviews. After that, Gamboa and Gilberto Luque made their way to the ring. Burnett-Thompson would be the last fight of the night.

While Gamboa-Luque was being contested, DiBella told Hamilton and Burns that he wanted to cut Kevin's bout to four rounds. Both men objected. They figured that Thompson would be in the fight for two rounds; and after that, Kevin would dominate.

"We have a contract for six," Hamilton told DiBella.

End of discussion.

The bell for round one of Burnett-Thompson rang at 11:00 P.M. Kevin had been in the arena for six hours, five of them with his hands taped. Only a few diehard fans remained.

The first stanza was a feeling-out round for both men, with Burnett seeming a bit tentative. Thompson attacked in round two, and Kevin responded with his most effective jabs of the night followed by a series of thudding right hands to the body.

Thereafter, Burnett controlled the fight when he jabbed and was less impressive when he didn't. There were times when he looked hittable, but Thompson didn't do it much. Rather, he allowed Kevin to wind up on his right hand (which didn't do as much damage as one might have thought) and rest when he wanted to. Burnett won all six rounds, although one of the judges (who was probably tired) gave him only four.

So . . . Where does Kevin Burnett stand in his quest to become a force in the heavyweight division? He has a "Class A" trainer and "Class A" management. The jury is still out on whether he'll be a "Class A" fighter.

"I don't have a real handle on where Kevin is right now," Hamilton says. "He's coming along a little more slowly than I envisioned because he started in such poor physical condition and it took a long time to turn that around. The loss and the draw are cause for concern, but I can look past them on the theory that Kevin was working his way into shape and just beginning to learn how to fight when they happened. He has good instincts. He likes boxing and works hard. Now he needs a better understanding of what his gifts are, and he has to develop those gifts and use them when he fights. Larry Holmes never got bored with hitting an opponent in the face thirty-five times a round with his jab. If Kevin keeps winning, we'll see to it that everything else falls into place."

"This is a great time to be a young heavyweight," Burns adds. "It's not a good time for the public as far as the heavyweights are concerned. But for a young heavyweight with potential, it couldn't be better. There's not much out there now, and there are very few good young guys coming up in the system. Given where Kevin was with his shoulder and being as out-of-shape as he was, it's hard to get a fix on how he'll develop as a fighter. But he works hard; he wants to be successful. Obviously, he has to keep learning and he has to get stronger. But if things work out right, in two years he'll have an impact on the heavyweight division."

That leaves the fighter himself to be heard from.

"Boxing isn't what you think it will be before you start," Burnett notes. "On TV, you see the fights and hear how much money some of the heavyweights are making. But it's a long road to the top. A lot of things are harder than I thought they'd be, and nothing has been easier. But I love boxing. You have to love it to be dedicated and to do things right. And the more I learn, the more that love grows."

"My jab is my best offensive and defensive weapon. A year ago, I thought I had a good jab; but I've learned so much since then. How to throw it different ways; how to defend myself better when I throw it. My jab is faster, stronger, and better now than it was before, and the rest of me is improving."

Then Burnett turns to the future. "There's so much I want out of boxing," he says. "I'd love to be champion and build a legacy. I want to be able to give things to my mom that she never had before," Kevin smiles. "My mom has never seen me fight and she won't see me fight. She doesn't want to see me get hit, and she doesn't want to see me hit anyone else."

Kevin smiles again. "I can imagine people from my past seeing where I am now and saying to themselves, 'I never knew that quiet guy had dynamite like that in him.' I just have to stay healthy and keep learning, and everything that's supposed to happen will happen. Time is on my side."

John Duddy is one of my favorite people, in or out of boxing . . .

John Duddy: The Challenge Ahead

John Duddy sat on a chair in dressing room #5 at Madison Square Garden and bowed his head. An hour earlier, he'd been on the same chair, readying to do battle against a club fighter named Walid Smichet, who'd been chosen in the belief that his style and limited ring skills would make Duddy look good. Their fight was presumed to be the final step on the journey to a lucrative match-up between John and middleweight champion Kelly Pavlik.

Now Duddy looked as though a biker gang had stomped on his face. Both of his eyelids had been ripped open. There was another cut beneath his left eye. "I'm sorry," he said. "I let a lot of people, including myself, down tonight."

Duddy has the makings of a fantasy fighter. He's smart, well-spoken, and movie-star handsome. When he steps into the ring, women fear for his safety and wish there were a way they could help protect him. He's famous enough now that fans intrude upon private moments more often than he'd like. But he has a kind word for everyone who approaches him. As Jack McGowan wrote in the *Belfast Telegraph* last year, "Duddy, Derry born and bred, is riding a magic carousel. He's impulsive, high-spirited, and a risk-taker; Irish-handsome and Irish exciting."

Every Duddy fight is an event. His personality and action-packed ring style make him a highly marketable fighter. John himself says, "When I fight, there's lots of action in the ring, and lots of singing and drinking outside it." But while others party, the fighter gets hit. Duddy is the one who walks through the crowd and up the steps into the ring to engage in dangerous and potentially lethal combat.

"Boxing is a serious business," Duddy observes. "When it comes to boxing, I don't play games." Nor does he cut corners, complain, or lie. Not to himself and not to anyone else. That was clear in September 2006, when he prevailed in a brutal twelve-round war against veteran Yory Boy Campas. John never complained to referee Hubert Earl about Campas's tactics, which included low blows, hitting on the break, and pushing John's head down while punching at the same time.

"When a fighter complains," Duddy said in his dressing room after that bout, "all it means is he doesn't want to fight."

Then John was asked about a trip Campas took to the canvas that the referee had ruled a slip.

"It was a knockdown," Harry Keitt (Duddy's trainer at the time) interjected. "I saw it."

"I saw it better," John said. "He was on the way down when my glove brushed against him. It was a slip."

The victory over Campas was one more triumph in a career that was on an upward arc. It moved John's record to 18-and-0 with 15 knockouts. But there was a problem. While Duddy was winning convincingly at the club fight level, he lacked imagination in his attack. He was predictable with too few surprises for opponents. And his defense was flawed.

Defensively, John didn't move his head enough or bend enough at the knees. When he retreated, he tended to move straight back while stand-ing straight up. Too often, he carried his hands low. Clan Duddy was aware of the flaws. "I know that I still have a lot to learn," John said. But he didn't seem to be learning it. And inevitably, attention focused on trainer Harry Keitt.

On March 16, 2007 (St. Patrick's Day eve), Duddy won a technical decision over Anthony Bonsante in a fight that was cut short when Bonsante was badly cut by an accidental clash of heads. Once again, John had been hit too much. Several days later, Eddie McLoughlin (Duddy's promoter) discussed the matter with his brother, Anthony McLoughlin (John's manager), matchmaker Jim Borzell, and former featherweight champion Barry McGuigan (a hero in the Duddy household when John was growing up). Then Eddie broached the issue directly with John, who agreed to consider a change in trainers. For one week, Duddy worked with Don Turner (who trained Evander Holyfield for sixteen fights over the course of nine years). Then he went back to Keitt.

"Everybody has their opinion," John said at the time. "But I've got to do what's right for me; not what other people think is good for me. I've tried what was offered and what other people suggested. Now I'm going back to what I want to do. I'm the one who's getting in the ring and doing it."

An uninspiring ten-round decision over Dupree Strickland followed. Three days later (on May 21, 2007), Duddy met again with the McLoughlins, who pressed for a change in trainers. Finally, John agreed. Eddie offered to break the news to Keitt, and Duddy said, no, he'd do it himself. John told Harry the next day in a face-to-face meeting at Gleason's Gym.

"It's one of the hardest decisions I've had to make in my life," Duddy said afterward. "I should have been putting on a better display in the last two fights. I need to reinvigorate myself. I wasn't doing Harry justice. He was a fantastic coach. I was letting Harry down with my performance."

"Maybe John doesn't have it in him to get to the next level," Eddie McLoughlin added. "But I think Harry has taken him as far as he can. I would say that Harry took John from a 'C' fighter to a 'B' fighter, and I honestly think he took him there about four fights ago. I don't think John has improved since then. No disrespect to Harry," McLoughlin continued. "Maybe Harry is doing the job right and John simply hasn't been responding. Either way, it doesn't look as though John and Harry can make it to the top as a team. We could always keep Harry and cut John loose, but that wouldn't leave us with much, would it?"

In June 2007, Duddy began training with Don Turner on a fulltime basis. Having fought all of his previous professional fights in the United States, he returned to Ireland and scored knockout victories over Alessio Furlan and Prince Arron. In December 2007, he was matched against Howard Eastman. Many observers considered the fight an unnecessary risk. The thirty-seven-year-old Eastman had seen better days, but is an experienced boxer who'd gone the distance with Bernard Hopkins and won 42 of 47 bouts. Duddy prevailed on a ten-round decision.

The victories were mounting; 23 in a row. Now even Duddy's detractors conceded, "Yes; John can fight a bit." The plan was to match him against middleweight champion Kelly Pavlik at Madison Square Garden on June 7, 2008. John's purse for that fight was the subject of ongoing negotiation. But whatever the amount, it would be a lot of money.

The final step was a tune-up bout against Walid Smichet on the undercard of Wladimir Klitschko versus Sultan Ibragimov at Madison Square Garden on February 23rd. In the dressing room prior to facing Smichet, Duddy was quiet and self-contained. He rarely talks in the hours before battle.

"I've heard a lot about you," a well-wisher who'd been granted brief access told him.

"I hope it's all good," Duddy responded. Then he retreated into his own thoughts; not wanting to be rude but focusing on the perils ahead.

Meanwhile, at ringside, negotiations for Pavlik-Duddy were moving forward. Eddie McLoughlin had originally demanded $2,000,000 on behalf of Clan Duddy. Bob Arum (Pavlik's promoter) had countered with an offer of $1,000,000. For weeks, both sides had held firm. Now the two promoters were sitting several rows apart. As the undercard progressed, Jim Borzell ran back and forth, relaying offers and counteroffers. Arum raised his bid to $1,200,000. McLoughlin instructed Borzell to aim for $1,500,000. Thirty minutes before John stepped into the ring to face Smichet, they settled on $1,450,000.

At roughly the same time, a bagpiper in Irish ceremonial garb asked Duddy if there was any particular music he'd like played during his ring walk.

John shook his head. "It doesn't matter. I don't hear it anyway."

For where Duddy should be in his career right now, the fight against Smichet was his worst performance ever. He got hit all night and the blows were solid. Walid swung from the heels and connected with punches that should never have landed. It was entertaining, but John is supposed to fight like a professional boxer, not a bar-room brawler.

As the fight evolved, Duddy began to box more and slug less. But basically, he was there to be hit, and it wasn't a pretty sight. He landed more punches than Smichet; but the heavier, more damaging blows (and there were a lot of them) belonged to Walid.

Duddy had never received a gift decision before, but one could argue that this was a present. Judge Frank Lombardi scored the bout even at 95–95. John McKaie and Don Trella were inexplicably generous, each scoring 98–92 in John's favor. One could make a case for 96–94 Duddy victory. 98–92 was beyond the pale of reason. Even some of the Irish fans in attendance booed the decision.

The aftermath of the fight was an odd counterpoint to Duddy's 2006 battle against Yory Boy Campas. That night, the veteran had exposed John's flaws, rocking him with punches from all angles and ripping open a horrible gash above his left eye. It was a bloody war with each fighter standing his ground. Duddy won the decision, and deservedly so. Afterward, in his dressing room, he was euphoric. "I'm under no illusions," he said at the time. "I got hit a lot; I have a lot to learn." But his eyes had sparkled and he seemed exhilarated by it all. "This is what boxing is all about," he'd said. "This was more than I've ever experienced. It was one of the best personal experiences I've had in my life."

There was no such joy after Duddy-Smichet. Once again, John's eyelids had been ripped open. The cut on his left eyelid was a horrible gash that required twenty-two stitches to close. It was in the same place as the cut sustained in the Campas fight; only this wound was longer, wider, and deeper. The slice on his right eyelid needed another ten stitches.

Duddy is a harsh self-critic, and he was brutally honest in appraising his work. "I didn't fight like a professional tonight," he told the members of his team who'd gathered around him. "I fought with my heart instead of my head. I got the win. A bad win is better than a good loss, but it was a step backward. Kelly Pavlik will be laughing after he sees this one. It was a mediocre performance, and I should get mediocre ratings for it. I'm very disappointed in myself."

John took a deep breath and let it out slowly. "I'm a better fighter than this," he said. "But boxing is an unforgiving sport."

A few tears mingled with the blood that seeped from the cuts above his eyes.

Putting matters in perspective, the Smichet fight exacted a heavy toll on Duddy. The first hurt is physical. John was cut badly and will be out of action for five to six months while his wounds heal. Also, he was hit 220 times by a professional fighter and many of those blows were hard punches to the head. As a matter of health, he simply can't keep getting hit like that.

Second, there has been a significant financial loss. John won the fight on the judges' scorecards. He remains marketable. Bob Arum still wants to promote Pavlik-Duddy sometime in the future. But the $1,450,000 payday slated for June 7th at Madison Square Garden is gone, and no one knows what the future holds.

"It's not over by a long shot," Eddie McLoughlin says. But in the next breath, McLoughlin acknowledges, "John needs another nice performance before he fights for the title to make it a more credible fight for the fans."

That leads to the third hurt. Being game is different from being good. One bad fight shouldn't define Duddy's career or dictate the rest of it. But February 23rd was the most discouraging night of his professional career and it raised doubts as to how good he can be.

The positive view is that John fought stupidly against Smichet in the early rounds, got caught up in a brawl, took too many punches, and eventually wised up enough to box his way to a decision. The negative view is that he fought like a club fighter and won't be competitive at a world-class level.

There's no doubt that Duddy has a good chin. But it doesn't matter how good a fighter's chin is. If he takes multiple punches flush on the jaw from opponents like Kelly Pavlik and Arthur Abraham, he'll be knocked out.

Duddy is twenty-eight years old now. He has been fighting professionally since age twenty-four, and his face is starting to look older. Part of that is the demands of his trade. His nose has been broken. The Campas and Smichet fights led to 56 stitches being embroidered around his eyes. He has limitless potential as a person. He might be a limited fighter.

One of the hardest things for an athlete to accept is that he loves his sport but might not have what it takes to get to the highest level. There are thousands of basketball players who were stars in high school, the best ever in the city they lived in. And no matter how hard they work, they simply don't have the physical ability necessary to make it to the NBA. Ditto for baseball. Yeah; he's a great centerfielder and hits with power but the requisite hand-eye coordination isn't there.

Boxing is about more than a good support team, dedication, and heart. It requires God-given physical talent. Duddy is fighting to win the middleweight championship of the world; not to be a contender. There's honor in the way he has conducted his career so far, but he's not satisfied yet. He wants to play in the Super Bowl and win it. "I started boxing to find out how good I am," he says. "If I didn't see myself fighting and beating the best someday, there wouldn't be any sense in my continuing as a fighter."

Is the brass ring out of reach? Don Turner thinks there's hope.

"John is a smart kid, but he's not a smart fighter," Turner posits. "He has a good boxing brain, but he doesn't always use it. The best fighters know when to box and when to turn it on. John tries to impose his will at the wrong time and there are technical things he does wrong."

"That's the bad stuff," Turner continues. "The good stuff is that John is a hard worker, he's not afraid, and he's a fighter. His work ethic and determination remind me of Evander. If John could fight the last few rounds against Smichet the way he did after taking all those punches, then he could have done it earlier. He knows what to do. The question is whether or not he's disciplined enough to do it consistently. If he is and if he fights to his full potential, we could have some fun and make some money. It doesn't have to come out the way I feel. I've been wrong before. But I still think that John is going to surprise a lot of people."

Meanwhile, Duddy doesn't want to hear about what a good person he is and how much courage he has. That's like being told by the woman of your dreams, "I think you're wonderful, but I'm marrying someone else." He wants to be a championship-caliber fighter. In the wake of Duddy-Smichet, he's asking himself a lot of hard questions. There are no right or wrong answers; only what's right for John.

*In the first half of 2008, boxing's "elite" heavyweights kept stumbling
along.*

The Heavyweight Follies

"The greatest tragedy for heavyweight boxing," James Lawton of the
Independent has written, "is not so much the decline so visible in the rem-
nants of a once compelling trade, but the way what is left of the carcass is
still fed upon so ravenously."

Two recent fights (Wladimir Klitschko versus Sultan Ibragimov and
Oleg Maskaev against Samuel Peter) exemplify that phenomenon.

Klitschko-Ibragimov was trumpeted as "the first heavyweight title-
unification fight" since Holyfield-Lewis in 1999. But let's get real.
Holyfield-Lewis was for all the marbles. Klitschko (IBF) versus Ibagimov
(WBO) matched two of four beltholders; that's all. Klitschko, despite his
accomplishments, is perceived by many as a flawed fighter. And the WBO
belt has *never* been carried into the ring by the true heavyweight champion of the world.

The first WBO heavyweight beltholder was Francesco Damiani, who
won the bauble by knocking out Johnny DuPlooy in 1989. Other WBO
titlists included Ray Mercer, Tommy Morrison, Michael Bentt, Herbie
Hide, Henry Akinwande, Corrie Sanders, Lamon Brewster, Sergei
Liakhovich, Shannon Briggs, and Ibragimov. Michael Moorer, Riddick
Bowe, Vitali Klitschko, Wladimir Klitschko, and Chris Byrd also held
the WBO crown. But in each instance, it was when someone else was
acknowledged to be boxing's true heavyweight champion. For example,
Vitali won the WBO belt by beating Herbie Hide at a time when Lennox
Lewis was the WBC-WBA-IBF king. And Vitali's brief reign with the
WBO hardly set the world aflame. His only successful "title" defenses
were against Ed Mahone and Obed Sullivan.

Klitschko-Ibragimov didn't set the boxing world on fire either. As
their February 23rd match-up at Madison Square Garden approached, a
series of press releases advised the public that fans were "snapping up

tickets at a breakneck pace" and anticipation was reaching "a fever pitch." Tom Loeffler of K2 (Klitschko's promoter) proclaimed, "We are on track to sell out the Garden," while Leon Margules of Seminole Warriors Boxing (Ibragimov's promoter) declared, "I would advise any fight fans that want to see this historic fight live to get to the box office as soon as possible because we expect a sellout."

Meanwhile, more than one writer compared Ibragimov's appearance to that of Barney Rubble of *The Flintstones*. At the final pre-fight press conference, Tim Struby of *ESPN: The Magazine* mistook Sultan for a limo driver.

On fight night, the mezzanine at the Garden wasn't open. So much for "sellout" and "fever pitch." Klitschko entered the ring as a 4-to-1 favorite. At 6-feet-6 inches, 238 pounds, he's an imposing presence and towered over Ibragimov (who was generously listed as five inches shorter and weighed 219 pounds).

The fight was pretty boring (although there's no truth to the rumor that, during the middle rounds, fans circulated a petition asking that it be cut from twelve rounds to ten). Wladimir is a safety-first fighter, which isn't necessarily a bad thing. But boxing (like all sports) is a form of entertainment, and Klitschko-Ibragimov wasn't very entertaining.

According to CompuBox, through the first three rounds, Klitschko threw a grand total of three "power punches" and landed NONE. And keep in mind; according to CompuBox, a "power punch" is any punch other than a jab. Then Wladimir upped the ante, landing a total of three out of eleven power punches (one per stanza) in rounds four, five, and six.

The crowd had come to cheer Klitschko, but wound up booing and jeering instead. Ibragimov fought as well as he could (which wasn't very). Each time Sultan tried to jab, Wladimir slapped the southpaw's right hand down with his own left in a modified form of Patty-cake. Meanwhile, Ibragimov was rarely able to move past Klitschko's jab. And on the few occasions when Sultan did get inside, Wladimir simply darted away.

The best action occurred in round ten, when Ibragimov body-slammed Klitschko to the canvas. But before he could go for the pin, referee Wayne Kelly intervened. Wladimir also landed some good right hands in the second half of the fight. But Ibragimov took them well and Klitschko opted not to go for the kill.

Before the final round, Emanuel Steward told Wladimir, "Unless you knock him out, it's not good at all. You have to try to knock him out. Otherwise, it's gonna be bad."

It was bad. Klitschko won a unanimous decision, but the reviews were not kind. A sampling of headlines on both sides of the Atlantic told the tale:

> *New York Daily News:* "It Was a Fight to Stay Awake"
> *New York Times:* "Klitschko Wins Fight Marked by Inaction"
> *Boston Globe:* "Effortless Win by Klitschko"
> *The Associated Press:* "Clunker of a Heavyweight Title Fight"
> *The Guardian:* "Cautious Klitschko Claims Title but Few Plaudits"
> *The Telegraph:* "Wladimir Klitschko's Forgettable Victory"

In other words; Klitschko-Ibragimov was supposed to be a coronation but wound up resembling an abdication. A charitable appraisal would be that Wladimir's defense was impenetrable and he fought like Lennox Lewis might have during an intense sparring session. Don Turner (who once trained Evander Holyfield and Larry Holmes) offered a lesser view, opining, "Klitschko looked like a giant who was afraid of a midget."

Then the scene shifted to Cancun, where, on March 8th, Oleg Maskaev defended his WBC heavyweight belt against WBC "interim champion" Samuel Peter. Don King promoted the fight (having won a purse bid as Peter's co-promoter). WBC president Jose Sulaiman presided as circus ringmaster.

Ten days before the fight, Dennis Rappaport (Maskaev's promoter) said he was "extremely concerned" that Oleg wouldn't receive fair treatment from the referee and judges. "There's no doubt," Rappaport maintained, "that with the WBC picking the officials, the cards are stacked against us."

That engendered a lengthy response from Sulaiman, who declared in part, "Mr. Dennis Rappaport is mercilessly attacking the WBC and myself after owing almost every penny that he has made in boxing to the WBC's support. By Rappaport putting on my back so many accusations of libel and slander, he is betraying the support, trust, and friendship that I have given him through a quarter century. Oleg Maskaev should know that the WBC would never betray its priority of justice. I promise and commit myself to Oleg Maskaev that the WBC will stand by unwavering right-fulness and that there is nothing to substitute our backbone principle that the winner in the ring will be the winner on the cards. The referee [Guadalupe Garcia] is one of the best ten of the world; one judge [Daniel van de Wiele] among the absolute best in Europe; the second judge [Ken Morita] the very best in Japan; and the third judge [Herman Cuevas] the absolute best in Mexico."

Here, it should be noted that Ken Morita ("the very best" judge in Japan) had Mike Tyson ahead of Buster Douglas when that fight ended after nine rounds in Tokyo.

There was little of the sweet science in Maskaev-Peter. Samuel has a well-deserved reputation for being lazy in training camp and came into the ring looking like the winner of a pie-eating contest. At 251 pounds, he was eight pounds heavier than Oleg. But the relevant numbers were thirty-nine (Maskaev's age) and five (the number of times that "champion" Maskaev previously had been knocked out).

The fight boiled down to two big guys lumbering around the ring like World War II tanks slogging through the mud. Peter's signature blow is a clubbing right hand to the back of the head. He also paws occasion-ally with his jab. It ended in the sixth round with Maskaev still on his feet but absorbing too many blows.

Looking to the future, Wladimir Klitschko will be the focal point of the heavyweight division in the near term. He's physically-gifted, uses his height well, and (despite his showing against Ibragimov) has the potential to turn out the lights with one punch. Emanuel Steward (Klitschko's trainer) says, "I consider Wladimir one of the best heavyweights in his-tory." Of course, before Taylor-Pavlik I, Steward told the world, "In all the years I've been training fighters, I've never had a fighter in better shape mentally or physically than Jermain is now. Even if I was Marvin Hagler or Sugar Ray Robinson, I wouldn't want to be fighting this Jermain Taylor."

Unfortunately, Wladimir has taken the easy road as of late. His activ-ity for 2007 consisted of fights against Ray Austin and Lamon Brewster. 2006 saw him against Chris Byrd and Calvin Brock. The Brewster fight was particularly unappealing. Lamon was on medical suspension in the United States at the time it occurred. And two of his sparring partners told Keith Idec of the *New Jersey Herald News* that, prior to fighting Klitschko, Brewster (who had previously suffered a detached retina on at least two occasions) had difficulty seeing out of his left eye.

It's precisely because Wladimir is the best of the current heavyweights that he should be held to a higher standard than the one he has adhered to as of late.

HBO is hopeful that it can facilitate title unification in the heavy-weight division in the not-too-distant future. But that's a misplaced goal. In today's world of multiple sanctioning bodies, title vacancies, mandatory defenses, and stripped titles, the belts don't mean much. The focus now should be on the best fighting the best. The biggest problem with Klitschko-Ibragimov (and HBO's support for it) was that it gave credibility to the sanctioning bodies and their belts. Just because someone has a belt doesn't mean he's a champion.

Ruslan Chagaev is now the WBA heavyweight beltholder. Most fans wouldn't recognize Chagaev if he sat next to them in a restaurant. Few, if any, knowledgeable insiders think that Chagaev would beat Klitschko. So forget Klitschko-Chagaev.

As for a rematch between Klitschko and Samuel Peter, Samuel's improvement has been minimal since he lost a unanimous decision to Wladimir in 2005. Indeed, he might have regressed because his chin seems to have been rewired for the worse since then. And let's not forget; five months ago, Peter was life and death with Jameel McCline (who lost ten of twelve rounds to John Ruiz on the undercard of Maskaev-Peter).

In truth, the most interesting heavyweight fight right now would be Klitschko against 7-foot-2-inch, 320-pound Nikolay Valuev.

Valuev is slow, and Wladimir's mobility would give him trouble. Also, Nikolay has never been hit as hard as Wladimir would hit him. But Valuev is a composed fighter. He takes a good punch and has never been on the canvas. His skills are improving and his size would pose considerable prob-lems for Klitschko (who is used to controlling fights with his own size and tends to wear down late).

Meanwhile, the heavyweight throne is still vacant and the theory of intelligent design remains inapplicable to boxing.

★   ★   ★

(A note on the October 11, 2008, fight between Samuel Peter and Vitali Klitschko)

Samuel Peter versus Vitali Klitschko for the WBC heavyweight belt shaped up on paper as an interesting fight. Of course, as Tom Gerbasi wrote, "That's a problem in and of itself. If the prospect of a brittle thirty-seven-year old with almost four years of ring rust on him taking on a crude brawler who was sent to the canvas three times by Jameel McCline represents the best of heavyweight boxing circa 2008, the game may be in more trouble than we've imagined."

The 6-foot-7-inch Klitschko won a WBC belt in a 2004 bout against thirty-eight-year-old Corrie Sanders (for the title vacated by Lennox Lewis). In an earlier championship reign, he'd claimed the WBO crown by beating Herbie Hide. Injuries forced Vitali to retire in 2005. Prior to facing Peter, he'd never beaten an elite heavyweight. His most impressive showing was a TKO loss to Lewis in 2003.

Peter has brute strength and not much more. His signature wins were two decisions over an out-of-shape James Toney and an inartful clubbing of Oleg Maskaev earlier this year to annex the WBC crown.

At an August 27th press conference in New York, Klitschko proclaimed, "I have studied many fights of Samuel Peter. He is a big puncher, but his style is good for me and I can punch a little bit. I think I will knock him out."

Then Vitali was asked to comment on claims by the Peter camp that Samuel had become a much better fighter since losing to Wladimir (Vitali's brother) in 2005. "You saw the fight against Wladimir," Vitali said with a smile. "You saw the fight against McCline. You can decide."

Klitschko trains like a serious professional. Peter trains like a petulant child. Everyone understood prior to the fight that Vitali would be in the best shape possible (whatever that might be) and Samuel wouldn't. That was good enough to make Klitschko a 2-to-1 favorite.

When fight night arrived and the bell rang, Peter looked fat (253 pounds) and sluggish. He showed little skill and less heart, waddling around the ring, rarely throwing more than one ineffectual punch at a time. At some point before quitting (which he did after round eight, imploring his corner to "stop it"), Samuel should have swarmed Klitschko and thrown punches anywhere, everywhere, all over Vitali's body. After all, Klitschko has broken down in training several times and his shoulder failed him against Chris Byrd. But Peter gave up his belt without a fight.

Vitali won every minute of every round. He might have won every ten-second segment of every minute. Showtime blow-by-blow commentator Steve Albert labeled the bout "a glorified sparring session." An "inglorious sparring session" would have been more accurate. Samuel's performance (as Al Bernstein put it) was "dreadful." And it further exposed the heavyweight division.

Peter was better than Toney who, in his last outing, was better than Hasim Rahman. David Haye is a cruiserweight with a questionable chin. Chris Arreola might improve, but right now he's an overweight club fighter with the potential to become world-class. The mandatory challengers for the four sanctioning-body belts are J. C. Gomez (WBC), Kali Meehan (WBA), Alexander Povetkin (IBF), and Alexander Dimitrenko (WBO). That augurs poorly for the future.

As Vitali noted after beating Peter, "There's one more belt not in the Klitschko family." That would be the WBA bauble currently shared by Nikolai Valuev (the "champion") and Ruslan Chagaev (the "champion in recess"). Look for Wladimir to go after the smaller Chagaev and leave the 7-foot-2-inch, 325-pound Valuev for Vitali. Wladimir is the better boxer, but Vitali is the better fighter.

Meanwhile, the Klitschkos are the class of the heavyweight division, and there will be no title-unification bout as long as they reign. As Vitali says, "Anyone who thinks they can make Klitschko against Klitschko, tell them to negotiate with our mother."

Bernard Hopkins versus Joe Calzaghe shaped up as a study in contrasts.

Hopkins–Calzaghe:
When Push Comes to Shove

Visually, the upcoming fight between Joe Calzaghe and Bernard Hopkins looks like a confrontation between a concert violinist and a street thug. The combatants' personalities are vastly different too.

Conversing with Hopkins is like clocking time of possession for a football team that has a dominant ground game. At the end of an hour, Bernard has talked for fifty-seven minutes and the other person for three.

Hopkins is self-reverential. Respect is enormously important to him, but he also wants to be liked. He's one of boxing's best self-promoters, speaking his mind and then some. Unlike some people in the business, he understood the power of the Internet a long time ago. "The reality show got big for me the last couple of years," he says.

Listen to Bernard for even a short time and a self-portrait emerges: "I'm an argumentative person . . . People respect me, not only for my accomplishments in boxing but because I'm a humble man . . . Fighters all got egos. Some are in check and some aren't . . . I'm a different fighter than any other fighter that came in my era . . . Come April 19th, people are going to have to put me in a whole new different category; maybe that icon thing. Legend, I already got. Icon would be really special to me."

In the ring, Hopkins projects an aura of invincibility. He's still fighting at age forty-three and doing it well. "What makes me different from other athletes my age," he says, "is that the desire is still there. I don't drink; I don't smoke. Being in the gym is my intoxication."

Does Hopkins need boxing to impose discipline on his life? Is it a necessary release for the demons within him? No one (except possibly Bernard) knows for sure. But late last year in quiet conversation, he offered a window onto his psyche. "I got $20,000,000 in the bank," he told this writer. "And outside of harm to my family, there's only one thing that I'm afraid of. Going broke."

Calzaghe, in contrast to Hopkins, is soft-spoken with an almost gentle manner about him. He conjures up images of a guitarist in a British rock band more than a professional fighter. Looking at him, it's hard to imagine that he has been undefeated as a boxer in the amateur and pro ranks over the past seventeen years.

"I grew up in a secure world," Calzaghe says, when asked about issues beyond the ring. "It frightens me to think what my children and grandchildren will face. We're destroying the world. Global warming is a terrible threat. I disagree with what's happening in Iraq. Too many innocent people are being killed. For what? I believe in fighting terrorism; but our being there only provokes more terrorism, not less."

As for his family (Calzaghe shares custody of two sons with his ex-wife), he says, "Joe [the older boy] wants to be me, but I'd rather he not fight. Boxing is a hungry sport, and he's not hungry."

Calzaghe is boxing's longest-reigning current champion. As with Hopkins, his most impressive credential is his longevity.

Bernard won the IBF middleweight title with a seventh-round knockout of Segundo Mercado in 1995 and made twenty successful title defenses before losing to Jermain Taylor in 2005.

Calzaghe won the WBO 168-pound crown with a twelve-round decision over Chris Eubank in 1997 and has made 21 successful title defenses. He has fought his entire career as a super-middleweight (although the Hopkins bout will be contested at 175 pounds). The level of Joe's opposition has been largely undistinguished. Super-middleweight is not one of boxing's "classic" divisions, and there have been few inquisitors for him to face. Still, he's 44–0 with 32 knockouts. His signature victories were a twelve-round shut-out of Jeff Lacy in 2006 and a dominant decision triumph over Mikkel Kessler in 2007.

"In the 1960s and '70s," Calzaghe observes, "there wasn't much money and there was only one title. You had to mix it up every few months and get busted up. Now it's easier to be a world champion, but the belts don't mean as much. This fight is for the money. After years of plugging away, I'm getting the rewards I deserve. But this fight is also about my legacy. People talk about pound-for-pound, but talking about who's the best in the world pound-for-pound is fantasy. No one knows, really. A legacy is something else. A fighter secures his legacy by winning difficult fights against tough opponents, and that's what I plan to do against Hopkins."

Hopkins-Calzaghe can only add to Bernard's legacy. If he wins, it gets bigger. If he loses; hey, he's forty-three years old.

Calzaghe has more at stake. If he loses, his legacy will be diminished. And if he wins?

Hopkins fills in the blanks. "I'm fighting a champion," Bernard says. "Calzaghe is fighting a legend. To have my name as a victory on his resume does more for him than having his name on my resume does for me. He could have an American icon on his resume."

"He calls himself a legend," Calzaghe responds. "He's old enough to be a legend. On April 19, we'll see who the legend is."

And there has been one more twist in the pre-fight build-up. An ugly one.

For Hopkins, every fight starts early. This one started before the contracts were signed. On December 7, 2007, (the day before Mayweather-Hatton), Hopkins and Calzaghe came face to face in the media center at the MGM Grand Hotel & Casino in Las Vegas. Initially, the banter was good-natured and revolved largely around who was ducking whom and who would win if they fought one another. Face to face became nose to nose. Joe was unrattled. Bernard turned to walk away, then turned back and declared, "I would never let a white boy beat me." An hour later, he tried to engage Calzaghe in further dialogue onstage at the Mayweather-Hatton weigh-in, but Golden Boy personnel stepped between them.

Calzaghe made light of the exchange. "It was good fun," he said afterward. "Hopkins's comment wasn't in good taste. But Hopkins isn't a good-taste person, is he?" Later, Joe added, "I don't think he's a racist. I think he said a stupid remark that made himself look stupid."

Others were less charitable. Summoning up righteous indignation, Frank Warren (Calzaghe's promoter) proclaimed, "I've heard some disgusting trash-talk in my thirty years in boxing, but that's the lowest of the lows."

The British press had a field day, wondering what the reaction would have been had Calzaghe said, 'I would never let a black boy beat me." And inevitably, Richard Schaefer (the CEO of Golden Boy, which promotes Hopkins) was drawn into the fray.

Prior to the 2006 fight between Oscar De La Hoya and Ricardo Mayorga, Schaefer was disturbed by Mayorga's homophobic rants and noted, "I'm not pleased to be associated with a person like Mayorga, but this is boxing so I guess we have to do it." Now, in response to Hopkins's comment, Schaefer acknowledged, "It was not appropriate, and I wish it hadn't been said."

However, one person refused to distance himself from the remark. Hopkins has an extensive vocabulary, but the phrase "I was wrong" doesn't appear to be in it. "What I did in Puerto Rico [throwing a Puerto Rican flag on the ground prior to fighting Felix Trinidad] and what I said to Joe are all part of boxing," Bernard declared.

That was followed by, "People say the world has changed, but not that much. I'm just telling it like it is. I don't regret saying what I said. I was right; and I was profoundly right."

Finally, at a press conference in London, Hopkins advised the media, "I said what I said. People who know me, know me. It doesn't matter what I regret or what I don't regret. Come April 19th, it's up to Joe to prove me a liar."

Meanwhile, Bernard was moving away from "I would never let a white boy beat me" to focus on the United States versus the United Kingdom. "I'm not just representing myself," he announced. "I'm also representing my country. I'm gonna make this thing so patriotic; every-one's gonna say, 'We've got to team up and support the American.'"

Still, the residue of Hopkins's "white boy" comment lingers. We're now at a point in the racial dialogue where neither side should get a free pass on comments of that nature. And it's disappointing when Bernard drops to that level because he's capable of so much more. Unlike some trash-talkers, he's smart enough and verbal enough that he doesn't have to fan the flames of prejudice to express himself. And more significantly, he holds himself out as a role model.

If Bernard wants to be a role model, he shouldn't talk like a bigot. As John Dillon wrote in the *Sunday Express,* "A full retraction and an apol-ogy would have been the wholesome course."

As for the fight; Calzaghe opened as a 2-to-1 favorite and the odds have risen slightly since then. Part of the reasoning behind that is Bernard's age and part of it is Joe's skills.

Calzaghe is a southpaw with quick hands and a good sense of antici-pation. "I throw more punches and I land more punches," he says. "That's what it comes down to. That's the basics of boxing."

Against Mikkel Kessler, Joe showed a solid chin and his non-stop assault was particularly impressive in light of the seven-year age differen-tial between them. The thirty-six-year-old Calzaghe didn't just rely on experience and skill against Kessler; he relied on his heart.

Calzaghe isn't taking Hopkins lightly. "He's forty-three," Joe says. "But he's still an excellent fighter. You can't take that away from him. Against Winky, the last fight [in July 2007], he moved very well and he used the right shots at the right time. He retained a lot of good movement. His work rate wasn't bad. The guy can still fight."

Still, over the past few months, the prospect of a Calzaghe victory over Hopkins has been stated most forcefully by Joe himself:

> • "Hopkins is not as good as he thinks he is. He knows what it's like to lose. He's lost four times. I'm a winner, a champion, undefeated for seventeen years. I've beaten everyone they put in front of me. I'll domi-nate the fight."
> • "Hopkins is a bully; simple as that. He's a messy fighter; he's a dirty fighter. But I'm not intimidated by him. I just find it funny that a grown man carries on the way he does. He can be the bad guy now, but I'm going to be the bad guy come April 19. Let's see who's doing the talk after the fight."
> • "Sometimes you win pretty; sometimes you win ugly. I go with the flow in each fight. I've always done better against tall guys, so that works in my favor. I normally carry around fourteen stone [196 pounds], so [moving up to 175 pounds] should give me more punch-ing power and I won't have to struggle to make weight."
> • "He's confident, but so am I. I don't just want to win. I want to put on a show and smash him to bits. He's never been in the ring with someone like myself with my hand-speed and my work rate. I don't see how he can possibly beat me. I would have beaten him ten years ago and I'll beat him now. Joe Calzaghe is better than Bernard Hopkins."

Calzaghe's prediction of victory is backed by two men who have been mentioned as possible future opponents for each combatant. "I think Calzaghe beats Hopkins," says Kelly Pavlik. "He'll throw too many punches for Bernard to handle."

"Calzaghe is a good fighter," adds Roy Jones Jr. "He's very busy and he knows what he's doing. To beat Calzaghe, Bernard will have to knock him out; and Bernard doesn't have the power to do that."

Hopkins knows that he's in for a tough fight. "Calzaghe has made twenty-one title defenses," Bernard says. "I don't care if it was against twenty-one Charlie Browns or Donald Ducks. I know what he had to do within himself to get up for those fights. I know what it takes to maintain that mental strength. I'd be a fool to not respect a guy who made all those defenses."

And Hopkins concedes that his age is a factor. "Every fight a fighter fights takes something out of him," he acknowledges. "That's true of me too. We all lose a step here and there. You know how much you've aged when you look at a tape from ten years ago. I can't do the things now that I could do when I was thirty, but the sand hasn't run out of the glass yet. I'm an old man, but I'm an old man that can still fight."

To prove it, Hopkins has put together a team that includes lead trainer Freddie Roach, Naazim Richardson, John David Jackson, and Mackie Shilstone. The addition of Shilstone is significant because he was instrumental in building Bernard from a middleweight to 182 pounds (which was what Hopkins weighed on fight night when he defeated Antonio Tarver).

"I can't delude myself about the fact that I'm a 43-year-old athlete," Bernard says, explaining Shilstone's presence. "I can't just sit back and say, 'I work hard and I'm special.' So rather than wait until my age bites me in the ass in the middle of a fight, I'm working with Mackie so I don't see those signs of age after the bell rings."

Calzaghe thinks he can beat Hopkins with activity and speed, not unlike the way Roy Jones did years ago. But Jones brought very different gifts to the table in 1993 than Calzaghe does now. And Hopkins has learned since then how to blunt that type of attack.

"I'd fight Roy Jones differently if I had that fight to do over," Bernard says. "I tried to box with Roy, and that was a mistake. I should have put him against the ropes, roughed him up, mauled him, and kept him there. That's a fight I could have won."

"I'm always learning," Hopkins reflects. "As long as I'm in this game, I have to re-invent myself. Once you believe as an athlete that you don't have to re-invent yourself, you're the walking dead. You're done, because the other guys are planning every day. They're watching you, figuring out ways to beat you, figuring out how to avoid your punches, to counter whatever you do. I don't fight every fighter the same. There's a strategy for every opponent. Calzaghe is in for an ugly surprise. I'm not Jeff Lacy, who avoided guys that know how to fight. I'm not Mikkel Kessler, who stands straight up and comes right at you. There's a lot of number-one contenders that could have been champion but Bernard Hopkins was in the way."

Calzaghe hopes to make Hopkins fight at a fast pace and increase his work-rate beyond a level that the forty-three-year-old champion can sustain. Then again, that's everyone's plan against Hopkins. To be sure; fighters of a certain age can get old in the ring overnight. But Team Hopkins thinks that could happen just as easily to Calzaghe.

Here, the thoughts of Naazim Richardson are instructive. "Joe Calzaghe is an outstanding athlete," Richardson acknowledges. "He's tough physically and mentally, and Bernard understands that. If there's a round where nothing much is happening, Calzaghe can steal it by throwing more punches."

"But a lot of things that Calzaghe does," Richardson continues, "he won't be able to do against Bernard. He might start off firing a hundred punches a round; but against Bernard, he won't hit much. You score punches based on accuracy, not activity. And Calzaghe's hands can't be in two places at once; so if he's punching, he's not defending himself. Calzaghe is used to fighting guys who stand right in front of him and don't make him pay when he misses. Timing beats speed, and anyone who throws a punch at Bernard gets something back. Bernard will be throwing punches in between Calzaghe's punches. You don't make Bernard do what he doesn't want to do. Nobody has ever been able to make Bernard fight at a pace he doesn't want to fight at. So when Calzaghe's activity starts to cause him pain, he'll slow it down on his own. There's nobody that fights like Calzaghe, and there's nobody that fights like Bernard. Neither one of them has fought a guy like he'll be fighting on April 19th. The difference is that Bernard has been in the darkness before."

Hopkins is better than any fighter that Calzaghe has ever fought. And while Joe is a very good fighter, he has yet to prove that he's great. One thing is certain. On April 19th, when push comes to shove, Hopkins will shove back.

"Hopkins-Calzaghe," many people said, "will be a great writer's fight until the bell rings." It was a pretty good fight afterward too.

Joe Calzaghe: The Legend Beater

In boxing today, fighters fight for bogus world championship belts bestowed upon them by money-hungry sanctioning bodies in exchange for sanctioning fees subsidized by television networks that demand "title" fights.

Joe Calzaghe versus Bernard Hopkins was a fight for the real light-heavyweight championship of the world.

Hopkins-Calzaghe moved front and center on boxing's radar screen last November when, moments after defeating Mikkel Kessler, Calzaghe declared, "Bernard Hopkins; let's do it. He wants a big fight. Fight me. I'm here, man."

At the post-fight press conference, Frank Warren (Calzaghe's promoter) seconded the challenge, saying, "Hopkins can pick the weight. He can pick the date. He can pick the site. We don't care; we want this fight. We'll fight him in his backyard, if that's where he wants it."

A week later, the forty-three-year-old Hopkins responded, "I'm excited and elated that a guy who is supposedly at the top of his game wants to call out an old man. So after I picked up my cane and put my teeth in, I got up and stood in the middle of the room and thought, 'Well, maybe I still got it a little bit.'"

The posturing had begun.

The first issue to be resolved was where the fight would be held. Hopkins voiced the view, "I've accomplished some profound things in my career, but beating Joe Calzaghe in Yankee Stadium would be super-duper." That sounded good to Bernard. However, the would-be promoters (Golden Boy and Warren) understood that a less ambitious venue was in order.

Calzaghe had never fought in the United States before, but it was clear from the start that the fight would be in America. Bernard stated as much when he proclaimed, "I'm not Charles Brewer; I'm not Byron Mitchell [two Americans who fought Calzaghe in his native Wales]. Me, go across the pond? For what? There's an edge when one guy stays home while the other has to come across the ocean. I've fought my whole career to gain home-court advantage. I'm not about to give it up now to Calzaghe."

Then, for good measure, Bernard added, "Joe's known but he's not well-known, and there's a difference. You've got to leave your neighborhood and fight the best guy in another neighborhood to prove you're the toughest guy out there. Calzaghe is a neighborhood champion. So he has to step out of his crib in Wales, where he's got his bottle on one side and his pacifier on the other, and set foot on my soil so that we can get this on."

The other issue, of course, was money.

"My offer," Bernard announced, "is sixty-forty; fifty-fifty being out of the question. But we can talk."

So they talked.

"I'll give it to Ol' Popkins," Calzaghe said. "He's the king of talk. He's boxing's version of Oprah Winfrey. They should give him his own TV show because he loves the sound of his own voice. The guy can talk forever but that's all he can do. How about putting a little bit of fighting behind those words."

In the early negotiations, Calzaghe priced himself out of the fight and Golden Boy wasn't offering enough money to make the deal work. "Hopkins wants to have home-field advantage," Joe reasoned. "He has to give up something financially to get it."

"Besides," Calzaghe added in a private moment, "it's bargaining, isn't it? You can always come down and ask for less. But it's hard to turn around in the middle of a negotiation and ask for more."

Then Mayweather-Hatton happened and Hopkins made his infamous "I'll never let a white boy beat me" comment (which he later said was designed to stir interest in the promotion rather than a mark of prejudice). Presumably, Bernard thought that being a racial profiteer was somehow better than being a bigot (although the two often go hand in hand).

Regardless, Calzaghe later acknowledged, "Going to the weigh-in [for Mayweather-Hatton] and seeing the tremendous reception that

Ricky got; it was absolutely incredible, the sight of all those thousands of fans. I had a buzz off that. I wanted to get a bit of that for myself before I retired."

Negotiations in earnest followed with the Hopkins and Calzaghe camps settling on a fifty-fifty split. HBO agreed to pay a $6,500,000 license fee, while Setanta purchased UK television rights. Each network decided to televise the fight as part of its monthly subscription package rather than on pay-per-view. Planet Hollywood provided the most substantial piece of the financial puzzle when it purchased the live gate for $11,000,000. "In order to be taken seriously in the gaming industry," Robert Earl (Planet Hollywood CEO) told the media, "we have to get into the fight game."

Tickets were also a negotiated part of the contract, with Calzaghe-Warren accorded the right to buy 5,000 of them. That was in keeping with the theory that the fight would be a continuation of Mayweather-Hatton, where ticket-brokering engendered millions of dollars in side profits.

But Calzaghe's fans don't travel like Hatton's, and Bernard's fans rarely travel at all. Thousands of Brits came to Las Vegas to see Hopkins-Calzaghe, but the demand for tickets was finite. Thus, somewhere along the line, Golden Boy and Warren agreed to cut $2,000,000 off the $11,000,000 that Planet Hollywood had initially pledged. One explanation for the reduction was that Earl decided just before signing the contract that the price was too high and negotiated a lower number. An alternative scenario was that ticket sales were so poor that Golden Boy and Warren agreed after the signing that a refund was in order.

Either way, the battle was joined and Calzaghe acknowledged, "All great fighters want to fight in Las Vegas in a big fight. This is what I've been waiting for. It's a challenge in itself to go to America and win. It would be a shame never to experience it first-hand."

Then the build-up began.

Hopkins is a typical Welsh name. Unlike Anthony Hopkins (the Welsh-born actor who played Hannibal Lecter), Bernard doesn't claim to be of Welsh extraction. But he does display some Lecter-like qualities.

"Anytime someone signs a contract to fight me, it's personal," Bernard said. "Calzaghe got extradited to the United States. Pressure from the public and the media forced him to come here. So let's not dance around this matter. I have a license to kill Joe Calzaghe. I'm not saying that's what I want to do, but it happens. This is not something I take lightly. It's what we've both chosen to do. You don't have to be forty-three years old to get hurt in boxing. You can get hurt anytime.

One of Hopkins's many boasts is that he has "never lost a press conference to anyone." He also gives the impression that there is no line he won't cross as long as he feels he can get away with it. And he observes, "People don't get in Bernard Hopkins's face."

But as the fight neared, Calzaghe put him to the test. Among the words of wisdom that Joe offered were:

> • Hopkins tries to get into opponents' heads. I've seen him do it in the past. But believe me, he's barking up the wrong tree with me. It may work against a 22-year-old kid who's in awe, but not against me.
> • He's not a legend. He's a B-side fighter, who depends on big-name opponents to attract fans to his fights. I'm quite tired, really, of all his talk. And that's all it is; talk. He's a St. Bernard; all bark and no bite. All of his blathering sounds like he's trying to convince himself he can beat me. Let's see if he can back it up on Saturday night.
> • Look at my face. It tells you, doesn't it? I always seem to come out right. His nose is flat across his face. So much for a great defense. He must have walked into a lamp-post to get a nose like that.
> • He thinks he can intimidate me because he's been to prison for robbery. So what? So you burgled somebody, you brave boy. That makes you a thug, not a fighter. It makes you an idiot.

Enzo Calzaghe (Joe's father and trainer) seconded his son's confidence. "Hopkins can think what he wants about himself," the elder Calzaghe said. "Everyone is entitled to his own opinion about himself. But Joe is faster; Joe is younger; Joe has more moves and power. Let Hopkins think that Joe slaps. That's what Jeff Lacy thought. How much power does Hopkins have? One knockout [against Oscar De La Hoya] in five years."

"Boxing is music," Enzo continued. "Music is timing and notes and how you express them. Boxing is timing, a few punches, and how you express them. In the ring, Joe makes beautiful music. One way or another, Joe will win."

Team Hopkins, of course, had a different view. Bernard is a fistic marvel. The first thing a fighter loses isn't his speed or reflexes. It's his desire to train hard. As a boxer succeeds, he also learns how to cut corners and is less likely to stay in shape between fights than he was before. Hopkins is always prepared, physically and mentally, and leaves as little as possible to chance.

"It's not magic that I'm doing," Bernard says. "It's discipline. It comes from the way I treated my body; not just now, but when I was in my twenties and thirties. I haven't had a beer in twenty-three years. I haven't drunk alcohol in twenty-three years."

Mackie Shilstone (the conditioning expert who Hopkins brought in to work with him in the weeks leading up to the Calzaghe fight) bolstered that thought and told the media, "I've had the pleasure of experiencing more than three thousand pro athletes. I have never met a more disciplined man than Bernard Hopkins. Bernard is 43 years in age, but that doesn't equate to a performance age. His age is much younger from the standpoint of performance; probably in the neighborhood of 27 to 28 years old."

Freddie Roach (Hopkins's lead trainer) further stated the case for victory. "The name of the game is hit and don't get hit," Roach said. "It took me a while to figure that out when I was a fighter, but now I know. Bernard is a textbook fighter. Hands up, chin down, perfect balance. Now look at Calzaghe. He throws wide punches and punches over the top, which leaves openings for a good counter-puncher. And Calzaghe is predictable; his style isn't hard to figure out. When Bernard makes certain moves, Joe will make certain moves in response and Bernard knows what they are. Bernard will control the fight."

There was extra pressure on Calzaghe because, during the previous month, the other two champions trained by his father (Gavin Rees and Enzo Maccarinelli) had both been knocked out in title fights. And two other Brits (Ricky Hatton and Clinton Woods) had failed in recent championship outings.

There was also the matter of the referee.

"Hopkins is a dirty fighter," Calzaghe has said. "I'm more concerned about being head-butted than being hit with his punches. And there are other things Hopkins does, like hit on the break, hit low, and use his shoulder on the inside."

Initially, it was thought that Jay Nady would referee the fight. Nady had handled both Hopkins-Taylor encounters and, after studying tapes of their first bout, ran a tight ship in the rematch. Then, for reasons that were unclear, Joe Cortez was designated as the referee for Hopkins-Calzaghe.

Calzaghe was familiar with Cortez. He'd been the third man in the ring when Joe won his first title against Chris Eubank in 1997. More recently, Cortez had aroused the ire of British boxing fans by his handling of Ricky Hatton versus Floyd Mayweather Jr. The opinion in some circles was that he had improperly interrupted the flow of Hatton's attack while allowing Mayweather to do pretty much what he wanted to do.

"No issue," Calzaghe said when Cortez was chosen. "He's an experienced referee, and the world is watching. I don't do holding and mauling. I come to fight and Joe is aware of that, so I'm sure he'll let me get on with my job. You have to have faith in the system."

Still, there was concern in some quarters as to how Cortez would call the fight. A hostile crowd is child's play compared to a hostile referee. Indeed, there was a school of thought that Calzaghe was like a poor soul who walks into a bad neighborhood oblivious to the fact that he's about to be mugged. He knows it's a rough neighborhood, but he hasn't really come to grips with the reality of it.

"I'm not in denial about what Joe can do," Hopkins said several days before the fight. "But Joe is in denial about what I can do. Trust me. I'm going to show him things he's never seen before. I'm a scientific boxer and fighter. You can't pity-pat with me like Calzaghe does. Wide punches, slapping punches; that's the kind of opponent I like. With Calzaghe, I'll go straight down the middle and smash his face. Every time I fight, sooner or later, you hear people say, 'The other guy is fighting Bernard's fight.' This fight will be no different. I'll take away what Calzaghe wants to do and make him fight my fight."

One day before the bout, each fighter weighed in at 173 pounds. At the ritual staredown, Hopkins leaned into Calzaghe and, referencing his years in prison, muttered, "D-block, D-block. I'm taking this to the streets."

On fight night, Calzaghe was the de facto hometown fighter. "It's amazing," he said. "Brits are the best supporters in the world. You wouldn't get ten thousand Americans to come over to the UK to watch a fight no matter how big you are."

Ten thousand Americans didn't go to the Thomas & Mack Center either. The announced attendance was 14,213. But a lot of tickets were given away, while others were sold by Planet Hollywood at a steep discount.

The WBC, in its never-ending quest for truth, justice, and sanctioning fees, offered to designate the fight a "special attraction" and give the winner a WBC "achievement" medallion. Golden Boy CEO Richard Schaefer asked how much that would cost and was told $25,000. He declined the honor. Meanwhile, as the bell for round one rang, the WBC was still seeking sanctioning fees from Calzaghe and Warren despite the fact that no WBC title was at stake. By night's end, no agreement on that issue had been reached.

The fight started badly for Calzaghe. "Joe is used to winning," Hopkins had said at the final pre-fight press conference. "I have to change that mindset early."

He did. One minute into the first stanza, Bernard landed a short sharp right hand, and Calzaghe went down for only the third time in his career. He rose quickly ("It was a flash knockdown; I wasn't hurt"). But it was an inauspicious start and, at round's end, Joe was down by two points.

Round two was more of the same. Hopkins dictated the pace; fought hard in spurts; and got off first. The lead right was his money punch. Calzaghe seemed cautious and unable to penetrate his opponent's defense.

Then the tide turned. Calzaghe kept coming forward. His hands were faster than Bernard's and he was physically stronger than Hopkins had expected.

By round four, Hopkins was getting chippy. "I know every second where the referee is at," Bernard has said. "That's ring generalship." In this case, "ring generalship" included following through with his head or shoulder after punching and numerous infractions in clinches.

"He was head-butting me," Calzaghe said afterward. "Hitting me with low blows, hitting on the break, holding me with one arm on the blind side of the referee, sticking his head in my face. He's a dirty fighter, but I expected that. I had to keep my composure because I knew that, if I retaliated, I might get a point knocked off."

But despite Hopkins's tactics, Calzaghe didn't get frustrated. And before the eyes of the world, Bernard finally got old in a boxing ring.

Usually, the second half of a fight belongs to Hopkins. This one was different. In the second half of Hopkins-Calzaghe, Bernard showed his age. He circled away from his oncoming foe, trying to lure him in for occasional right hand leads but, in reality, doing little offensively. He fought like a pick-pocket, not a mugger, and slowed the action to isolated engagements while Calzaghe sought an ongoing fire-fight.

"Around the seventh round," Joe said later, "I knew he was fading. He was struggling to breathe and couldn't handle the pace."

With that in mind, Calzaghe kept the pressure on and hit Hopkins with more clean shots than Bernard is used to being hit with. Hopkins blunted much of the attack with a defense that was largely punch and run, punch and hold, hold and run some more. At times, he looked a bit like John Ruiz.

Then, thirty seconds into round ten, Calzaghe threw a left to the body. Hopkins pulled Joe's head down at the same time, causing the blow to go low. And Bernard turned thespian; grimacing, limping, and groaning his way through a two-minute "time out" given to him by Joe Cortez.

"What a crap actor," Calzaghe said afterward. "He looked like he'd been shot in the balls, not hit. He basically cheated and took three [sic] minutes off when he needed a rest. Joe Cortez should have been firmer. I was worried they might say he couldn't continue and we'd get a technical draw or something. He was gasping for air, and the referee gave him a break."

The break interrupted Calzaghe's rhythm and momentum. At 2:28 of round eleven, Hopkins repeated the performance, claiming another low blow that no one saw. That earned him a 12-second respite.

Through it all, Calzaghe maintained his composure. Nothing deterred him; not the knockdown, not the fouls, and not the conduct of the fight by the referee. Joe was as strong mentally as Hopkins was and physically stronger than Bernard had thought he'd be. It wasn't pretty, but Calzaghe got the job done. He made the fight; he won the fight. And his superiority becomes clearer when one examines the "punch-stats" compiled by CompuBox.

Calzaghe outlanded Hopkins over the course of the bout by a 232 to 127 margin. Bernard landed ten punches or less in each of the first five rounds and twelve or less in all but three rounds. More telling, Calzaghe outlanded Hopkins in total punches landed and power punches landed in every round.

Adalaide Byrd scored the fight 114–113 for Hopkins. Chuck Giampa (116–111) and Ted Gimza (115–112) saw things more clearly, giving the victory to Calzaghe. This observer scored it 115–113 in Calzaghe's favor.

As for what Hopkins-Calzaghe means in terms of the larger picture; Bernard won his first world title in 1995 but didn't get full respect until 2001 when, at age thirty-six, he toppled Felix Trinidad. Calzaghe has been a champion since 1997 and is now the same age that Hopkins was when he beat Trinidad.

Most likely, Joe will enter the ring next against Roy Jones this autumn. "I've been boxing for twenty-six years," he says. "That's a long time. I'd like this to be my last year. The money's great, but what I really want is to retire without having tasted defeat. It's easy to have one fight too many."

How good is Calzaghe?

"I won't call myself a legend like some people do," he says. "But I'm very proud of what I've accomplished."

That's good enough.

As for Hopkins; there's only one thing that he hasn't done in boxing: get beaten up. With that in mind, now would be a good time for him to retire. At the post-fight press conference, he indicated that he would. "You can't play with age," he said. "I want to be able to speak and talk like I am now, so why push the envelope? I got a chance to sit back and smell the roses."

But Bernard has retired and unretired before. It wouldn't be a surprise to see him in the ring again.

Hopkins's place in history is secure. It might not be as exalted as he'd like it to be, but he would have been competitive against any middle-weight in any era. The saddest thing about Hopkins-Calzaghe is that it afforded Bernard the opportunity to leave boxing as a sportsman in addition to having been a great fighter, and he failed the test. If rounds one and two of the fight showed him at his best, the post-fight press conference revealed him at his worst.

Hopkins was conspicuously ungracious after the fight. "I got beat tonight," he told the media. "But it wasn't by Joe Calzaghe." He then demeaned Calzaghe as a fighter and questioned the accuracy of the punch-stat statistics. Finally, a reporter asked in frustration, "Aren't you going to give Joe any credit for winning the fight?"

"I don't think he won, so how can I give him credit for winning the fight," Bernard answered.

Calzaghe took the words in stride (as he'd taken all of the verbal barbs that Hopkins fired in his direction prior to the fight). "I didn't expect him to be a gracious loser," Joe said. "He's still crying about Jermain Taylor. Hopkins should watch the tape and accept that he lost. There were three American judges, and he still lost. He's just a spoiled little girl, isn't he?"

It goes back to the streets. In the world that Bernard Hopkins comes from, a good loser is a loser.

But a sore loser is a loser too.

Kelly Pavlik was one of boxing's ongoing stories in 2008.

Kelly Pavlik: The Journey Continues

Former middleweight champion Tony Zale grew up in the steeltown of Gary, Indiana. In the late-1940s, he won two of three slugfests against Rocky Graziano in boxing's bloodiest championship trilogy.

A photograph of the U. S. Steel plant in Gary taken years ago tells of the world that Zale came from. A large sign outside the plant reads, "Days Since Last Disabling Injury." Beneath that is the notation:

Power and Fuel Division   998 days
Blast Furnace Division   403 days
Sheet-Pin Hot Roll Division   8 days

"When a guy don't want to go back to a certain thing," Zale said late in life, "that's what makes him fight."

HBO commentator Jim Lampley once observed, "The notion that you don't give up your body to make a living and support your family is an elitist white-collar notion. In the blue-collar world, people do it every day. Laborers who put up high-voltage power wires face constant physical danger. The lungs of coal miners in Appalachia tell a tale of creeping death."

Kelly Pavlik comes from Youngstown, Ohio; a factory town in the heart of America's "rust belt." It's an area rich in coal and iron that was once the center of steel production in the United States. In the 1970s, the local economy went bad. Steel mills shut down. Youngstown and the surrounding communities never fully recovered.

Pavlik is a professional fighter. That's how he provides for himself and his family. In the past year, he has beaten Edison Miranda and Jermain Taylor (twice) and annexed the middleweight championship of the world. He is a source of civic pride and Youngstown's biggest sports hero.

"It's weird, the way things happened," Kelly says. "One day, I was ignored; and the next day, people were calling me a savior. I haven't changed, but a lot of people are treating me different. Go figure. I'm just doing my job."

On June 7, 2008, Pavlik's job took him to Boardwalk Hall in Atlantic City, where he defended his crown against Gary Lockett. At present, Pavlik has two belts (WBC and WBO) in addition to the *Ring Magazine* bauble. Lockett was the WBO's mandatory challenger, although at a March 27 kick-off press conference in New York, the Welshman acknowledged, "I don't know how I got to number one."

The fact that Frank Warren is his promoter helped. Lockett's status within the WBO had far more to do with Warren's admirable lobbying skills than Gary's fistic accomplishments. As Showtime boxing analyst Steve Farhood observed, "Mug an old lady and, if you have the right connections, the WBO will rank you seventh."

Lockett (whose largest previous purse had been $60,000) was pleased to be in line for a $250,000 pay-day against Pavlik. That left open the issue of whether or not the WBC would sanction the fight. After all, the challenger was unranked by the WBC in February 2008.

No problem. There was a sanctioning fee to be had. In March, Lockett (who had never been ranked in the top forty by the WBC) found himself in the #15 slot and thus eligible for championship competition.

Pavlik said all the right things in the build-up to the fight. "It wasn't that long ago that I was the number-one contender," he told the media. "I know the hunger Lockett has for my title."

It was also noted that Lockett had only been on the canvas once in his career (in a 12-round decision win over Ryan Rhodes in 2006). And there was talk that Gary was a "big puncher" with a puncher's chance.

But being a big puncher in the school playground isn't the same as being a big puncher on an elite championship level. And nothing on Lockett's record suggested that he posed a serious threat to Pavlik.

Kelly would be entering the ring with 33 victories in 33 fights, 29 of those wins coming by way of knockout.

Lockett had similar numbers (30–1 with 21 KOs). But his opposition had been suspect and he'd fought only once in the previous thirteen months (against an opponent from Finland named Kai Kauramaki, who'd lost seven of his previous eight bouts and been knocked out nine times).

The challenger was hardly a study in confidence. "I'm a massive underdog," he acknowledged. "I know that. But if I lose, I'll have given it my best shot." That was followed by, "I'm under no illusions. The odds are greatly stacked against me, but it's not impossible. Maybe I'll catch him at

the right time. Maybe they're underestimating me. Maybe this, maybe
that. Who knows?" Next came, "There are a lot of people who think I
don't deserve the shot. Well, I got here the hard way; fighting on small hall
bills for very low money. Anyone who knows me won't begrudge me my
shot." And finally, "Before [the Pavlik fight] came along, I seriously contemplated retirement. I had better things to do with my life. Boxing is like
a job to me. I know a lot of people think you should love boxing, but I
don't. I fell out of love with the sport a long time ago."

In the absence of a compelling match-up between the fighters, the
promotion turned to the trainers for drama.

Pavlik is trained by Jack Loew, whose credentials were questioned
before Kelly dethroned Jermain Taylor last year (at which point, Loew
became a candidate for "trainer of the year" honors). Lockett is guided by
Enzo Calzaghe, who won the "trainer of the year" award and works with
numerous fighters (most notably, his son Joe).

An April 30th press release quoted Loew as saying, "I see where
Lockett has become inspired by Joe Calzaghe's victory over Bernard
Hopkins and is predicting the same result against Kelly. Maybe Enzo
Calzaghe can teach Lockett to slap like a girl, just like Joe. You can get
away with that style of fighting against a 43-year-old geezer, but don't try
that against Kelly."

Then Loew sat back and waited for the fallout, which was fast in
coming.

"I had to go on the Internet because I'd never even heard of this person, Jack Loew," Enzo Calzaghe responded. "All I found was that he paves
driveways. When Pavlik is world champion for ten years and has made 21
title defenses, then I will listen to Loew. Pavlik hasn't even held his title
for a year yet."

For a while, things escalated. It was suggested that, at the final pre-
fight press conference, the staredown should be between Loew and
Calzaghe. Then Mike Pavlik (Kelly's father and no-nonsense co-manager)
proclaimed, "Kelly's not a real big advocate of trash talk. Kelly works hard
to keep his image clean and he never says anything against fighters. I think
it's time to put a stop to the talking."

When the final pre-fight press conference came, each trainer expressed
nothing but admiration for the opposing camp. Although Loew did won-
der aloud, "Why should I have to keep my mouth shut when everyone
else in boxing is allowed to say whatever they want? Besides," he added,

"I'm enjoying this. It's the first time I can remember that I've been taller than the other trainer."

"How tall are you?" Loew was asked.

"Five-seven-and-a-half," he answered. "And make sure you give me the half inch."

On June 7th, Pavlik arrived at Boardwalk Hall at 8:30 pm. Kelly is superstitious about certain things. At the request of his camp, he'd been assigned dressing room #115 (the one he'd been in on the night he seized the middleweight crown from Jermain Taylor eight months earlier).

A New Jersey Board of Athletic Control physician came in to conduct a cursory last-minute physical examination.

"You should be taking my blood pressure, not Kelly's," Mike Pavlik told the doctor. "I'm a nervous wreck."

The room was hot and humid. Some fighters like it that way. Kelly doesn't. Mike asked a maintenance man to bring the temperature down.

Thereafter, Kelly followed a familiar routine. He sat on a chair in the middle of the room, put his legs up on a chair in front of him, and began reading text messages from well-wishers.

Earlier in the month, Mike had told Jason Lloyd of the *Lake County News-Herald,* "Who could have imagined it leading to this? It's like having a kid out in the back yard throwing a football. You can't ever imagine him winning the Super Bowl." Then he'd confided to Joe Scalzo of the *Youngstown Vindicator,* "You go to a newsstand or a supermarket and you see Kelly's picture in the sports section and it doesn't sink in. You see him on the national news. This has definitely been beyond what I ever expected. You can't prepare for this. There's no courses to take and no literature to read."

Now Mike was in his son's dressing room before yet another battle for the middleweight championship of the world. "I'll never get used to this," he said. "I've been at every one of Kelly's fights, and I've been nervous before all of them."

"Which was the toughest for you?" he was asked.

"The first Jermain Taylor fight."

Kelly looked up from his Blackberry. "I don't know about you," he told his father. "But Edison Miranda scared the shit out of me."

The conversation turned to other sports, with Jack Loew joining in. "Who's the greatest running back you ever saw?" the trainer queried.

"Jim Brown," Mike answered.

"The greatest baseball player?"

"Mickey Mantle might not have been the best, but he was my favorite."

At 9:30, referee Eddie Cotton came in to give the fighter his pre-fight instructions.

At 9:40 Loew began taping Kelly's hands.

Manager Cameron Dunkin entered and, referencing a rival fight card in Connecticut, announced, "Paul Williams just knocked out Carlos Quintana in the first round."

A champion dethroned.

At 9:55, the taping was done. Kelly sat down on the floor and began a series of stretching exercises.

Through it all, Mike Cox had stood quietly to the side. Cox is on the Violent Crimes Task Force of the Youngstown Police Department. He and Kelly are friends. On fight night, Mike serves as a cornerman and security guard for Team Pavlik. Now, on impulse, Cox dropped to the floor and did twenty-five push-ups. "Nervous energy," he explained.

At ten o'clock, Kelly stood up and began shadow-boxing. Then he put on his protective cup and powder-blue trunks.

Cox and John Loew (Jack's son) began the process of resolving how they'd carry Pavlik's championship belts to the ring; who would carry which belt and how they'd hold them.

Mike Pavlik massaged his son's shoulders and upper arms. "Feels like steel," he said admiringly.

Kelly pointed to his biceps. "These are the wicks," he told his father. "And these (holding up his fists) are the bombs."

At 10:20, Daniel Ponce De Leon versus Juan Manuel Lopez (the first HBO fight of the evening) began. Two minutes and 25 seconds later, it was over with Lopez (the challenger) winning on a first-round knockout. Another champion dethroned.

Kelly gloved up and began hitting the pads with Loew.

"Fight smart," the trainer told him. "Double the jab. Right hand behind it. He's gonna try to get close and come at you with an overhand right or hook. That's all he's got. Don't let him in. Now if he comes in at an angle like this—"

Loew simulated a move he expected Lockett to make. Kelly turned, taking the angle away.

"That's it; perfect. This guy wants to take everything you worked for away from you. Double jab. Right hand. Hook. There you go. One more time."

Kelly looked sharp and very strong.

Cutman Miguel Diaz greased down Pavlik's face.

An HBO production assistant came into the room and announced, "You walk in six minutes."

Moments later, HBO production coordinator Tami Cotel entered. "You've got five minutes," she said.

Kelly smiled. "Actually, it's five minutes and thirty seconds," he told her. "The other guy told us six minutes, and that was thirty seconds ago."

Cameron Dunkin's cell phone rang. "Unbelievable," he murmured.

"What happened?" Miguel Diaz asked.

"Sergio Mora just won a decision over Vernon Forrest."

Quintana, De Leon, and now Mora. Three champions dethroned in less than an hour.

"It's your night," Mike Pavlik told his son. "Hit him hard."

"It took me seven years to get here," Kelly promised. "I'm not giving it up now."

The fight that followed had the look of a grown man beating up a boy. Pavlik was sharp. He hadn't cut corners in training and, if need be, was in shape to go twelve hard rounds. "That's just the way I am," he said afterward. "How can you not get up for a fight when you know that someone is coming to punch you in the face?"

Meanwhile, Lockett was overmatched and everyone knew it. He didn't have the boxing skills to outbox Kelly or the power to knock him out. He landed only one blow of consequence the entire night. "I made a dumb mistake in the first round," Pavlik said afterward. "I got lazy with my jab, and he caught me with an overhand right. Other than that, I fought a good fight."

Midway through round one, a jab followed by a right hand to the temple wobbled the challenger.

In round two, a hard right to the body followed by two sharp rights to the head put Lockett in trouble. He took a knee to temporarily avoid further punishment, rose, was subjected to further beating, and took another knee at the 2:41 mark.

At that point, the fight could have been stopped. But referee Eddie Cotton and Enzo Calzaghe let it continue until 1:25 of round three, when Lockett went down for the third time and Calzaghe threw in the towel. In less than eight minutes, Pavlik landed 66 power punches. It was a world-class performance on his part and a terribly one-sided fight.

At the post-fight press conference, Bob Arum (Pavlik's promoter) called Kelly "a symbol of America" and "the best middleweight I've ever seen."

"I never saw Sugar Ray Robinson," Arum conceded. "But I saw Carlos Monzon; I saw Marvin Hagler; I saw Thomas Hearns. And Kelly Pavlik is better than any of them."

That's a bit hyperbolic. But right now, Pavlik is the best middleweight in the world. As Oliver Holt of the *Mirror* wrote, "He's a proper champion; not just an alphabet-soup titleholder."

Pavlik sets a fast pace and fights exciting fights. He's learning to be relentless without being reckless. He's likeable and someone who all boxing fans (not just fans from Youngstown) can root for.

Also, in terms of marketability, the color of his skin doesn't hurt. Earlier this month, Thom Loverro of the *Washington Times* observed, "Pavlik is a white American champion, virtually a museum piece in the sport. There hasn't been a white American champion of note in twenty years. And there hasn't been a white American middleweight champion of note since Joey Giardello more than forty years ago."

Arum would like to promote Pavlik against Joe Calzaghe at the Thomas and Mack Center in Las Vegas this autumn. But the fight that Calzaghe really wants is against Roy Jones at 175 pounds; not Pavlik at 168. Thus, it's more likely that Kelly will return to the ring against a less imposing foe, the most likely options being WBC mandatory challenger Giovanni Lorenzo, journeyman Marco Antonio Rubio, and John Duddy.

"It doesn't matter to me who the opponent is," Kelly says. "My job is to fight. I just get in the ring and do the same thing every time. If they tell me to fight Godzilla, I'll fight him."

But Pavlik needs more inquisitors like Jermain Taylor and Edison Miranda (not more sanctioning-body mandatory challengers) to prove his greatness. For now, it's premature to be thinking about his place in history.

As for Gary Lockett; he's now a line in the record book beneath Pavlik's name. And someday, he'll tell his grandchildren that, once upon a time, he fought for the middleweight championship of the world.

Miguel Cotto versus Antonio Margarito was, in my view (and the view of many), the best fight of the year. .

Cotto-Margarito: La Batalla

It was called "La Batalla."

On July 26, 2008, at the MGM Grand Garden Arena in Las Vegas, the eyes of the boxing world focused on the much-anticipated showdown between Miguel Cotto and Antonio Margarito.

Cotto-Margarito was marketed as a crucial chapter in the ongoing rivalry between Mexican and Puerto Rican fighters. Cotto has lived in Puerto Rico for his entire life. Margarito was born California, but his family moved to Tijuana when he was two years old and he has lived in Mexico ever since.

Before the bout, there was a lot of talk about Mexican fighters being known for an almost blind toughness. "Mexican tradition," wrote William Dettloff, "is you're not in the fight until you're bleeding; that if you don't have a hook to the liver, you're nothing; that if you're not moving forward, you're running away." Conversely, Puerto Rican fighters are often seen as stylists in the mold of Wilfredo Benitez and Hector Camacho.

In reality these stereotypes are belied by Puerto Rican punchers (such as Wilfredo Gomez and Felix Trinidad) and Mexican practitioners of the finer points of boxing (e.g. Marco Antonio Barrera). Indeed, for much of his career, Cotto has fought "like a Mexican fighter."

Regardless, passions between the two countries run deep. Before his 1992 victory over Camacho, Mexican icon Julio Cesar Chavez said, "The Mexican people will never forgive me if I lose. They will lynch me if I lose. I couldn't return to Mexico."

Margarito acknowledged, "Ever since I signed for this fight against Cotto, I was very aware that it is Mexican against Puerto Rican. That makes it a very important fight, a special fight." And Cotto observed, "Everybody knows about the rivalry. Now it's me against Margarito."

But in simpler terms, Cotto–Margarito promised to be a great fight, period. The combatants could have come from Slovakia and the Czech Republic and boxing fans would have eagerly anticipated the battle.

"Forget all the bullshit and phony events that HBO is into these days," promoter Bob Arum said at the May 22nd kick-off press conference. "Boxing done right is the most exciting sport there is. This is two honest, hard-working, real fighters."

Cotto is soft-spoken and polite. One has to move close to hear him speak. His English has progressed to the point where he now conducts entire interviews with the English-speaking media without an interpreter. He has come a long way since 2004, when he journeyed to Las Vegas to fight Randall Bailey. On that occasion, a security guard at Mandalay Bay saw him walking around the casino, evaluated him as an undesirable, and asked him to leave the casino floor.

At the start of 2008, Cotto was grouped with Floyd Mayweather Jr, Manny Pacquiao, and Joe Calzaghe at the top of most pound-for-pound rankings. His record stood at 32-and-0 with 26 knockouts. Victories over Paulie Malignaggi, Carlos Quintana, Zab Judah, and Shane Mosley had raised his profile to the point where many observers considered him worthy of a place in the pantheon of Puerto Rican boxing heroes alongside Benitez, Gomez, Trinidad, Carlos Ortiz, and Jose Torres.

"If you ask me to put me on a scale with other boxers," Cotto said when the subject was raised, "I cannot tell you that I deserve a ranking. I don't compare myself to the other greats. My job is to train and to box. I just try to do my work to win for me and my family and my country and the people who root for me. The people that write about boxing will decide my ranking and my legacy."

As for Margarito; a victory over Cotto would move him closer to the gods of Mexico: Chavez, Barrera, Salvador Sanchez, Ruben Olivares, Vincente Salvidar, and Erik Morales.

Margarito had five losses in 41 fights prior to meeting Cotto, but that statistic was deceiving. He'd turned pro at age fifteen. Three of his losses came when he was 16, 17, and 18 years old by decision against opponents with a 31-and-3 composite record.

There's nothing subtle about the way Margarito fights. As Jim Lampley observes, "Antonio is willing to get hit for the opportunity to hit you back."

"I'm the type of fighter who throws a lot of punches and puts a lot of pressure on my opponent," Antonio says. "My strength is my power and my stamina and my ability to be on top of my opponent all the time."

The odds opened with Cotto a 2-to-1 favorite and rose as high as 13-to-5 before returning to 2-to-1. The feeling among the boxing intelligentsia was that Miguel had been good to begin with and was constantly improving as a fighter. Having moved from 140 to 147 pounds, he was stronger and had even more stamina than he'd displayed earlier in his career.

Also, several of Margarito's previous fights cast doubt on Antonio's status as an elite fighter. In 2004, he was struggling against Daniel Santos when an accidental clash of heads ended the match. The fight went to the judges' scorecards with Santos winning a split decision.

Two years later, Margarito looked less-than-imposing in defeating Joshua Clottey, who suffered damage to his left hand in the fight. And in 2007, Antonio turned down a match against Cotto in favor of a WBO title defense against Paul Williams. But against Williams, he gave away the early rounds and, after rallying impressively, virtually disappeared in round twelve to lose a close decision.

Still, a realistic case could be made for Margarito beating Cotto. Miguel is used to being the brute. Antonio would be the most physically imposing fighter that Cotto had faced and the first who could be considered more physically imposing than Miguel.

Moreover, Cotto's greatest perceived vulnerability was his chin and his propensity to get hit on it. Margarito was expected to put that theory to the test.

"I think it's going to come down to whose rhythm do we dance to," Antonio said. "I have a lot more power than Judah and Mosley and a bigger heart than both of them combined. I know I have twelve good hard rounds in me. I'm not going to pace myself. I'm going to go hard and see if he can keep up with me. I've been waiting for so long to get to this place. This fight is my consecration."

And significantly, the relationship between Cotto and his trainer (his uncle, Evangelista, who had trained him from his first day in the gym) was strained. During a fight-week sitdown with the media, Miguel said that the problem stemmed in large part from the fact that the gym they train in is too-heavily trafficked and he has to wait to move from one training exercise to another. Miguel Diaz (Cotto's longtime cutman) added, "Evangelista has had control over Miguel since he was a boy, and there comes a time when Miguel wants to make his own decisions."

But a source in the Cotto camp pointed to other reasons for the estrangement. First, there had been a much-publicized falling out between Evangelista and Miguel's brother, Jose, who Evangelista also trained. Miguel tried to patch things up between them, but Evangelista wanted no part of it. And second, Evangelista had been critical of the way that Miguel separated from his wife and particularly the fact that Miguel had brought his girlfriend to the gym and exposed his children to her.

"It's like a marriage," Miguel said when pressed on the issue of his relationship with Evangelista. "We have our happy moments; we have our problems. It's not a hundred percent, but it's better now." As for his family life, Miguel said simply, "I'm not the best husband, but I want to be the best father."

Viewing the whole picture, it was clear that Cotto was a favorite at risk. And he deserved credit for fighting Margarito because, given his unbeaten record, Miguel had more to lose than Antonio by taking the fight.

A great fight isn't necessarily a big event: So much of boxing is illusion; how a fight is sold and how the result is spun afterward. Cotto-Margarito never became a big event. Arum put the bout in Las Vegas. Part of his motivation was that there's a huge pay-per-view market in the southwest and California that Cotto had been unable to penetrate. The theory was that a Vegas site would engender more media coverage in those markets and hence more pay-per-view buys.

The MGM Grand Garden Arena seats 16,000. A disappointing crowd of 10,477 attended the fight. Puerto Rico versus Mexico is still essentially an east coast rivalry. The bout would have been better attended had it taken place at Madison Square Garden or in Atlantic City. But Arum's judgment was vindicated by the first post-fight pay-per-view numbers, which indicated that there were close to 500,000 buys.

The fight itself lived up to its billing and then some. As it unfolded, everyone in the arena understood that they were watching greatness. There were virtually no clinches and the pace never slowed over ten-and-a-half exhilarating brutal rounds.

Each man had weighed in at 147 pounds, but Margarito was three inches taller with a six-inch reach advantage. Cotto could have negated those numbers by going inside, but it seemed as though that was the last place he wanted to be. From the early moments on, it was clear that Miguel respected Antonio's punching power more than Antonio respected Cotto's. Miguel is used to being the fighter who applies pressure, but here it was the other way around.

One has to marvel at a fight plan that calls for beating Cotto by walking through his punches. But essentially, that's what Margarito strategized. He was the aggressor throughout, moving inexorably forward and forcing exchanges whenever he could. "Pressure, pressure, pressure," he said afterward. "That was the plan. I knew he was a better boxer, but I am the heavier puncher."

Cotto's only road to victory was to outbox Margarito. He couldn't out-tough him. And Miguel had never been in a situation like that before. He had faster hands and was the better boxer. He did his best to be elusive, circling away and landing sharp crisp hard counters. He won five of the first six rounds by getting off first and hit Margarito with punches that had caused other fighters, good fighters, to crumble. But Antonio shrugged them off and kept moving relentlessly forward, digging to the body with thudding blows and going upstairs when the opportunity presented itself.

Margarito had the better chin. That was the difference. It enabled him to beat Cotto down with constant pressure and brutal punching power, just as Miguel has done to so many fighters in the past. As early as round two, Cotto was bleeding from the nose. He suffered a cut on his left eyelid in round three. By round six, he was bleeding from the mouth.

By then, it was clear that, even though Cotto was ahead on points, Margarito was imposing his will. "In the sixth round," Antonio said afterward, "I felt him weakening and I knew the fight was mine."

From round seven on, Margarito beat Cotto up. Miguel's facial features were remade. He fought back, but the smothering assault continued. Cotto's counters became less about causing damage than simply keeping Antonio off. And Miguel's punches were losing their sting, which took away the only defense he had against Margarito's assault.

It's an axiom of boxing that any fighter can lose and any fighter can be broken. In round eleven, Cotto was broken. A barrage of punches punctuated by a vicious left uppercut put Miguel on the canvas at the 1:20 mark. He rose, but his face was a bloody mess and he bore the look of a thoroughly beaten man. Another barrage of punches, this one lasting twenty seconds, backed him into a neutral corner. Then, what had once been unthinkable happened.

Miguel Cotto took a knee.

Referee Kenny Bayless began to count and Evangelista Cotto, white towel in hand, intervened.

It was a great fight that left hardened observers in awe of what they had seen. "This was Margarito's night." Cotto said afterward. "He did his job better than I did."

As for the future; Margarito's victory muddies the waters a bit. If Cotto had won, he would have stood alone atop the welterweight division and been a serious contender for the mythological "pound-for-pound" crown. Whatever Margarito was against Daniel Santos, he's a lot better than that now. But Antonio also lost to Paul Williams. Williams split two fights with Carlos Quintana. Quintana was destroyed by Cotto. And so it goes.

Meanwhile, Cotto–Margarito showed what boxing can and should be. Two elite fighters with exciting styles in the prime of their respective careers fighting each other in a competitive fight.

The sport is healthier now that it was ten days ago because of Cotto–Margarito. And boxing fans have served notice in the form of pay-per-view buys that they want to see more than good fighters. They want to see good fights.

I was in Kelly Pavlik's dressing room before and after each of his first three championship victories. But losing is also part of boxing.

Pavlik–Hopkins:
Boxing Is a Cruel Teacher

Boxing has its own version of The Golden Rule: "Do unto to others as they would do unto you." On October 18, 2008, Kelly Pavlik entered the ring at Boardwalk Hall in Atlantic City intent upon scoring a decisive victory over Bernard Hopkins. He didn't have to knock Hopkins out. But he was committed to fashioning a triumph that left no doubt as to which man was the better fighter. "I want everybody to know that I beat Hopkins," Pavlik said. "And I want Bernard to know that I beat him too."

That fit with the plan. Hopkins–Pavlik was supposed to be about Hopkins becoming a building block in the Pavlik legend. Instead, things evolved the other way around.

Pavlik was born and raised in Youngstown, Ohio. The national economy is now experiencing what Youngstown has endured for three decades. Since 1980, as jobs vanished, the city's population has dropped from 115,000 to 80,000. It has the lowest median income in the United States among cities with 65,000 people or more.

Pavlik has stayed close to his roots. He and his wife live with their twenty-two-month-old daughter in Boardman, a community adjacent to Youngstown. "If people are waiting for him to move to Las Vegas or California, it ain't gonna happen," says Kelly's longtime trainer, Jack Loew.

Within that milieu, Pavlik is the proverbial local boy made good. On September 29, 2007, he dethroned Jermain Taylor to become middleweight champion of the world. Another victory over Taylor and a third-round knockout of Gary Lockett followed. Not only was Kelly undefeated, he fought (as Tim Keown of *ESPN: The Magazine* wrote) "like a Marine taking a hill."

Pavlik never shies away from a challenge, is willing to go in tough, and is a nice guy to boot. He even has a self-effacing sense of humor.

During a recent conference call, a reporter asked, "Do you think that you can take the place of Oscar De La Hoya after De La Hoya retires?"

"It would be nice," Kelly answered. "But I've got a couple of things against me. First of all, there's my looks."

Pavlik's success in the ring has made him a celebrity at home. After winning the title, he got some endorsements in the under-$10,000 range. That's not big money. But if a fighter has been doing landscape work for ten dollars an hour (as Pavlik was in early 2007), it's a start. Greenwood Chevrolet gave him an SUV in exchange for some autograph sessions and a local commercial.

Ohio State football coach Jim Tressel telephoned and asked Kelly to address the team. Cleveland Browns coach Romeo Crennel also called. Pavlik was invited to throw out the first ball for an American League Championship Series game between the Cleveland Indians and Boston Red Sox.

"He was a little nervous about being in the clubhouse because he's a big Indians fan," Mike Pavlik (Kelly's father) recalls. "He walked in there kind of meek. And when the Indians saw him, they rushed up to him."

Later, Kelly told Joe Scalzo of the *Youngstown Vindicator,* "Things like that make you start thinking, 'I guess I did make it.'" Indeed, Pavlik's statewide appeal was such that his promoter, Bob Arum (an ardent supporter of Hillary Clinton) prevailed upon him to endorse the New York senator in this year's Democratic presidential primary in Ohio.

"I was at home and the telephone rang," Kelly remembers. "I picked it up, said 'hello,' and someone said, 'Hi, this is Hillary Clinton.' I'm like, 'Sure. Right. Uh-huh.' She's trying to convince me it's really her, and I'm wondering which of my friends is jerking me around."

There were indications that Kelly could go national. An endorsement deal with Affliction calls for the fledgling clothing company to pay him roughly $100,000 this year.

But there was also pressure. Ohio State has come up short in college football's last two BCS championship games. LeBron James has been unable to lead the Cleveland Cavaliers to the promised land. The Cleveland Indians haven't won the World Series since 1948. The Cleveland Browns have never won a Super Bowl. Kelly was expected to win every time he entered the ring.

After Pavlik knocked out Gary Lockett in June of this year, Jack Loew declared, "As long as Kelly stays in the middleweight division, this is what you're going to see." The question was, who would boxing fans see it against next? HBO turned down Marco Antonio Rubio, John Duddy, and Raul Marquez as opponents. It okayed Pavlik against Arthur Abraham, Paul Williams, and Winky Wright, but none of those fights could be made. Arum offered Team Pavlik a million dollars plus an upside to fight Rubio on an independently-produced pay-per-view card. But Kelly's purse had been $2,500,000 for the Lockett fight and he wanted to stay at that level.

Thus, Team Pavlik looked to opponents in higher weight divisions. Joe Calzaghe wasn't interested. Pavlik-Hopkins at a catchweight of 170 pounds followed. Each fighter was guaranteed a $3,000,000 purse. After paying 20 percent to his co-managers (his father and Cameron Dunkin), 10 percent to Jack Loew, sanctioning fees, other expenses, and taxes, Kelly would walk away from the fight with more than a million dollars. And his title wouldn't be at risk.

"When we looked and saw who was out there," Arum explained shortly after the fight was signed, "we realized this was the best fight for Kelly, both from a money standpoint and a notoriety standpoint. A victory over Hopkins will put Kelly in good stead. Nobody has beaten up Hopkins. If Kelly can knock Hopkins out or beat the hell out of him, he'll be on top of the world."

But that was easier said than done. Hopkins is one of boxing's most compelling personalities with skills to match. Bernard's life story is well known. In 1982, the year Pavlik was born, seventeen-year-old Bernard Hopkins began a much-deserved fifty-six-month stay at Graterford State Penitentiary in Pennsylvania. After his release from prison, he turned to boxing and lost his first fight.

"My friends were selling cocaine, which was big in the eighties," Hopkins recalls. "They were driving Jaguars and Mercedes, and you know they wanted me to work with them."

But Hopkins stayed clean. "You never can beat the system," he says. "You can only beat individuals. But I learned how to work the system and beat the people who run it at their own game."

A lot of people dislike Bernard. Patrick Kehoe has written, "Hopkins can desecrate a Puerto Rican flag and by implication the people for which it stands, invert the race card, and answer charges rightly leveled against his malice by streaming nonsensical rebuttals as if an arduous life gives him the license to say anything, anytime, anywhere."

Old allies such as Bouie Fisher and Lou DiBella have been turned into enemies. After winning a split-decision victory over Hopkins earlier this year, Joe Calzaghe declared, "He was a complete ass. Some fighters pretend to be an ass before the fight. But there's mutual respect afterward, always. That's a great part of the noble art of boxing. Try to knock each other out in the ring but be gentlemen afterward. [After the fight] I gave him his respect. He then showed the same disdain and disrespect he'd shown before the fight, continuing with this delusional attitude that he'd won."

Hopkins has a simple response for Calzaghe and everyone else who criticizes him. "I never second-guess my decisions," he says "because I think long and hard about the decisions I make before I say 'I do.' For twenty years, other than boxing issues—and some say I'm right, some say I'm wrong about them—no one has had any reason to question Bernard Hopkins. So love me, hate me, enjoy me while I'm here. Who are you gonna get a better sound bite from than Bernard Hopkins?"

There were plenty of sound-bites during the build-up to Pavlik-Hopkins. Surprisingly, few of them came from Bernard. At the August 5th kick-off press conference in New York, he told the media, "I respect Kelly Pavlik. I have nothing bad to say about Kelly Pavlik. Kelly Pavlik became middleweight champion of the world the right way. He earned it."

In response, Pavlik said, "I want my legacy to be as great as Bernard's."

Thus, this time, the sound-bites came from the Internet (the mainstream press having largely ignored the fight). For the most part, they were negative comments based on the belief that Bernard is now more belligerent outside the ring than in it.

Eric Raskin of ESPN.com opined, "Paying to watch Hopkins fight is like paying to watch a pitcher hold a runner on first." Steve Kim of Maxboxing.com declared, "The problem in selling this fight is the specter of seeing Hopkins do what he does best, which is to take away his opponent's preferred offensive weapon and suck the life and action out of any fight he's involved in. If this were hoops, he'd be in the four-corners all game and slow the tempo as soon as the tip-off."

"Sometimes the way I fight isn't pretty," Hopkins acknowledged. "I do what I gotta do."

Naazim Richardson (Bernard's trainer) concurred, saying, "A 43-year-old fighter is going to do the things he has to do. Muhammad Ali did the rope-a-dope to extend his career. Bernard has his tricks too."

But the bottom line was, the world expected a boring fight. And the near-unanimous assumption among the media was that Pavlik would win. Ergo, Kelly's assignment wasn't just to beat Hopkins. Jermain Taylor and Joe Calzaghe had already done that. It was to beat Hopkins decisively, thereby establishing himself as boxing's newest superstar.

That was a tough assignment. Pavlik is a middleweight. He fought the rematch against Jermain Taylor at 166 pounds because Taylor wasn't willing to make the sacrifices necessary to make weight. But the night of their rematch, both men were really over-the-limit middleweights.

Pavlik's size and strength are usually his biggest edge. Against Hopkins, he would be forfeiting that advantage. A crucial element of Kelly's fight plan would be to wear down Bernard with constant pressure. But in boxing, it's hard to wear down a significantly bigger foe.

And more significantly, Hopkins would be the smartest, most skilled opponent that Pavlik had faced. "You know how I fight," Kelly had told fans at an August 27th "pep rally" in Youngstown. "You know my style. Nothing's gonna change."

That was the problem. Hopkins knew exactly how Kelly fights. "This kid is so fundamental," Bernard told Naazim Richardson at the start of training camp. "If I can't beat him, I should retire."

"I know that Kelly walks you down with his jab," Richardson said the week of the fight. "I know that Bernard won't be able to coast. Kelly will force Bernard to fight. An ass-whipping means nothing to Kelly. Whatever happens, he'll keep trying and he punches hard enough that you don't want to get hit. But Kelly is going to realize early that he's in there with a fighter. He's been in there before against athletes who boxed a bit. Bernard is all about fighting, and there's a difference between a great athlete and a great fighter. Kelly has a shotgun for a right hand. But if you take away the shotgun, he ain't got nothing. Bernard might not have a shotgun; but he's got a switchblade, a razor blade, and a dagger. Bernard can't play basketball. Bernard can't rap. But Bernard can fight his ass off."

And Hopkins added, "Kelly Pavlik wants to knock Bernard Hopkins out. At least that's what he says. But I got the book on Pavlik. Comes straight forward. Jab. Good right hand. Determined. Lots of heart. Slow. Not a skilled boxer. Anyone who thinks that I'm just showing up for a payday on October 18 is wrong. The last time I fought in Atlantic City was two years ago against Antonio Tarver. I was a 3-to-1 underdog and Antonio was going to knock me out. Do you all remember that? Now I'm a 4-to-1, 5-to-1 underdog. But I'm not like any of those other guys that Pavlik beat. This fight is going to be two construction workers fighting on a pier when both of them is hungry but one of them is more skilled than the other. That's my kind of fight. It's going to be a rough tough fight. I'll take some career out of Kelly Pavlik."

That said; there were a lot of people who thought that Hopkins would take a pound-for-pound pounding. The image of Bernard sucking air and stalling for time in the late rounds against Joe Calzaghe convinced many that Pavlik was a lock. The prevailing view was that Hopkins had bitten off more than he could chew and that he could no longer do what he'd done against Tarver. Jim Lampley spoke for many when he opined, "Bernard Hopkins late in his career has become a master of the close decision loss."

Pavlik's greatest perceived advantage was the difference in age between the fighters. Bernard is forty-three; Kelly is twenty-six. Freddie Roach (who trained Hopkins for the Calzaghe fight) recalled, "At one time during training for Calzaghe, we asked Bernard to go a few more rounds, and he said 'no.' He said he knew his body and he didn't want to push himself anymore that day. Naazim said that had never happened before. And four times against Calzaghe, Bernard went to the wrong corner at the end of a round. I tried to talk to him about it after the fight, but he didn't want to listen."

"Bernard has had a great career," Roach continued. "He doesn't need the money. He has nothing to prove. I think he should retire, and I'd definitely rather that he not take this fight. Kelly Pavlik is a big puncher. He's a young strong guy, who backs people up well. Bernard isn't going to be able to lull him into a slow pace. Maybe Bernard is crafty enough to outbox him; but not the way he looked against Calzaghe in the last fight. This is a dangerous fight. I'm a bit worried. My concern is that Bernard might get hurt."

Jack Loew was in accord. "There comes a day when every old dog has to be put down," the trainer said. "This will be a good fight for six or seven rounds. Then I see it playing out like Cotto-Margarito. A fighter can back up and take shots for just so long. One way or another, whether it's the referee or a towel from the corner or Bernard himself, this fight will end early. I think Kelly will stop him in the late rounds."

As for the possibility of Hopkins seeking an edge by engaging in illegal tactics, Loew warned, "Don't be surprised if we put Bernard's nuts in this throat before he touches us low. We're just as rough as he is on the inside."

Pavlik covered the remaining bases, saying, "I'll go in there, throw punches, and make Bernard work all night. The weight is no big deal to me. At 170, I'll have more energy and snap to my punches. Bernard is a good defensive fighter, but he's not unhittable. Bernard gets hit, and I hit harder than Calzaghe. They say that Bernard gets in his opponent's head, but I get in my opponent's head too. I just do it a different way. Bernard will be thinking about me when he's lying in bed the night before the fight."

Joe Scalzo summed things up when he wrote, "Pavlik gets asked about his weight; Hopkins gets asked about his age. Pavlik gets asked about winning by knockout; Hopkins gets asked about losing his recent fights by controversial decisions. Pavlik gets asked about his next fight. Hopkins gets asked, 'When's your last fight?' Not surprisingly, Pavlik is a 4–1 favorite."

Indeed, rather than debate the outcome of the contest, some insiders openly wondered what would happen when (not if) Hopkins found himself in trouble. Would he (a) fight like a warrior to the point of going out on his shield; (b) foul to gain an edge and, failing that, be disqualified; or (c) feign injury and quit.

Even Hillary Clinton got into the act. The week before the fight, she telephoned Pavlik to thank him for his help in the primary and wish him luck. "The first call," Kelly noted afterward, "I mean, who would believe that you're sitting at home and Hillary Clinton calls. By now, it's not such a shock."

Meanwhile, as the fight approached, there was one final point to be considered. Pavlik had an 88 percent knockout percentage, but Hopkins had never been knocked out. In fact, Bernard had been on the canvas only twice in his career; both times against Segundo Mercado at high altitude in Ecuador in a bout that was declared a draw.

Thus, Top Rank matchmaker Bruce Trampler sounded a cautionary note when a conversation turned to big-money fights that lay ahead for Pavlik. "Before all that happens," Trampler warned, "'A' Kelly has to win the fight, and 'B' Kelly has to win the fight."

Team Pavlik arrived in Kelly's dressing room at Boardwalk Hall on Saturday night at 8:45. Several minutes later, Dr. Domenic Coletta of the New Jersey Athletic Control Board came into the room to administer the final pre-fight physical. Everything went according to form until Coletta asked, "Are you on any medication?"

"Yes, sir."

"What for?"

"Bronchitis."

"Did you have a fever?"

"Not today."

"Before today?"

"A hundred and one degrees."

"What have you been taking?"

Mike Pavlik handed a sheet of paper to the doctor. "Here's what they gave Kelly."

Coletta scanned the list. Mucinex, penicillin (one shot on Wednesday night), and ciprofloxacin (500 mg twice a day through the day of the fight).

"How do you feel now?"

"Okay."

Coletta finished his work and left. Over the next ten minutes, Mike and Jack Loew exchanged bad jokes. "That's a new low, no pun intended," Mike quipped after one of Jack's particularly bad offerings.

Then Mike turned pensive. "This has been an incredible journey and I'm glad to be part of it," he said. "But when it's over, I won't miss it. When your kids are little, you say, 'When they're older, I won't worry about them.' But you always worry. Little kids, little problems. Big kids, big problems."

Larry Merchant came in for HBO's ritual pre-fight interview. He was followed by Arturo Gatti, who wished Kelly well. In previous years, Gatti had been the standard-bearer for boxing in Atlantic City. Pavlik, it was hoped, would be his successor.

Kelly began doing stretching exercises on the floor.

On a television monitor in a corner of the room, middleweight prospect Danny Jacobs could be seen disposing of a mismatched opponent in the first round. "Jacobs fought better guys in the amateurs than he's fighting now," Loew said.

HBO production coordinator Tami Cotel entered and asked Kelly to weigh in on the "unofficial" HBO scale. Kelly complied.

The day before, Hopkins had weighed in at 170 pounds and Pavlik at 169. But those numbers were deceiving. Now, Kelly (wearing a track suit but no shoes) weighed 176. Minutes earlier, wearing sneakers, Hopkins had tipped the scale at 185. Bernard would have a considerable weight advantage.

The second pay-per-view fight of the evening (Marco Antonio Rubio versus Enrique Ornelas) began. The winner would be the mandatory challenger for Kelly's WBC middleweight belt. All eyes focused on the television monitor.

"Rubio gets hit an awful lot," Loew said.

Referee Benjy Esteves came in and gave Kelly his pre-fight instructions. "Are there any questions?" Esteves asked at the end.

There were none.

"The Hopkins corner said they were concerned about rough tactics from Kelly," the referee added.

That elicited a collective laugh from Team Pavlik.

"All right; just keep it clean," Esteves cautioned.

Rubio emerged with a split-decision triumph over Ornelas. "That's your mandatory," Loew told Kelly with a smile.

John Loew (Jack's son) went down the hall to watch John David Jackson tape Hopkins's hands.

Kelly took off his track suit, put on black ring trunks, and laced up his shoes.

At 10:20, Jack Loew told the control board inspector, "Tell the Hopkins people I'm starting to wrap. If they want somebody here, fine. But I'm starting."

Steven Luevano against Billy Dib (the final preliminary bout) began.

Naazim Richardson entered the room and looked on as Loew taped

Kelly's hands. When the job was done, Richardson left. Kelly moved to the center of the room and began shadow-boxing. More stretching exercises followed.

At eleven o'clock, Loew gloved Kelly up.

Fighter and trainer began working the pads. It was Kelly's first strenuous exercise of the night.

"Double jab," Loew instructed. "That's it. Chin down. Aggressive but patient."

Kelly began to cough.

"Stick to the game plan. Nice and easy. Double the jab."

The hard edge that had permeated the dressing room prior to Kelly's recent fights didn't seem to be there.

"That's it. Punish him. Hard to the body. If you hit him on the belt and he turns to the referee to bitch, jump on his ass."

Each time Loew took a break, Kelly went into the adjacent bathroom, coughed, and spat out phlegm. The third time he did it, Mike Pavlik turned away in a corner of the room, pressed both fists against the wall, and took a deep breath. A very deep breath. "Christ," he murmured.

Kelly returned from the bathroom and looked around the room at Team Pavlik: his father and brother (Mike Jr), Jack Loew, John Loew, Mike Cox (a Youngstown cop, cornerman, and friend), cutman Miguel Diaz, and Cameron Dunkin. "You guys are a nice team," he said. "But you're an ugly bunch."

Despite the shaky national economy, there was a near-capacity crowd in Boardwalk Hall. Pavlik entered the ring first to a roar of approval. Hopkins, wearing a hood and black executioner's mask, followed.

At the start of a fight, a boxing ring is like a chessboard with an infinite number of possible moves to be played. Bernard didn't play with Kelly, but there were times when it looked as though he was. He did everything right and fought more aggressively than he has in a long time.

The first two rounds set the pattern for the fight. Hopkins was faster. He moved in and out at will. Working off the absence of a left hook in Pavlik's arsenal, he circled to the right to avoid Kelly's right hand. Kelly's jab wasn't landing, which made his right hand even more ineffectual.

The best that could be said for Pavlik's performance after two rounds was that he was one point ahead of where Joe Calzaghe had been at a similar juncture in his fight against Hopkins (when Joe was knocked down in round one and lost round two as well). The questions now were (1) could Kelly make adjustments as Calzaghe had done; and (2) could Bernard keep it up for twelve rounds. The answers were "no" and "yes."

Pavlik simply couldn't get untracked. There were times when it looked as though he was fighting in slow motion. Hopkins was in control from beginning to end. He found the holes in Kelly's defense and exploited them with sharp precision punching. He was too big and too good. He outboxed Pavlik and he outfought him. He asked questions all night long and Kelly had no answers.

By round eight, it was clear that Pavlik needed a knockout to win. But Bernard is hard to play catch-up against and no one has ever knocked him out. In round nine, his punches opened an ugly slice on the outside of Kelly's right eyelid. Finally, in round ten, Pavlik maneuvered Hopkins into a corner and landed a right hand flush. Nothing happened.

"That's when I knew the fight was over," Richardson said afterward.

Hopkins outlanded Pavlik 172-to-108 with a 148-to-55 edge in power punches. Contrary to all expectations, he also threw more punches than Kelly in nine of the twelve rounds.

Referee Benjy Esteves deducted a point from Pavlik for hitting behind the head in round eight and from Hopkins for holding in round nine. Neither deduction was warranted; neither affected the outcome of the fight.

The judges scored it 119–106, 118–108, and 117–109. Hopkins fought a superb fight. No over-forty fighter has ever looked better.

"This was the best performance of my career," Bernard said at the post-fight press conference. "Better than Tarver, better than Trinidad, better than Oscar, better than my twenty-one defenses. It out-does everything I accomplished. I am extremely happy tonight."

As for what comes next; Hopkins's dream scenario has Roy Jones beating Joe Calzaghe on November 8th followed by a Hopkins-Jones mega-fight in 2009. "Fighters don't retire from the ring," Bernard says. "The ring retires fighters. I think people still want to see me and Roy Jones get together one more time. And I keep proving that I'm not ready to be retired."

But no matter what happens, Bernard has had quite a ride. His longevity violates the nature of the sport. It's like an object defying gravity, falling up instead of down. And his ring accomplishments are all the more remarkable when one considers that he has succeeded without a big punch.

Meanwhile, as Hopkins celebrated his victory, a markedly different scene was unfolding in Pavlik's dressing room.

"I felt weak," Kelly told the members of his team gathered around him. "I didn't have anything on my punches. I couldn't get off; it just wasn't there. He beat me to the punch all night long."

Kelly's wife, Samantha, moved to his side.

"Jermain Taylor is faster than Hopkins; and against Jermain, I never had that problem. The way I fought tonight, anybody could kick my ass."

Tears welled up in Kelly's eyes. He sat on a chair and began to cry. Samantha knelt at his knees and tried to console him.

"You didn't lose this fight," Mike Pavlik told his son. "The loss was my fault. I should have pulled it when you got bronchitis."

Kelly shrugged. "I lost it."

Domenic Coletta came in and administered a brief post-fight physical. Then it was time to decide what to do about the cut on Kelly's eyelid. "We can do stitches now or a butterfly now and stitches in the morning," the physician advised.

"Let's get it over with tonight," Mike Pavlik said.

"I'll call ahead to the hospital," Coletta offered. "They'll have someone ready to stitch it up."

At 1:00 A.M., Kelly left the dressing room with his father, Mike Cox, and a paramedic at his side. As they walked to a waiting ambulance, Kelly was approached by several fans who wanted him to stop and pose with them for photos. Each time, as his father and Cox did a slow burn, he complied.

"Good fight," one of the fans said.

"Actually, it wasn't so good," Kelly replied.

When they reached the ambulance, Kelly and his father got in back with the paramedic. Mike Cox sat up front with the driver.

Kelly sat silent and stared straight ahead during the ride. "When you start boxing," he'd said earlier in the week, "your first goal is to become a world champion. Once you accomplish that, you start thinking about your place in history."

But a fighter's dream is hard to fulfill. One day, he's on top of the world. And twelve rounds later, the sky has fallen. The cruel reality of boxing is that, no matter how good a fighter is, eventually he loses. Sooner or later, there comes a night when he can't solve the puzzle in front of them. It had first happened to Hopkins when he fought Roy Jones Jr fifteen years ago. As Jack Dempsey noted looking back on his own brilliant career, "Losing is an occupational hazard in boxing."

At 1:10 A.M., the ambulance arrived at the emergency room entrance to the Atlantic City Regional Medical Center. Kelly walked through the reception area into a small square room with a linoleum tile floor and hospital-green curtain drawn across the door. After he lay down on the bed, a nurse came in to check his blood pressure and temperature.

A second nurse followed.

"How much do you weigh?"

"172 pounds."

"How tall are you?"

"Six-two-and-a-half."

"Date of birth?"

"Four five eighty-two."

Address . . . Telephone number . . . Social Security number . . .

"Do you have a headache now?"

"No."

At 1:20, Dr. Eric Wolk entered the room, introduced himself, and examined the cut.

"I'm not a plastic surgeon," Wolk said. "But I can do this. I'd tell you if I couldn't."

Kelly nodded. "That's okay. I trust you."

"It's a very linear laceration. It will close up nicely."

"My grandmother was a nurse. She sewed me up lots of times when I was a kid."

Wolk filled a syringe with anesthesia.

"We're going to numb it first. Then we'll irrigate it. After that, we'll close it up."

At 1:30, the needle went in.

"Is anything else bothering you?" Wolk asked.

"Just my feelings."

Mike Pavlik patted his son's leg. "This is my fault," he said. "Every instinct, every intuition I had told me I should have pulled the fight when you got bronchitis."

Wolk crafted seven stitches.

"Can I take a shower when I get back to my room?" Kelly asked.

"No problem. Just don't rub the eye."

Kelly stood up. "Thanks, doc. I appreciate it."

"Feel better," Volk said.

Kelly took a deep breath. "I've lost once," he told his father. "Hopkins is a legend and he's lost five times."

Father and son embraced.

"I don't care about the loss," Mike said. "All I care about is that you're all right."

At 2:00 A.M., Kelly, his father, and Mike Cox walked out of the hospital into the chill night air. In five hours, the sun would rise over the Atlantic Ocean. Kelly's face would be bruised and swollen. It would hurt to know that he'd lost an important fight. But he'd fought with honor and finished on his feet.

It's easy to be a champion when all a fighter does is win. One measure of greatness is how a champion handles defeat.

A boxing ring is the best lie detector test in the world.

Joe Calzaghe versus Roy Jones Jr

The main arena at Madison Square Garden is a nice place to make history. On November 8, 2008, Joe Calzaghe and Roy Jones Jr did just that, although the results were far more gratifying to Calzaghe.

"The Battle of the Super-Powers" (as the bout was styled) marked the intersecting arcs that have defined the careers of two great fighters.

Jones was once mentioned in the same breath as Sugar Ray Robinson and other ring immortals. When he was in his prime, his performances had the look of an action hero in a video game. Years ago, George Foreman observed, "The better Roy is, the less people understand it."

Jones has been fighting professionally for two decades. He won his first world championship by outclassing Bernard Hopkins fifteen years ago. He went from blazing young prospect to champion to superstar, peaking in 2003 when he defeated WBA titlist John Ruiz to become the first former middleweight champion since Bob Fitzsimmons in 1897 to capture a piece of the heavyweight crown.

Jones dominated a lot of good fighters (e.g. Hopkins, James Toney, and Reggie Johnson). There were highlight-reel moments that encapsulated his brilliance. He knocked out Virgil Hill with a single punch; a right hand *under* the jab. Against Glen Kelly, standing with his back to the ropes and both hands behind his back, Roy flashed a right hand that put his opponent down for the count. In effect, he knocked Kelly out with his hands behind his back.

But like a modern-day Icarus (whose father fashioned wings from wax and feathers so they could escape exile on Crete), Jones flew too high and too close to the sun. The Ruiz fight was his greatest triumph, but it also held the seeds of his destruction.

Jones put on twenty pounds of muscle to fight in the heavyweight division. When he moved back to 175 pounds, his body was slow to readjust. He showed grit and heart in a 2003 victory over Antonio Tarver. Then he lost to Tarver, was brutally knocked out by Glen Johnson, and lost to

Tarver a second time. Jones was now beatable. Worse; in his own mind, his sense of invulnerability was gone.

Then Roy got old. He could no longer do the same things in the ring that he'd done before. He was left for roadkill by the boxing establishment. But as Angelo Dundee noted in explaining why Muhammad Ali and Sugar Ray Leonard kept coming back long after their time, "Nothing takes the place of being the best in the world at what you do."

Thus, Jones kept fighting. He resurrected his marketability with victories over Prince Badi Ajamu, Anthony Hanshaw, and Felix Trinidad. At age thirty-nine, reaching for the brass ring one more time, he signed to fight Calzaghe. "Continuing to fight is not by choice," Roy said recently. "It's in my blood; I was born to fight. My mother told me, 'Boy, you're getting older; you better quit fighting.' I say, 'I know; but I can't quit just yet.' I'll fight till I can't do it anymore."

Calzaghe joined the ranks of professional boxers four years after Jones turned pro and was little more than a footnote during the years that Roy reigned as boxing's pound-for-pound king. He had none of Jones's pedigree or promise. Rather, he was an obscure fighter from Wales with a neophyte trainer (who was also his father). "Dad talks like a raving lunatic at times," Joe says. "But he knows his stuff. We understand each other."

At first glance, Calzaghe is an unlikely fighter. It's hard to imagine him in a boxing ring. There's an almost fragile quality about him. But if Joe doesn't look like a fighter, surely he fights like one. "Joe has a heart second to none," Enzo Calzaghe proclaims. "The harder the fight, the better he performs."

Prior to facing Jones, Calzaghe was undefeated in 45 bouts. His signature performances were victories over Jeff Lacy, Mikkel Kessler, and Bernard Hopkins. Each of these triumphs was more impressive than the one before. But his credentials were still questioned. Lacy was "overrated." Kessler was "one-dimensional." Hopkins was "an old man."

Calzaghe was unfazed. "Either I'm doing something right in the ring or all my opponents are having off days," he said.

There was a school of thought that Calzaghe-Jones should have been in London or Cardiff (where 50,000 fans have turned out on a given night to watch Joe fight). But HBO (which was televising the bout on pay-per-view) wanted it in the United States and offered a three-part

"24/7" series in exchange for a domestic site. That was fine with Calzaghe, who'd always wanted to fight in Madison Square Garden. Jones, who was undefeated in five Garden fights, had no objection either.

Square Ring (Jones's promotional company) and the newly-formed Calzaghe Promotions agreed to a fifty-fifty split on all revenue and expenses. Roy suggested that the contract call for the fighters to weigh-in at 168 pounds so they could fight for Calzaghe's 168-pound title; then drink some water, step back on the scale, and weigh-in for Calzaghe's 175-pound *Ring Magazine* belt. Such is the credibility that attaches to titles in boxing today. Ultimately, the match was made at 175 pounds.

The fondness and mutual respect that the fighters had for each other was evident during the build-up to the fight. At the September 16th kick-off press conference in New York, one could all but hear the lyrics to *Mutual Admiration Society* wafting through the air.

"I've watched Roy Jones Jr his whole career," Calzaghe told the media. "I've been a Roy Jones fan for a long time. As far as I'm concerned, it doesn't get any bigger than fighting Roy Jones in Madison Square Garden."

Jones responded in kind, saying, "Joe is an outstanding person and a great fighter."

Indeed, at the close of the press conference when the fighters posed for the ritual staredown, the stare lasted for about a second. Then Roy's eyes twinkled, his mouth curled upward, and Joe's face broke into a broad smile.

But the fight was a hard sell. The press conference in New York took place one day after the Dow Jones industrial average plummeted 504 points and Lehman Brothers filed for bankruptcy. That was a bad omen. When tickets went on sale, an unusually high number of prospective buyers went online to Ticketmaster.com and looked but did not buy. The prices ($1,500 to $150) were too high.

Also, the November 4th presidential election sucked most of the air out of media coverage of the fight.

Last minute ticket sales boosted the gate. The announced attendance was a better-than-expected 14,152. But a lot of those tickets were sold at significantly discounted prices, and New York State Athletic Commission records show a paid attendance of 10,377. More significantly, a source at

HBO says that pay-per-view buys were "between dismal and a disaster." One inside estimate puts the number at "less than 225,000."

As for who would win; the first issue was age.

"Sooner or later," Lennox Lewis has observed, "age catches up with everyone." That's particularly true of a fighter like Jones, whose greatness was founded upon speed and reflexes.

Prior to facing Calzaghe, Roy maintained that the only concession he'd made to age was, "I'm a little more economical in the ring now than I was before." Then he'd added, "I'm a much smarter fighter now than I was before and I'm stronger mentally than I was before. I'm a new-born soul back at the top of my game. You saw that against Felix Trinidad."

But Jones's victory over Trinidad was a source of false hope. It had been a competition between two old athletes hoping to be young again. Calzaghe put it in perspective, saying, "Roy didn't turn back the clock to beat Felix Trinidad. With all due respect, Felix Trinidad was a blown-up welterweight who was well past his prime."

The most interesting facet of Calzaghe-Jones was that, in the past, each man had always been quicker than his opponent. This time around, Alton Merkerson (who coached Roy at the 1988 Seoul Olympics and has trained him for most of his pro career) acknowledged, "Calzaghe's hands are as fast as Roy's and he'll throw a lot more punches."

Thus, the Jones camp was relying on what it believed was Roy's superior punching power. "Roy has more snap on his punches," Merkerson said. "And his punches are more effective."

"I know that the quality of my punches will overcome his quantity," Jones added. "I would never be able to match the punch output that Joe will throw. But this is pro boxing, so I don't have to match his output. I am definitely the stronger puncher."

However, even assuming that was true, Calzaghe was presumed to have the better chin. Much better.

Then there was "the Bernard Hopkins factor." Hopkins was the one common opponent that the two men had faced, and each man beat him (although at different stages of their respective careers). Jones fought Hopkins in 1993 when Bernard was green and Roy was young. Calzaghe bested a mature Hopkins earlier this year.

"I thought he was a fool before the fight," Calzaghe said of Hopkins when Bernard refused to give Joe credit for the victory. "Now the only difference is that the whole world knows he's a fool. He's self-centered. He's got no manners and no appreciation for other people. The words 'cheating coward' sum him up best."

But worse from Calzaghe's point of view, his victory over Hopkins was diminished by the perception that Bernard was an old man. "Where is the respect?" Enzo Calzaghe raged. "It's always, 'Joe needs another fight to seal his legacy. Joe needs another fight to seal his legacy.'"

Then, on October 18th, Hopkins beat Kelly Pavlik over twelve one-sided rounds. That fight gave Calzaghe a huge boost. Suddenly, Bernard didn't seem so old anymore.

"I was happy with Hopkins's win," Calzaghe acknowledged. "I'm not friends with him, but I was happy he beat Pavlik because it showed how big my win over him was."

And finally, there were the intangibles.

"You find out what a man is made of by what he does when he's down," Jones says. "I've been down; and when I was, a lot of people said a lot of bad things about me. But I'm still here."

Signing to fight Calzaghe was an act of faith and a statement of Roy's belief in himself. But the reality of the situation was, in recent years, Jones has learned how to lose. He knows the feeling of being an undefeated fighter from past experience. Calzaghe is experiencing it now.

Thus, Calzaghe (who has never tasted defeat) confidently declared, "Roy Jones is still Roy Jones. He still has speed; he still has power. I'm not underestimating this guy. But I'm not really concerned with what Roy Jones brings to the table. I'm concerned with what Joe Calzaghe brings to the table. If I bring my 'A' game, then it's game over."

And several days before the fight, Enzo Calzaghe declared, "Roy Jones has been stopped before. He's a great fighter, but talk is cheap. It's the soul searching when the moment of truth comes that means the most."

Cus D'Amato (the legendary trainer who put a foundation under Mike Tyson) was fond of saying. "Great fighters in the twilight of their career often have one last great fight left in them."

That might sell tickets and pay-per-view buys, but it's rarely true. As fight night approached, Calzaghe was a 5-to-2 betting favorite. The feeling among boxing insiders was that Roy might "be Roy" for fifteen seconds a round. But Joe could give him those fifteen seconds and win the other two minutes forty-five seconds of each stanza.

Roy Jones entered his dressing room at Madison Square Garden at 9:18 on Saturday night and settled in front of a television monitor to watch the first pay-per-view fight of the evening; Dmitriy Salita versus Derrick Campos. A few minutes later, Daniel Edouard (who'd won an eight-round decision over Alphonso Williams in an earlier preliminary bout) knocked on the door and asked if he could come in. Permission granted.

"I just wanted to meet you," Edouard told Jones. "I've watched you fight ever since I started boxing. You're an icon. It's an honor to shake your hand."

"Thank you, man. I appreciate it."

Roy checked his cell phone for messages and chatted with members of his team who had gathered around him.

The room was hot. Throughout his career, Jones hasn't warmed up before fights in the conventional way. Rather, he sits in an almost sauna-like atmosphere, warming his body and conserving energy. He rarely stretches, shadow-boxes, or hits pads.

Salita-Campos ended. Roy drank a half bottle of orange juice and took a pair of high-topped orange-and-black Adidas shoes out of his gym bag. The shoes were new. The cardboard and tissue packing that came from the manufacturer were still in them.

McGhee Wright (Jones's business advisor) came into the room. They talked briefly. Roy went back to checking his cell phone messages; then took two sets of tassels from a clear plastic bag and tied them around the tops of his shoes. His mood was quiet, almost somber. He seemed detached from the storm ahead.

At 10:15, referee Hubert Earl came in and gave Jones the ritual pre-fight instructions. After he left, Roy turned again to the television monitor to watch Frankie Figueroa versus Emanuel Augustus. Augustus, as is his way, was gyrating and wobbling around the ring in exaggerated fashion. Roy shook his head when Figueroa imitated his foe. "They call that a drunken master," he told the room. "You don't play with a guy like that because he does it better than you."

Roy took a small container of Vaseline and greased up his own face; then put on a pair of orange trunks with black trim. Alton Merkerson taped his hands. Billy Lewis (a longtime friend from Pensacola) led the group in prayer. Merkerson gloved Roy up.

At 10:58, Jones began hitting the pads with assistant trainer Alfie Smith, throwing three, four, and five-punch combinations with fifteen seconds in between each burst.

There were cries of encouragement from around the room.

"They don't believe. We got to make some believers."

Jones joined in the commentary: "Old man fighting here."

Burst of punches.

From the chorus: "Oooooh!"

Jones: "I am an old man, but this old man is gonna bite him."

Burst of punches . . .

Chorus: "Yeah! It's showtime at The Apollo."

Jones: "Feels good to be back."

Chorus: "That boy is fast."

Alfie Smith flicked out his left hand and the edge of his pad caught Roy directly in the right eye.

Jones turned away and grimaced in pain.

Everything stopped.

Merkerson took a towel and wiped Roy's face.

Then the action resumed, coming in five, six, and seven-punch combinations.

Jones: "It ain't over. I'm bringing it back."

Burst of punches.

Chorus: "Oooooh! The magic is back."

Jones: "Don't want to cool off now."

Burst of punches.

Chorus: "It's a Roy Jones night."

The padwork lasted for a full half-hour.

"It's whatever Roy feels," Merkerson said when it was over. "He hasn't done it like this before. He just feels like doing it now."

The worlds of Roy Jones Jr and Joe Calzaghe were hurtling toward one another, about to collide.

The fight started auspiciously for Jones. With 48 seconds left in round one, he formally introduced himself to Calzaghe with a jab followed by a quick righthand. The latter glanced off Joe's cheek and ear onto his shoulder and put him down. Calzaghe rose and charged straight back at his foe. But when he returned to his corner at the end of the round, blood was flowing from the bridge of his nose.

"I really didn't see the punch coming," Joe said later. "Roy stunned me. But I didn't panic. I composed myself, got back up, and started to fight again. Anyone can fall on the floor. How you recover is what matters."

Round two was fairly even with an edge to Calzaghe (who landed far more punches, although Jones's were the sharper blows). Thereafter, Joe beat Roy at his own game. He did to Jones what Roy used to do to other fighters; dominating with speed, calculated aggression, showman-ship, and flair. His stamina was remarkable. When they traded, it was Calzaghe throwing four and five punches to Jones's one. "I always felt I was a step ahead of Roy," he said afterward. "I knew what Roy was going to do before he did it."

There's sadness in watching a fighter who was great when he was young grow old. Jones now fights off the memory of what he used to do. But he can't do those things anymore. His reflexes have slowed. His legs are old. He's still capable of impressive work. Against Calzaghe, the right-hand lead was his most effective punch. But Joe has a good chin. When the blows landed, he took them well. And he made Jones fight for three minutes of every round. Too often, Roy retreated to the ropes, raising his gloves to eye level in a defensive posture. When a fighter positions his hands as "earmuffs," he sends a message to his opponent: "Hit me."

The middle rounds were target practice for Calzaghe. In round seven, a sharp right hook opened an ugly gash on Jones's left eyelid. It was the first time ever that Roy had been cut in a fight. "I couldn't see out of my left eye," he said later. "It was swollen up and the blood was coming in."

"The cut looked a lot worse than it was," Barry Jordan (chief medi-cal officer for the New York State Athletic Commission) said after the fight. "It's just that, for whatever reason, Roy's corner couldn't stop the bleeding between rounds."

Meanwhile, Calzaghe kept coming forward, relentlessly forcing the pace, never giving Jones a moment's rest. His quiet manner outside the ring belies the fact that he's a mean tough son-of-a-bitch in it. He didn't just win rounds; he won them big; outworking, outboxing, and outfight-ing Roy.

Jones is fond of saying that a one-eyed rooster is dangerous. But long before the bout was over, he looked like a beaten fighter. It was clear that he needed a knockout to win. But Roy hasn't knocked out an opponent since Clinton Woods in 2002. And Calzaghe has never lost, let alone failed to go the distance.

The late rounds were like watching Muhammad Ali against Larry Holmes or Sugar Ray Leonard against Terry Norris. The only weapon left in Roy's arsenal was his heart. "I thought of stopping it," Merkerson said later. "But in a fight of this magnitude, that's hard to do and Roy wanted to keep fighting."

Each judge scored the bout 118–109, giving Calzaghe all but the first round. He outlanded Roy 344 to 159 and had an edge in every "punch-stat" category.

Great fighters in their prime have an aura of excellence about them. During the past year, Calzaghe has secured his reputation as one of the United Kingdom's greatest fighters. John Lumpkin put things in perspective when he wrote, "Calzaghe is a better fighter than most give him credit for. He has honed his craft in much the same fashion as Bernard Hopkins did over his long title reign, taking on a series of top-ten contenders and producing victories over a wide variety of styles."

There will always be doubters. Comparing Calzaghe to Jones, Lumpkin continued, "Like Roy Jones Jr. the majority of his foes lacked the credentials to be credible threats to his championship. Unfortunately for Calzaghe, unlike Jones and Hopkins, none of his super-middleweight opponents were future hall-of-famers in their prime. And the two hall-of-famers he did beat were so far past their prime that their significance on his resume is substantially reduced."

Still, Calzaghe was well within his rights when he told the media at a post-fight press conference, "I'm so happy. This year, I beat two legends in Hopkins and Jones, and I came to the United States to do it. I took the risk. They didn't come to me. I came to them to make it happen."

Joe is a "young" thirty-six. Now would be the ideal time for him to retire. He talked a lot about the possibility before facing Jones, saying, "I've been boxing for twenty-five years and I just feel like I don't want to fight anymore after this fight. It's difficult to stay motivated as you get older. Physically, I feel just as good as I felt five years ago; but mentally, it's more difficult to fight. To win my last fight in Madison Square Garden against one of the greatest fighters ever would be the perfect ending for me."

Indeed, at an August 14th press conference in Cardiff, Joe declared, "As long as I win and win in style, this will be my last fight. I've achieved everything I can in boxing. I love boxing and I love what the sport has given me, but it's important for me to end at the top. Hardly any fighter has managed to do that. To be undefeated for forty-six fights would be amazing."

Some observers point to Calzaghe-Jones as proof positive that Joe should continue in the ring. After all; he looked superb. But the best argument for Calzaghe's retirement was right in front of him on November 8th. Roy Jones showed us what happens when a great fighter stays on too long. One hopes that Calzaghe-Jones was the last fight for both men.

Meanwhile, as Calzaghe basked in the glow of victory at the post-fight press conference, a very different scene was unfolding in Jones's dressing room.

Roy sat in a far corner of the room on a folding metal chair with his head down. His twin sons (Deshawn and Deandre, age seventeen) were fighting back tears. His youngest son (Roy Jones III, age eight) stood to the side with tears streaming down his face. Raegan Jones, her hair beaded, as cute as a four-year-old can be, moved to her father's side and put her arms around him.

"I'm a big girl, daddy," Raegan said. "I don't cry."

Roy smiled and gave her a hug.

Alton Merkerson pressed an Enswell against Roy's swollen left eye.

"I forgot my game plan," Roy said. "I was on track pretty good. Then, after the first round, I started loading up, trying to knock him out instead of moving in and out like we planned."

Maybe. Or maybe Roy went for the knockout because he realized early in the fight that the best chance he had was a puncher's chance.

Bernard Hopkins came into the room. Roy rose to greet him.

"Are you all right?" Hopkins asked.

"Doing fine."

The two men hugged.

"It's all about respect," Roy said. "You got yours, man."

"You too, baby."

Bernard left.

There were scattered conversations around the room.

"Calzaghe's a good fighter," Merkerson said. "He was ready and he came to fight. He has some of the abilities that Roy had. He has good upper-body movement. He's hard to hit. He's a good counterpuncher. He can get off first and his punches are sharp. He measures distance and speed and how fast you punch and what you do when he punches extremely well. He knows what's coming the same way Roy used to know."

It's too bad they didn't fight when Jones was younger.

Roy stood up, took off his shoes and robe, and sat down on the chair again. He looked much older than he'd looked several hours earlier. His face was battered and swollen with a mixture of sadness and pride in his eyes. It was the face of a fighter. And it conjured up thoughts from long ago.

In 1892, James Corbett conquered John L. Sullivan. Thirty-three years later, during the reign of Jack Dempsey, Corbett observed, "Champions come and go. I have seen many climb to the top, fall, strive futilely to climb back, then pass out of the picture. It's a hard road to the top and he stands there for now. But he will fall in the dust like all the others and a new man will be hailed as the greatest of them all."

2008 ended on a down note for Paulie Malignaggi.

Hatton–Malignaggi:
The End of a Dream

In today's era of devalued titles, it's not enough to be a "champion." To be fully recognized and make big money, a fighter has to be a star.

On November 22, 2008, Paulie Malignaggi fought Ricky Hatton at the MGM Grand Garden Arena in Las Vegas. Entering the ring, Paulie knew that the hopes and dreams and hard work of twenty-eight years would be distilled into a handful of three-minute segments. Everything in his life had led up to this moment. Everything in his future would be influenced by it.

"If I fail in boxing, what do I do?" Paulie had wondered aloud earlier this year.

When Malignaggi turned pro and signed with Lou DiBella in 2001, he was clear about his goals. "I'm not just going to be a champion," he told his promoter. "I'm going to the Hall of Fame."

It was more than talk. Paulie genuinely believes in himself. He's a gifted boxer with a good work ethic who seems to sense everything as it unfolds in the ring. His Achilles heel is a lack of power; five knockouts in 27 career fights. He also has a fragile right hand that has been broken multiple times. Larry Merchant calls it "as brittle as uncooked spaghetti."

All of that has led to a lack of respect for Paulie in some circles. "You see articles about prospects all the time," he says. "Prospect of the Year; Prospect of the Month. There wasn't one prospect article written about me. Cuts and broken bones heal. Disrespect doesn't. It hurts to be written off."

Malignaggi craves attention and styles himself to get it. He puts a lot of time and effort into his appearance. In his mind, looking good means feeling good which translates into fighting well. But more than seeking attention for his style, Paulie wants recognition for the substance of his work. That led to his challenging Miguel Cotto at Madison Square Garden on the eve of the 2006 Puerto Rican Day parade.

"It was like fighting the devil in hell," Malignaggi recalls. In round one, Paulie suffered a bad cut from a head butt. In round two, he was knocked down. He left the ring that night with the first loss of his career and broken bones in his face that took six months to heal. But he'd fought valiantly, went the distance, and won four rounds (five on one judge's scorecard). That was important from a marketing point of view and also as a matter of pride.

"I came up short," Malignaggi said afterward. "But having gone through the experience and knowing it didn't break me tells me that I can walk through the fire again. There's no price that I won't pay to achieve my goals."

Fifty-three weeks later, Paulie shut out Lovemore N'dou with a masterful performance over twelve one-sided rounds to claim the IBF 140-pound crown. He successfully defended his title against Herman Ngoudjo and won a contractually-mandated rematch against N'dou. But by his own admission, he looked ordinary each time.

The second N'dou fight was notable for an act of monumental stupidity. Paulie came into the ring wearing long braided hair extensions which were tied and theoretically secured behind his head. But he'd never sparred with them to see what might happen during a fight. Why trainer Buddy McGirt allowed him to enter the ring under those circumstances is a mystery.

The hair extensions came loose in round one. Despite repeated efforts by Malignaggi's corner to tape them, they obscured his vision throughout the fight. Finally, after round eight, cutman Danny Milano took a scissors and cut them off, making it the first time in boxing history that a combatant had been given a haircut between rounds of a world championship bout.

"I love Paulie," Lou DiBella said afterward. "But sometimes he's an idiot."

Worse, during round six of the fight, Paulie broke a knuckle on his right hand, necessitating the fourth surgery on his hand in less than six years.

Prior to facing Malignaggi, Hatton had a career record of 44 wins with 31 knockouts against a single loss. Until 2005, Ricky had been widely thought of as a "protected" fighter. Then he stopped Kostya Tszyu in eleven rounds to annex the IBF junior-welterweight crown. Victories over Carlos Maussa, Luis Collazo, Juan Urango, and Jose Luis Castillo solidified his claim to being a legitimate world champion.

More significantly from an economic point of view, Hatton is the most popular fighter in England, with rabid fans who will follow him anywhere on the globe.

In December 2007, Ricky reached for the stars. He signed to fight Floyd Mayweather Jr. But when fight night came, he was forced to battle both boxing's pound-for-pound king and the one-sided refereeing of Joe Cortez. Mayweather knocked him out in the tenth round.

"I'd rather give credit to Floyd than blame the referee," Hatton said afterward. "But this is not just me feeling sorry for myself and finding something to complain about. I thought I could have won the fight. Yet it got to the point where I thought, 'I'm scared of hitting him in case I get warned.' Floyd would be turning his back and I'd be saying, 'Where do you want me to hit him when he's doing that?'"

The silver lining (actually, it was platinum) was that Hatton's contract for the Mayweather bout called for him to receive $6,000,000 plus British television rights. Initially, those rights were thought to be worth about $3,000,000. But despite the fact that the fight was on British television at the ungodly hour of 4:00 A.M., there were well over one million UK pay-per-view buys. That sweetened Ricky's take by more than $20,000,000.

Still, Hatton took the loss hard. "I don't want my last fight to be me on my back getting counted out," he said afterward. "I wouldn't be much of a champion if I gave up after my first-ever defeat, would I?"

He returned to the ring with a unanimous twelve-round decision over Juan Lazcano. Training for that fight, Hatton was hindered by a persistent chest infection. Be that as it may; Lazcano hurt him late and Ricky looked exceedingly vulnerable.

Hatton-Malignaggi followed. Ricky has always wanted to fight as the headline attraction at Madison Square Garden. This seemed like an ideal opportunity to do it since Paulie is from New York. But Golden Boy (Hatton's promoter) thought that the bout would be more profitably contested in Las Vegas. Thus, it purchased Malignaggi's services from DiBella Entertainment for $1,700,000. Paulie's purse was $1,200,000.

The fighters would be facing off after two consecutive less-than-stellar performances by each of them.

"After the Mayweather fight, I was down in the dumps," Hatton acknowledged. "Then, after Lazcano, I started asking myself, 'Am I past it? Have I seen better days? Have I had too many hard fights?' I thought about quitting a couple of times. The warning signs were there. I've had two fights in which I didn't produce a vintage Ricky Hatton performance. I'm a sensible lad and you need to be honest with yourself in this sport. I should beat Paulie. If I don't beat him, I'll have to start looking at things a little closer."

Malignaggi had a similar view. "I'm a perfectionist when it comes to boxing," he said. "And my last two performances were unacceptable. I should be criticized for them. They weren't anything like what I did to win the championship. They were a lot less than what I can do."

And like Hatton, Malignaggi had doubts about his future. Paulie isn't a kid anymore. His body has filled out and his boyish face has given way to the visage of a man. "I don't feel like I'll last much longer," he said after his second win over N'dou. "I keep breaking my hand and there are other problems on the physical side. I know I'll have arthritis and maybe worse later in life. The question is, 'How much worse will things be if I keep fighting and what risks am I willing to take?'"

But there was a major difference between Malignaggi and Hatton. Ricky had been to the mountaintop and beyond. Paulie had yet to visit the promised land.

"Every year, I start out hoping that this will be the year I make it big," Paulie said after the contracts for Hatton-Malignaggi were signed. "So far, it hasn't happened. The Cotto fight could have done it, but I came up short. Beating Ricky Hatton can get me to where I want to be. Ricky has a lot on the line too. He's fighting to stay on top. But this fight can get me recognized as the best junior-welterweight in the world. This fight can make me a star."

Hatton-Malignaggi would be Paulie's first fight in Las Vegas and his second high-profile bout on a world stage (Cotto being the first). To get it, he had to relinquish his IBF title rather than fight a rematch against Herman Ngoudjo, who'd returned to the "mandatory-challenger" slot after losing to Paulie in a mandatory challenge earlier this year.

"It's total stupidity that I have to give up my title," Paulie said of the situation. "I worked hard to win it, and I've never heard of a champion being required to fight the same boxer as a mandatory twice in the same year. But I'll do what I have to do to get to where I want to be."

In Las Vegas, Malignaggi was within reach of what he wanted. His face was on room keys at the MGM Grand. The world press was there. "Think of Paulie as John Travolta in *Saturday Night Fever*," Larry Merchant suggested. "He's a kid from Brooklyn who's dancing his way into the bigtime."

Malignaggi was long on confidence. "When I fought Cotto," he proclaimed, "I was excited but it was naïve excitement. Now I've been there. And don't compare Hatton with Cotto, because they're not on the same level. Ricky is an average fighter. In England, he was pampered against club-fighter opponents. He's been very ordinary over here. I think he's regressed, or maybe he was never that good to begin with."

"Hatton has flaws that I can take advantage of," Paulie continued. "They're always there. I've seen them all through his career. When you're fast, you can hit anybody. I'm fast, and Ricky isn't a good defensive fighter. My A-game is better than Ricky Hatton's A-game. It's going to be a very frustrating night for Ricky. He'll be catching a lot."

"Paulie thinks he's a good talker," Hatton said in response. "But he tends to come out with a lot of bull. You're not going to see Ricky Hatton doing the Ali Shuffle. But you will see more head movement and a few other things that I know how to do and haven't done as often as I should lately. And you'll also see what I always do; constant pressure and body punching."

In truth, the Hatton camp felt that Paulie was made for Ricky. The 12-to-5 odds in their man's favor supported that view. Former heavyweight champion Lennox Lewis (one of British boxing's greatest standardbearers) was in accord, saying, "Malignaggi will have to hit Hatton hard to keep him off, and Hatton's head is like a brick wall. So most likely, either Paulie won't hit Ricky hard or he'll hurt his hands."

But in Paulie's mind, he wasn't the underdog. If Hatton planned to pressure him, he intended to frustrate his foe.

"Speed kills," said Lou DiBella. "And speed particularly kills Ricky. It's not punchers that give Ricky trouble; it's speed. Look at his fights against Floyd Mayweather Jr and Luis Collazo."

There was also a question as to whether Hatton could work effectively under the aegis of his new trainer, Floyd Mayweather Sr. In late-

July, Billy Graham (who'd trained Ricky for every one of his professional fights) was fired. In announcing the move, Ray Hatton (Ricky's father) said, "There has been no falling out. It's Billy's decision that he's retiring. He has found it harder and harder physically to look after Richard. He has been having to have pain-killing injections in his hands and his elbows before every pad session, and that was doing him no good at all. When the injections wore off, Billy would be in agony."

Graham responded by saying that he'd been fired and that the move ("a huge blow") was instigated by Ray as part of an effort to deprive him of his fair share of monies from past fights.

That brought Ricky into the fray with the declaration, "Billy thinks other people conspired for him to leave, but I'm the boss and make the final decision. How do I know how hard or correctly I'm punching when Billy cannot feel his hands when we're on the pads? I don't want to hear from my trainer, who's taking so much medication to ease the pain, 'Don't worry, Rick, I'll get through this training session.' If he thinks anything of me, he'll have a good look in the mirror and admit 'I'm falling to bits; I'm physically done.'"

There was a school of thought that Hatton would miss Graham both in the gym and in his corner on fight night. And more significantly, there was the issue of Ricky's lifestyle. If Malignaggi's underlying weakness was his hands, Hatton's was perceived to be the abuse of his body between fights.

Ricky is a drinker; a heavy drinker. Some think that, ultimately, his drinking will cause him more harm than the blows he takes in the ring. He's also a ravenous eater and typically gains forty to fifty pounds between fights.

Naazim Richardson (who has worked with Bernard Hopkins for years) observes, "Fights between elite fighters aren't won in training camp. Fights at the highest level are won on lifestyle. People make a joke out of Hatton blowing up, gaining forty, fifty pounds between fights. And then they say, 'Look how hard he works when he's training.' But think about how much better he'd be if he stayed in shape all year long."

Hatton made light of the situation. On a teleconference call after training camp began, he told the media, "I've been stepping out at five-thirty in the morning to run for five miles, which is a big change from the usual routine of getting in at five-thirty in the morning after a night on the town."

But in recent fights, Hatton has tended to fade in the championship rounds. Collazo, Mayweather, and Lazcano all hurt him late. And conditioning became even more of an issue when nutritionist and conditioning coach Kerry Kayes quit Team Hatton in protest over Graham's dismissal.

Thus the question: What had a hedonistic lifestyle coupled with the aggressive practice of a brutal sport taken out of Hatton? Would Hatton-Malignaggi be the fight when Ricky was suddenly too old to do what he does well?

Hatton is thirty; Malignaggi is twenty-eight. But because of Ricky's lifestyle, he was thought of as a much older fighter. The feeling in Malignaggi's camp was that Hatton was ripe for the taking.

Paulie likes to get to the arena early when he fights and give himself time to settle in. He wouldn't be in the ring until 8:00 P.M., but he arrived at his dressing room at five o'clock sharp preparatory to his battle against Hatton.

Team Malignaggi was with him. Trainer Buddy McGirt, assistant trainer Orlando Carrasquillo, cutman Danny Milano, Umberto Malignaggi (Paulie's brother), Pete Sferazza (a close friend), attorney John Hornewer, and Anthony Catanzaro (who mentors Paulie outside the ring).

While the others engaged in quiet conversation, Paulie sat on a chair and listened to music through a pair of headphones. It was impossible to know what doubts and fears he harbored. Perhaps Paulie wasn't even sure what lurked beneath the surface as a consequence of his experiences in the ring; particularly the beating he'd suffered against Cotto. But one thing was certain. Paulie knew the taste of defeat. Its sour residue had been in his mouth for two years. He never wanted to taste it again.

Over the next few hours, Malignaggi stretched, put on his shoes and trunks, had his hands taped, shadow-boxed, and listened to referee Kenny Bayless's pre-fight instructions.

Lou DiBella came in and wished Paulie well. "He's ready," DiBella opined. "Before Cotto, Paulie had his game face on but it was the ego and arrogance of youth. Now he's more purposeful and focused. For Cotto, Paulie was a kid. Now he's a man."

At seven o'clock, Malignaggi went into an adjacent room with Orlando Carrasquillo to warm up and hit the pads. Buddy McGirt stayed in the main dressing area to watch James Kirkland versus Brian Vera (HBO's first televised fight of the evening) on a television monitor.

At 7:15, Sylvester Stallone and Chuck Zito entered the dressing room and made their way to Paulie and Carrasquillo.

"You look good, man," Stallone told Malignaggi. "Better than I ever looked."

"I'm ready. The plan is to bust him up."

"Have a good one."

In less than a minute, Stallone and Zito were gone. For the next half-hour, Paulie alternated between hitting the pads with Carrasquillo and sitting on the arm of a worn paisley-covered sofa with his head down. More than any of the people around him, he was processing the reality of how dangerous and contingent the next hour would be.

As boxing insiders had speculated might be the case, a fighter got old in the ring during Hatton-Malignaggi. But the fighter was Paulie.

Malignaggi had a slight edge in round one as a consequence of his footwork and jab. But he wasn't particularly effective with either, which was a precursor of things to come. He let Hatton get into a rhythm early and never got into a rhythm of his own.

In round two, Hatton became more aggressive and, with a half-minute left, stunned Paulie with a chopping right hand. Thereafter, Malignaggi seemed to abandon his game plan and waged an almost impatient battle. He fought like a fighter with a puncher's chance instead of a boxer who's only road to victory lay in putting together punch after punch to win point after point round after round. And he didn't have a puncher's chance because he isn't a puncher.

Hatton was physically stronger. Paulie's primary defense was movement. He didn't have the power to keep Ricky off. When he landed, Hatton simply walked through the punches to get inside. And there seemed to be a disconnect between Paulie and Buddy McGirt in the corner. A trainer doesn't get his fighter to relax between rounds by shouting, "Relax!"

At times, Malignaggi seemed frozen; unable to punch or get out of the way of Hatton's punches. Contrary to all expectations, he allowed Ricky to get off first for much of the night.

"My neck felt like it had a stinger," Paulie said afterward. "Like there was a hundred pounds on it. I couldn't move the way I usually move. One time, I ducked and it felt like I was stuck. I guess that's what Ricky does to you. But the referee did a good job. I've been in fights where the referee was a spectator. Kenny Bayless did his job right."

Hatton took advantage of what Bayless gave him. On occasion, he jammed an elbow into Malignaggi's throat or raked a glove across Paulie's face. But overall, he fought a clean fight. It was Malignaggi, not Hatton, who initiated most of the holding.

In the middle rounds, Hatton stepped up the pace, going to the body with telling effect. By round nine, Paulie was fighting to survive.

During round ten, Lou DiBella went to Malignaggi's corner and told McGirt, "He's not doing anything. Maybe it should be stopped." McGirt said no. But he did tell Paulie between rounds that, if he kept taking punches without throwing back, he'd stop the fight.

In round eleven, Malignaggi took a hard body shot and DiBella returned to the corner. "If you don't stop it, I will," he told the trainer.

Twenty-eight seconds into the stanza, McGirt waved the white towel of surrender. The CompuBox statistics credited Hatton with a 124-to-91 edge in punches landed. The fight was more one-sided than that. Each judge gave Malignaggi one round, which was a more accurate measure of the contest.

After the fight, Paulie sat for a long time on the sofa in his dressing room. The back of his robe was pulled up and forward over his head, completely covering his face. Finally, he lowered the robe.

"They shouldn't have stopped the fight," he said.

There was a distraught look on his face.

"You were getting hit."

"But I wasn't taking big shots. I wasn't hurting that bad. There was less than two rounds left. How bad could it have been? This will bother me forever."

"You were behind on points, and you weren't going to knock him out."

"He wasn't going to knock me out either. Losing is bad. Having it on my record that I got stopped is worse."

"No one wanted to see you get hurt."

"Against Cotto, I got hurt worse. Against Cotto, I could have understood someone stopping it, although I'm glad they didn't. Tonight; oh, man; no way it should have been stopped."

The door to the dressing room opened and Ricky Hatton entered. Paulie rose and the fighters embraced.

"It was a good fight, mate," Hatton said. "You weren't that far behind me. Most of the time, you were causing me murder."

There were more compliments. Then Hatton left.

Paulie kicked a towel that was on the floor. "The most important fight of my life and I didn't finish. I'm better than being stopped."

"You didn't get stopped. Someone else stopped it."

"Yeah; but that's not what the record book will say. The record book will say 'TKO by 11.' It goes down in history now; Paulie Malignaggi got stopped."

"You fought a good fight."

"No, I didn't. I fought like I was forty years old. I saw openings, but my mind and hands wouldn't connect."

"Did your hands give you trouble?"

"My hands are fine. How could I hurt my hands? I didn't hit him all night."

As for what comes next; for Ricky Hatton, the dream lives on. He can expect a historic payday in his next fight; most likely against the winner of Oscar De La Hoya versus Manny Pacquiao or a rematch against Floyd Mayweather Jr.

For Malignaggi, the future is more complicated.

One can argue either way as to whether or not Hatton-Malignaggi should have been stopped. Paulie was losing. He wasn't going to knock Hatton out. Rounds eleven and twelve are the rounds in which fighters who are behind and fading tend to take the most punishment.

But Paulie has a lot of pride. And a fighter's mental state is often as important as his physical wellbeing. The belief here, with the advantage of twenty-twenty hindsight, is that, until there was a knockdown, he should have been given the opportunity to finish.

Malignaggi is still a good fighter. In today's world of multiple champions in each weight division, he could win a title again. Herman Ngoudjo and Juan Urango will fight for the IBF 140-pound belt on January 30, 2009. Paulie has beaten Ngoudjo and, given the opportunity, would be competitive against either man. Ditto for Malignaggi versus Timothy Bradley, Andreas Kotelnik, and Kendall Holt (the other sanctioning body title claimants).

But none of these would be big-money fights. The dream of super-stardom as a fighter and the riches that come with it is all but gone. And more to the point, Paulie says, "If I can't be the best, I don't know that I want to fight anymore."

Putting his career in perspective; Malignaggi has had two world-class performances. When he beat Lovemore N'dou in 2007, he did more than win a belt. He fought with the skill of a true champion. And against Miguel Cotto, Paulie showed a heart as big as any fighter ever. No one can take those performances away from him. Like his loss to Ricky Hatton, they're part of boxing history.

But Hatton-Malignaggi was the third fight in a row that Paulie fell short of his own expectations. Now he's facing the hard reality that fighters who rely on quickness and speed peak early. His prime years are nearing an end. His career is analogous to that of a baseball or football player who's good enough to start on a team that wins the World Series or Super Bowl. That player might not make it to the Hall of Fame, but he has earned his championship ring.

Thus, three thoughts to close on:

You can't be in boxing if you're not willing to risk having your heart broken.

No matter how badly a fighter wants it, his opponent wants it too.

As a fighter, Paulie Malignaggi has exceeded everyone's expectations but his own.

This was the first of two articles I wrote in 2008 about boxing's "event of the year."

De La Hoya–Pacquiao:
A Weighty Issue

The promotional spots for the December 6th mega-fight between Oscar De La Hoya and Manny Pacquiao proclaim, "Pacquiao is younger and faster. De La Hoya is stronger and more experienced."

There's no mention of the adjective that most likely will determine the outcome of the fight. De La Hoya is bigger. Much bigger.

Pacquiao began his pro career as a 106-pound junior-flyweight. He has been knocked out twice by men weighing 112 pounds. Obviously, he has gotten better since then. He's a wonderful fighter. But until this year, he'd never competed above the junior-lightweight level.

De La Hoya has fought at weights as high as 160 pounds. Generally, on fight night, he refuses to get on the "unofficial HBO scale." But Freddie Roach (who trained Oscar for his fight against Floyd Mayweather Jr and now trains Pacquiao) says that De La Hoya gained ten pounds after weighing in at 154 to face Mayweather. Roach expects a similar gain on December 6th.

The disparity in weight between De La Hoya and Pacquiao has led to complaints that boxing's Golden Boy is buying a gold-plated mismatch. Oscar is in danger of being seen as a schoolyard bully who, having lost to fighters his own size, is now picking on tough little guys.

Roach says that Pacquiao will win with speed and that the weight differential "won't be that important." But Golden Boy CEO Richard Schaefer concedes that weight is an issue and, on August 5th, acknowledged, "You have two camps. The camp which is against the fight seems to be bigger than the one for it."

That balance can be expected to change as a consequence of the high-powered marketing campaign that has been put in place for the fight. But at the moment, critics abound.

The two best welterweights in the world at present are Paul Williams and Antonio Margarito. Obviously, each of them would like to fight De La Hoya. And just as obviously, Oscar has no intention of fighting either one of them.

"Oscar will stop Manny within three rounds," says Williams. "I don't want to take anything away from Pacquiao, but his punches won't hurt De La Hoya. Manny is just too small, and Oscar is just too big. That's why we have the different weight classes. The size and weight difference makes it a bad fight."

Margarito is more scornful, declaring, "Now Oscar is getting brave with a 135-pound fighter and is trying to convince everyone that it's a tough fight. He's getting brave with a great fighter, but a fighter who fights at 135-pounds. He wants to show the world that he can pull the trigger against a 135-pounder. What a man! What a hero!"

WBC president Jose Sulaiman has also gotten into the act. "What are they going to do?" Sulaiman queries. "Stuff Manny with tamales and beans, and reduce Oscar in the steam bath to bring them together? It's ridiculous. It's absurd. It's a fraud to the public. The only reason why the fight was made was money."

One presumes that the WBC will not be receiving a sanctioning fee for De La Hoya–Pacquiao.

How relevant is the weight differential?

One of the reasons that De La Hoya ended negotiations with Felix Trinidad for a rematch this year was that Trinidad wouldn't agree to come down to 160 pounds (Oscar's previous high). The discrepancy in size between De La Hoya and Pacquiao is greater than the difference between Oscar and Felix.

De La Hoya is the size of an average man. Pacquiao started his career 21 pounds below weight for a jockey in the Kentucky Derby. The chart below demonstrates their true difference. It lists the average comparative weight that each man has fought at since 1995 (the year Manny turned pro) and the differential between them on an annual basis. There is no 2005 entry for Oscar because he was inactive that year:

	De La Hoya	Pacquiao	Differential
1995	135	108	27
1996	140	113	27
1997	145	113	32

1998	147	113	34
1999	147	116	31
2000	147	120	27
2001	154	121	33
2002	154	121	33
2003	154	124	30
2004	158	125	33
2005	–	130	–
2006	153	129	24
2007	154	129	25
2008	150	132	18

"Wait a minute," you say. "Oscar is older than Manny, and one expects a fighter to gain weight as he gets older. At a certain point, the weight differential will even out."

Not so. The next chart lists each fighter's weight and the differential between them at the same age in their respective pro careers. Pacquiao turned pro at age sixteen and is now twenty-nine, while Oscar turned pro at age nineteen and is now thirty-five. Thus, ages nineteen through twenty-nine are the best ages for comparison.

	De La Hoya	Pacquiao	Differential
16	–	108	–
17	–	108	–
18	–	113	–
19	133	113	20
20	134	113	21
21	133	121	12
22	135	121	14
23	140	121	19
24	147	124	23
25	147	125	22
26	147	130	17
27	147	129	18
28	154	129	25
29	154	132	22
30	154	–	–
31	158	–	–
32	–	–	–
33	153	–	–
34	154	–	–
35	150	–	–

In other words, De La Hoya was, is, and always will be a much larger man than Pacquiao. Would anyone match Pacquiao against Paul Williams or Antonio Margarito?

Ultimately, curiosity and marketing will sell De La Hoya–Pacquiao. Manny's skill and determination will salvage it as entertainment. But the match-up will only be competitive if Oscar has nothing left as a fighter.

On December 6, 2008, Manny Pacquiao turned the business of boxing upside down. Or rightside up, depending on one's point of view.

De La Hoya–Pacquiao and the Business of Boxing

It's hard to know how future generations will evaluate Oscar De La Hoya.

Oscar is more than a name. He was once a very good fighter, but that time has come and gone. He has lost four of his last seven fights. One can argue that he hasn't beaten an elite opponent since a split-decision victory over Ike Quartey on February 13, 1999. Since then, De La Hoya has defeated Oba Carr, Derrell Coley, Arturo Gatti, Javier Castillejo, Fernando Vargas, Yori Boy Campas, Felix Sturm, Ricardo Mayorga, and Steve Forbes. That's nine wins in a decade. Yet during that time, Oscar has become a boxing legend as a consequence of his status as a marketing icon.

Fighters are paid for their marketability, not their ability (although the two are often related). De La Hoya was the right man in the right place at the right time. Initially, the sweet science embraced him as "the anti-Tyson." Then he benefited from the absence of a true heavyweight champion that the sport could rally around.

There have been slips. In 2001, after besting Bob Arum in an ugly court battle, De La Hoya boasted of defeating "one of the biggest Jews to come out of Harvard." And he was stung by the embarrassment of the now-infamous fishnet photos (Oscar contests their authenticity) that exploded upon the public last year.

But for the most part, outside the ring, De La Hoya has been boxing's consummate politician. Every word from his mouth seems carefully chosen to maintain his image and commercial viability. One wishes at times that he would strip away the layers of varnish and reveal the "real" Oscar. He seems, at his core, to be a good person.

Meanwhile, with the guidance of Richard Schaefer (CEO of Golden Boy Enterprises) De la Hoya has built a financial empire. And he has continued to fight; both for financial reasons and because it's an affirmation of who and what he is.

Over the years, De La Hoya has engaged in nineteen pay-per-view fights that have generated the staggering sum of $698,400,000 in pay-per-view revenue. On May 5, 2007, he was beaten by Floyd Mayweather Jr in a bout that engendered 2,400,000 pay-per-view buys with a domestic gross of $134,000,000. Those numbers exceeded anything in boxing history.

Thereafter, Oscar announced his intention to fight three times in 2008 and retire at the end of the year. The plan was to face Steve Forbes in May followed by a rematch against Mayweather in September and a farewell extravaganza in December.

"There's going to be no 2009," De La Hoya said during an April 2008 conference call. "I want to have these three fights and go out like a champion. I know it's the last time I will step inside the ring in December." One month later, Oscar declared, "There are no thoughts whatsoever about fighting after 2008. I've given Richard the marching orders. I have prepared everybody. This is my last year in the ring. There's no dinero that will bring me back, no amount of moolah."

De La Hoya–Forbes took place as planned. Then, in June, Mayweather announced his "retirement" from boxing. That led to cancellation of the proposed September fight and sent Team De La Hoya scrambling to find a big-money opponent for December.

The first option to be considered was Manny Pacquiao. Initially, the negotiations went poorly. De La Hoya wanted the contract weight to be 150 pounds; Pacquiao (who had weighed 129 for his junior-lightweight title defense against Juan Manuel Marquez earlier in the year) would go no higher than 147. Oscar wanted the bout to be contested with ten-ounce gloves; Manny preferred eight-ounces. And De La Hoya wanted as much money as he could get, while Pacquiao wanted as much money as he could get.

On August 13th, Schaefer and Bob Arum (Pacquiao's promoter) confirmed that Oscar had given in on the issues of weight and gloves but that negotiations had broken down over the division of revenue. Team De La Hoya was seeking a 70–30 split in its favor. Team Pacquiao would go no further than 60–40.

Meanwhile, Oscar was telling the media, "I want to go out with a big bang. I want to show everybody around the world that boxing is alive and well. I want them to say, 'Look at this big event.'"

But De La Hoya was tap-dancing around the issue of why he wouldn't fight Antonio Margarito, Paul Williams, or Miguel Cotto.

"Margarito had a great win against Cotto," Oscar acknowledged. "That's wonderful for him. I wish him all the best. I just feel personally that Margarito has some unfinished business to take care of against Paul Williams. We cannot forget about Paul Williams."

Okay; so fight Paul Williams.

That didn't work either. Williams wasn't "a big enough name." Or maybe he was too big in stature. And Oscar had once said that he wouldn't fight Cotto because he'd promised his wife (who is from San Juan) that he'd never fight a Puerto Rican.

Margarito spoke for many when he declared, "What happened with 'I want to fight the winner between Cotto-Margarito?' What happened with 'I'll fight anyone?' I hear nothing but excuses. 'I can't fight Antonio because the Mexican people will not like me.' Oscar needs to stop deceiving the people. He cannot continue being dishonest to the fans."

But those who wanted to see De La Hoya fight Margarito or Williams (or even Cotto) were missing the point. Oscar didn't want to end his career with a "KO by." And because of the size differential between De La Hoya and Pacquiao, a fight against Manny was perceived as giving Oscar a built-in edge. Thus, on August 21st, Golden Boy sweetened the pot by offering a 67–33 revenue split and Team Pacquiao accepted.

De La Hoya announced the fight (slated for December 6th at the MGM Grand in Las Vegas) in an August 28th conference call. "Manny Pacquiao is considered the best fighter in boxing today," he told the media. "And I always want to fight the best. These are the kind of events that get me fired up. To this day, I say to myself, 'Can I really beat the pound-for-pound champion?'"

The fight was styled "The Dream Match." A six-city promotional tour began at the height of the electoral battle between Barack Obama and John McCain. That was appropriate because the marketing of De La Hoya–Pacquiao had all the earmarks of a national political campaign.

The October 1st kick-off press conference was held on Liberty Island in New York. Standing near the Statue of Liberty, Richard Schaefer proclaimed, "With the global economy crumbling and the world financial system on the verge of collapse, we all need a moment to dream."

HBO Sports president Ross Greenburg helpfully added, "HBO is going to make sure that everyone in this great land of ours knows about this fight."

Not to be outdone, De La Hoya declared, "As the son of immigrants, being able to announce this fight at the Statue of Liberty, America's greatest symbol of freedom and opportunity, is a dream come true for me."

Then a question was put to Oscar: "You've chosen a very patriotic tone to market this fight and you have a great deal of influence in the Hispanic community. Will you stand up publicly for what you believe and tell us who you're voting for in this year's presidential election?"

He wouldn't.

Later in the press conference, De La Hoya was asked about the quality of the pay-per-view undercard that would be aired with the main event. "I promise you," he answered with sincerity in his voice. "We're going to have a really great undercard."

Wrong.

One can make a case for the proposition that De La Hoya's recent outings have become like the fights Mike Tyson had late in his career in that Oscar's level of achievement no longer justifies the extensive media coverage that he receives. That said, De La Hoya–Pacquiao was backed by a wave of press conferences, press releases, advertisements, and other marketing ploys that added up to what Richard Hoffer of *Sports Illustrated* called "the single most cynical promotion of [Oscar's] era."

In 2006, De La Hoya had sought to woo Pacquiao away from Bob Arum by giving Manny a briefcase filled with $300,000 in cash over dinner in a private room at a Los Angeles steakhouse. Pacquiao signed a promotional contract with Golden Boy that night but later had second thoughts. After ugly litigation, a settlement was reached. Top Rank (Arum's promotional company) retained rights to Pacquiao (although since then, Golden Boy has received a percentage of Top Rank's profits from Manny's fights).

With that history, Oscar proclaimed, "This fight is very personal for me. I respect Manny Pacquiao as a fighter but not as a man. When we looked into each other's eyes and shook hands, I felt we had a deal and he betrayed me. Where I come from, you don't do that. Your word is your bond. He's going to pay for that on December 6."

The promotion also sought to capitalize on friction between De La Hoya and Freddie Roach. Roach has trained Pacquiao for nineteen fights over the course of seven years. In 2007, he trained Oscar for the Mayweather fight.

"I learned a lot during that eight-week period with Oscar," Roach said. And Freddie claimed to have learned more when De La Hoya fought Steve Forbes. More specifically, the trainer maintained, "Oscar's skills are slipping badly. He can no longer pull the trigger. His best years are behind him."

"When Oscar read Freddie's comments," Richard Schaefer said later, "he was like, 'What the hell is that?' Oscar feels challenged now. He honestly feels that Freddie and Pacquiao have been disrespectful. Oscar will show them how he can pull the trigger. Pacquiao is being Freddie Roach's puppet, and Oscar wants to teach a lesson to them."

Oscar claimed to be similarly aggrieved, declaring, "Freddie Roach didn't train me properly. I went into the Mayweather fight as a one-dimensional fighter. When Freddie trained Bernard Hopkins, he told him after the loss to Joe Calzaghe that he had to retire. When he trained Israel Vazquez, he told him [after the loss to Rafael Marquez] 'you have to retire.' He trained me, and now he's telling me I have to retire. So you have Hopkins beating Pavlik without Freddie; Israel beat Marquez without Freddie. And now I'm going to beat Pacquiao without Freddie. I'm going to destroy his pupil."

Roach took the assault in stride, saying, "The game plan we had for the Mayweather fight was working well in the early rounds. Then Oscar abandoned the game plan; we ended up losing the decision; and about a month ago, he started blaming me for the loss. But he's always blaming somebody, so he can blame me for this one too."

A press conference was held to announce that Nacho Beristain had been hired as De La Hoya's trainer for the Pacquiao bout. Then Angelo Dundee was brought into camp as a much-heralded adviser. The world was told that Oscar was eating deer meat and kangaroo meat ("This diet is very effective," he said). One half-expected a press release announcing that De La Hoya had broken his training regimen to enjoy a couple of Tecate beers ("I know I shouldn't drink when I'm training. But Tecate is the lead sponsor for the fight. And Tecate tastes so good, I couldn't resist.").

[The deer-and-kangaroo-meat quote is real. The Tecate beer quote isn't.]

Then, in the midst of it all, De La Hoya reversed course and revealed, "I have no plans to retire. My reflexes and speed are still there. Physically and mentally, I can still compete at the highest level. I'll continue to fight as long as I can do it."

That declaration elicited less-than-universal joy. In some parts of the boxing world, "Oscar fatigue" was setting in. Matthew Hurley voiced the thoughts of many when he wrote, "Every De La Hoya smile, every pose, and every utterance looks and sounds rehearsed. Even when Oscar grits his teeth and tries to come off as angry and intense, you can't entirely take him seriously. His presentation to the public and the media is immaculately calculated and ultimately hollow. No matter how well-packaged the image, there is a residue of phoniness encapsulating it. The litany of Oscarisms over the years makes each archived interview interchangeable from year to year and fight to fight . . . 'This is the hardest I've ever trained in my life . . . This is my life. This is what I do. This is who I am . . . Now I'm actually really focused because this fight is so important to my career . . . This trainer is the greatest trainer I've ever worked with. I've learned so much.'"

Meanwhile, Pacquiao was readying for battle.

Manny is unpretentious and confident with an aura of innocence and little artifice about him. His journey to boxing's upper echelons contrasted markedly with Oscar's. De La Hoya came out of the 1992 Olympics as boxing's "Golden Boy" with million-dollar signing bonuses dangled in front of him. Pacquiao turned pro in his native Philippines for a handful of pisos at age sixteen. Six years passed before he fought outside of Asia.

Pacquiao today is the most famous person in the Philippines and the idol of a nation. De la Hoya is perceived as living apart from the people. He is a celebrity who seems torn between the divergent worlds of East LA, chic LA, and Puerto Rico. When Manny wins, there is unbridled joy throughout his native land. When Oscar loses, there are few tears in the barrios of East Los Angeles.

Pacquiao is "one of us." People light up when they see his face. He stirs passionate adulation.

"You have to understand," Bob Arum explained shortly before De La Hoya–Pacquiao. "An entire nation of ninety million people is focusing on Manny's every move. It's the most important topic of conversation in the Philippines. The Senate and Congress in the Philippines are going to close this week. They won't have a quorum because senators and congress people are flying over here in tremendous numbers. Nobody that I ever promoted was as popular as Muhammad Ali, but it wasn't the same. It wasn't one country, almost as one person, rising up and making it such a national issue as they do for Manny. Some of these stories in the newspapers about Manny and how much the Filipino people love him are so beautiful, they make you cry."

Arum professed optimism with regard to Pacquiao's chances against De La Hoya. During a November conference call, the promoter promised, "We're going to shock the world, because Manny is going to not only defeat Oscar but knock Oscar out."

Later, in a more reflective moment, Arum observed, "You don't put somebody in a fight that you believe he can't win just for money. I would not have allowed this fight to happen if I didn't feel in my heart of hearts that Manny could win. That doesn't necessarily mean that he's going to win."

Freddie Roach also thought Pacquiao would win. "We're going to break this guy down and win each round one at a time," the trainer said. "That's our goal. We have to get past Oscar's jab. That's going to be our toughest opposition, and we're working on that. I've got some great sparring partners with better jabs than Oscar. We're going to fight the whole time and just burn him out. And if Oscar tires like he normally does, we'll stop him. Manny is already a great fighter. This is going to be the icing on the cake."

Pacquiao's biggest edge was thought to be speed. There was also the fact that Nacho Beristain was the sixth trainer that De La Hoya had worked with during his pro career. In that regard, Arum opined, "I think it's very difficult when you change trainers as frequently as Oscar has. It's the same as a football team where the coach changes every year or two and there's flux in the organization and they can't get used to a particular system."

And most significantly, Oscar was getting old. Critiquing his performance against Steve Forbes, Steve Kim wrote, "De La Hoya not only didn't
look as good as he has in the past; he looked as though he has regressed
physically from May 2007, when he was defeated by Mayweather. His
reflexes weren't quite as sharp. He only showed brief moments of the
explosion and acceleration that marked his prime. He never really came
close to stopping a guy who was about ten pounds past his optimum
weight class. Don't let the HBO and Golden Boy rhetoric fool you. The
De La Hoya of 2008 is not even the De La Hoya of May 5, 2007."

Still, the consensus view was that Pacquiao was the perfect opponent
against whom Oscar could rebuild his reputation as an elite fighter and
make tens of millions of dollars in the process. Yes, Manny was faster. But
De La Hoya had a significant edge in size and, with that size, power.

No matter how the bout was packaged, Pacquiao would be fighting
above the weight class that was best suited to his pound-for-pound standing. Oscar's previous nine fights had been contested in divisions that were
19 and 25 pounds heavier than the highest weight class that Manny had
ever fought in.

The October 18th encounter between Bernard Hopkins and Kelly
Pavlik (which the heavier Hopkins dominated) had put weight differen-
tials between elite fighters in perspective. "Oscar and Pacquiao will be
competitive until Manny gets hit," Bernard predicted. "Then Manny will
feel something that he's never felt before and he's not ready for."

De La Hoya was coming down slightly in weight for Pacquiao. But
that didn't seem to bother Oscar. "What I found out," he said toward the
end of the pre-fight build-up, "was, what was I doing at 154? What was I
doing at 160? This is where I feel comfortable."

Freddie Roach was steadfast in maintaining, "I don't think the size is
that big a deal. If a guy has a height advantage or a reach advantage, Manny
has the style to take that away. He's aggressive, he comes forward. And when
you get close to a guy with long arms, it crowds their punches."

But Roach conceded, "Things are easier said from the corner than
done in the ring." And the prevailing view among the media (this writer
included) was that Pacquiao had been seduced into an ill-chosen fight by
the siren call of money and glory beyond the once-unimaginable heights
that he'd already attained.

De La Hoya–Pacquiao, critics said, would be "David without a sling-shot against Goliath" . . . "A con job; not a fight." It was suggested that "The Dream Match" be retitled "The Final Rip-Off" or "The Golden Fleece."

"It's a promoter's fight; not a fight fan's fight," Showtime boxing analyst Steve Farhood said. "And that's perfect because Oscar is now a promoter more than a fighter."

Still, the odds were remarkably close. De La Hoya opened as an 8-to-5 favorite at the MGM Grand Sports Book. Initially, the online bookies had Oscar favored at 3-to-1, but that gap quickly narrowed. Thereafter, the betting line consistently favored De La Hoya, but only between 3-to-2 and 2-to-1. People kept waiting for the "smart" money to come in on Oscar.

Expectation and reality are two different things. The smart money was already coming in. But it was coming in on Pacquiao.

Throughout fight week, Manny was gracious and polite. He posed for photographs, signed countless autographs for fans, and resisted the "Mexicutioner" label that the promotion sought to pin on him as a consequence of his victories over Marco Antonio Barrera, Erik Morales, and Juan Manuel Marquez.

"To me, it's nothing personal," Pacquiao said. "It's my job to do my best in the ring and beat my opponent. It's a big responsibility for me. Millions of Filipinos will be rooting for me and watching this fight."

When asked about the war of words between De La Hoya and Roach, Manny responded, "I don't have a comment about that. I'm out of that. That's between my trainer and Oscar." But when pressed, he added, "For me, I would never blame my trainer if I lost."

One day before the fight, Pacquiao weighed in at 142 pounds (about what was expected). Surprisingly, De La Hoya tipped the scales at 145 (two pounds beneath the 147-pound limit). At the staredown following the weigh-in, Manny was wearing high-soled shoes while Oscar was in his stocking feet. That made them look closer in height than the four-inch differential between them.

The assumption was that De La Hoya had dried out considerably more than Pacquiao to make weight. One night later, just before the fight, Oscar got on the "unofficial HBO scale." He had gained only two pounds. That was strange.

Meanwhile, the fight-week buzz in the media center was as much about marketing, ticket sales, and pay-per-view buys as it was about the fight.

Boxing's economic model is more vulnerable than that of other sports in the face of today's economic crisis. Most sports (such as baseball, football, and basketball) draw on a local fan base for their live gate. By contrast, the people who attend big fights get on a plane, spend several nights in a hotel, and shell out sometimes-exorbitant sums for tickets. Fans can watch the World Series and Super Bowl on television for free. Boxing's big events are on pay-per-view.

Two weeks before De La Hoya–Pacquiao, the November 22nd fight between Ricky Hatton and Paulie Malignaggi at the MGM Grand had posed a troubling wake-up call. Half of the tickets went unsold. On November 23rd, there were empty seats on planes leaving Las Vegas and it took less than five minutes to go through airline security checkpoints. That "never" happens on a Sunday in Las Vegas.

Thereafter, Richard Schaefer observed, "De La Hoya–Pacquiao is still the big one, but we have to redefine 'big.'"

There were two means of definition. The first was ticket sales.

When tickets for De La Hoya–Pacquiao were initially allocated, there was a feeding frenzy. Everyone remembered the ticket-scalping that had accompanied De La Hoya–Mayweather and everyone wanted to make a killing. Seconds after going on sale, tickets for De La Hoya–Pacquiao sold out (or so it was announced). The live gate would be just under $17,000,000, placing it slightly behind the $18,419,200 generated by De La Hoya–Mayweather.

But the truth was more complicated. One source says that tickets for De La Hoya–Pacquiao were allocated as follows:

(1) The MGM Grand = 5,500 tickets.
(2) Top Rank = 5,000 tickets (Pacquiao bought 1,000 of these and was given thirty more. Another 1,500 tickets from this allotment were set aside for sale in the Philippines).
(3) Golden Boy = 3,500
(4) Sponsors = 350
(5) HBO = 150
(6) Public sale = 1,500

Then problems arose. The MGM Grand's high rollers didn't respond to invitations as expected. The hotel lowered its criteria as to who constituted a "high roller" and still had tickets left, which it started packaging with deluxe rooms at prices below market value.

Some of the people who'd purchased tickets from Golden Boy and Top Rank had been acting as brokers. The tickets they'd bought were non-returnable. But the resale market was soft and they couldn't re-sell them at face value. Those tickets, too, started selling at a discount.

Next, the reneges started coming in. The WBC had ordered eighty tickets but declined to follow through on the purchase. According to Arum, when WBC president Jose Sulaiman arrived in Las Vegas to attend the fight, Golden Boy, Top Rank, and the Nevada State Athletic Commission all refused to credential him. Sulaiman had to buy his own ticket and sit several dozen rows from ringside.

On fight night, Las Vegas was surprisingly quiet. Cars flowed freely up and down the Strip. Some gaming tables at the MGM Grand weren't even open. Ten minutes before the bell for round one of De La Hoya–Pacquiao, there were blocks of empty seats in the arena. And they didn't belong to high rollers who had yet to filter in.

The second measure of economic success was the pay-per-view tally.

Sources say that, when De La Hoya–Pacquiao was first signed, HBO thought that it would engender a minimum of 1,500,000 buys. Arum (who had guaranteed Pacquiao $11,000,000) needed one million buys to break even. But it wasn't long before optimism was replaced by an unsettling fear that pay-per-view sales would be weak.

Pavlik-Hopkins on October 18th and Joe Calzaghe versus Roy Jones Jr on November 8th were back-to-back pay-per-view disasters. Part of the problem was the slumping economy. And part of the problem was piracy.

Internet piracy has evolved in recent years from delayed "resampling" to the live streaming of pay-per-view fights. Host sites post URLs that offer one-click access to content free of charge. Under the Federal Communications Act, a host site is required to have a "takedown" tool to deal with illegal content. But it takes time to effectively utilize the tool, and the law offers "safe harbor" to host sites as long as a takedown tool is in place.

For Calzaghe-Jones, HBO had forty "takedowns" on one site alone (Justin.tv). And more significantly, new sites sprang up on fight night like mushrooms in the dark.

HBO hired two outside companies to combat Internet piracy as it related to De La Hoya–Pacquiao. During fight week, a command center monitored sites that it thought would facilitate theft. On fight night, the center sought to shut down sites that illegally showed the pay-per-view card. But it was clear that Internet pay-per-view piracy had caught up with digital technology.

As for the fight; Jerry Izenberg wrote afterward, "Manny Pacquiao won one for everyone who was ever told he was too small to play with the big boys; for every kid who ever gave up his lunch money in the schoolyard because he was told not to mess with the bully; for everyone everywhere who was told 'no, you can't' when something deep inside him whispered, 'I think I can.'"

The maxim that most people were quoting before the fight was, "A good big man beats a good little one." It would have been more appropriate to prophesy, "A great fighter in his prime beats a fading old one." What many thought would be akin a man beating up a boy turned into a young man beating up an old one.

On this particular night, Pacquiao was a boxer-puncher and De La Hoya was neither. Oscar was in the wrong place against the wrong opponent at the wrong time. Forget about his not being able to pull the trigger. He didn't even have a gun.

In the opening round, the difference in height and reach between the fighters was obvious. So was the fact that De La Hoya's reflexes and legs were shot. After a relatively cautious opening stanza, Pacquiao became more aggressive; circling, attacking, darting in and out, staying off the ropes, and attacking again with a left-hand lead that was effective throughout the fight. Manny won on the inside and he won on the outside. His speed and southpaw stance gave De La Hoya fits.

By round three, Oscar's face was puffing up. His punches were tentative and his jab had become little more than a pawing stay-away-from-me flick. The beating accelerated in round four. By round six, Pacquiao was defiantly trading shots. In round seven, he battered De La Hoya around the ring, outlanding him 47 to 7. Forty-five of those blows were calculated by CompuBox as "power punches." Each judge scored the round

10–8 in Manny's favor. Oscar wasn't saved by the bell. The bell simply prolonged his suffering.

After eight rounds, Nacho Beristain stopped the bout with De La Hoya's consent. Oscar lost every minute of every round and was thoroughly beaten round-after-round. Pacquiao outlanded him 224 to 83 and, more significantly, connected on 195 of 333 power punches.

"You were right," De La Hoya told Roach when the carnage was over. "I don't have it anymore."

After the fight, Arum was ecstatic. De La Hoya–Pacquiao was the biggest installment in the ongoing war (sometimes cold, sometimes hot) between Golden Boy and Top Rank, and his guy had won. The victory gave him back much of the leverage he'd lost when Bernard Hopkins beat Kelly Pavlik and Miguel Cotto was defeated by Antonio Margarito.

"I'm walking on air," Arum said. "The only other time I felt like this was when George Foreman knocked out Michael Moorer. You can believe me or not, but this wasn't about personal vindication. I was really emotionally invested in Manny winning. It was big because it was against Oscar, but I have no hard feelings against Oscar."

Of course, later in the evening, Arum added, "At Top Rank, we develop fighters. We've been doing it for years. Golden Boy steals fighters that someone else has developed. All Richard Schaefer knows how to do is get TV dates from HBO and maybe make a site deal. Golden Boy doesn't know how to develop fighters."

Manny Pacquiao is now the face of boxing, and Arum has him. You'd better believe; Schaefer knows when Top Rank's contract with Pacquiao expires.

Meanwhile, Pacquiao's win is good for boxing. He's not unbeatable. He and Juan Manuel Marquez were separated by only one point after twenty-four rounds. But Manny has become a complete fighter; possibly the best fighter ever to come out of Asia. His victory over De La Hoya was the sort of performance that one puts in a time capsule to define a fighter. He'll be hard to beat at 135 or 140 pounds.

And he's a nice man. "The best thing for me about fighting," Pacquiao says, "is to make people happy."

In other words, Manny likes the happiness he brings to people; not just the adulation he receives as a consequence of winning. He gives boxing an exciting new face at a time when the sweet science needs one.

The challenges ahead for the business of boxing are enormous. De La Hoya–Pacquiao was the last big fight in what has been a lousy year for the sport. Television ratings dropped. Pay-per-view buys nose-dived. The heavyweight division is still a mess. Kelly Pavlik and Miguel Cotto (who were supposed to lead the next generation of superstars) lost.

Most likely, pay-per-view piracy on the Internet will continue to grow. Combating it is a labor-intensive job; and right now, the pirates are winning. As host sites emerge in countries that don't recognize U.S. and British copyright law, the problem will worsen. For the tide to turn, new service companies that view combating piracy as a profitable growth industry need to emerge. It's possible that, in the absence of new technologies, De La Hoya–Pacquiao (which HBO says engendered 1,250,000 buys) will be one of boxing's last blockbuster pay-per-view shows.

There also might be fewer big fights in Las Vegas in 2009 than has been the case in recent years. The high rollers didn't come in like they were expected to for Hatton-Malignaggi and De La Hoya–Pacquiao. If the casinos stop buying tickets for their high rollers, Sin City will become a lot less attractive to promoters.

As for Oscar; the best service he can perform for boxing now would be to retire from the ring.

There are those who say that De La Hoya's career as an elite fighter ended a long time ago. Whether or not he fights again, it's over now. Oscar would be well-advised to follow the example of his assistant trainer, Daniel Zaragoza. After a 1997 knockout loss at the hands of Erik Morales, Zaragoza (a champion in his own right) retired with the acknowledgement, "I didn't have it tonight, and I won't be any better tomorrow."

That leaves the issue of De La Hoya's legacy. It is what it is. His record is devoid of that one glorious night when he prevailed against a great fighter in his prime. In too many moments of truth, he came up short. Four of the six fights he lost were fights that, arguably, he could and should have won.

Still, Oscar has fought honorably for two decades. And with all the glitz and hype that accompanied his career, casual fans who cheered him on might have overlooked the essence of a prizefight. In the ring, there's no make-believe. The show is unscripted; the violence is real. Every time that Oscar De La Hoya stepped into the ring as a fighter, he was honest and on his own.

Round 2
Non–Combatants

If you can't write well about Don King, you can't write.

Don King: The Lion in Winter

I met Don King for the first time in autumn 1983. I'd just started researching a book entitled *The Black Lights,* which was my initial foray into boxing writing. Bill Cayton and Jim Jacobs (who co-managed WBC lightweight champion Edwin Rosario) invited me to lunch. I arrived at their office, and Bill told me, "Don King will be joining us."

I thought that was great. It would be a chance to interview the most powerful person in boxing. And obviously, it would be fun to chat with King over a pastrami sandwich. We went to Reuben's (a delicatessen on the corner of Madison Avenue and 38th Street). And the first thing that Don said to me was . . .

Nothing. Not a word.

I was a lawyer and writer delving into the inner workings of boxing. King was there because he'd be negotiating a contract with Bill and Jim later in the afternoon. He wanted nothing to do with me. That day, I learned that Don King can be very quiet.

Thereafter, my impressions of King were largely negative. I understood that he was one of the smartest, hardest-working, most charismatic men on the face of the earth. But in my view, he exploited fighters.

That belief was infused in the pages of *The Black Lights* and *Muhammad Ali: His Life and Times* (which I authored six years later). A comment I made in 1992 also received a fair amount of attention. Joseph Maffia (once the chief financial officer for Don King Productions) had been subpoenaed to appear before a United States Senate subcommittee that was investigating corruption in professional boxing. Maffia retained me as his attorney. Thereafter, he was questioned by Daniel Rinzel (counsel for the Senate subcommittee).

"Is Don King tied to organized crime?" Rinzel queried.

"You don't understand," I interjected. "Don King is organized crime."

And so it went. I wasn't King's favorite person (particularly after he was indicted by a federal grand jury on the basis of Maffia's testimony).

But somewhere along the line (long after a jury found him "not guilty"), there was a thaw in relations between us. A day in March 2003 stands out in my mind. A documentary crew had been following Don around during the build-up to Roy Jones versus John Ruiz. He and I were standing in the lobby of Caesars Palace, talking about the fight.

"Why don't you interview him," King told the producer, nodding in my direction. "That's the guy who got me indicted."

"You're surprisingly nice to him," the producer noted.

"He did his job," King said. "I respect that. Then he let it go, and I respect that too."

Later in the day, Don and I were talking in the media center. "I never thought I'd say this," he told me. "But you're all right."

Which leads me to the point at hand. I never thought I'd say this; but I think that Don King is now good for boxing.

In *Sunset Boulevard,* Norma Desmond (the faded star played by Gloria Swanson) harkens back to Hollywood's silent-screen era and proclaims, "We didn't need dialogue; we had faces then."

King is blessed with both a unique gift for rhetoric and a remarkably camera-friendly face. Over the years, he and Muhammad Ali have been boxing's two greatest showmen. Like Ali, Don became part of the fabric of the sport. He brought major championship bouts to the third world, nurtured some spectacular fights, and was a magnet for interest in boxing.

As a representative of the sweet science, King has met with Nelson Mandela, Mikhail Gorbachev, Leonid Brezhnev, Vladimir Putin, Pope John Paul II, Pope Benedict XVI, Tony Blair, Jacques Chirac, Silvio Berlusconi, Fidel Castro, Ferdinand Marcos, and seven presidents of the United States. Also, as he recites, "most of the people who have been president of a country in Africa, some Chinese heads of state, every president of Mexico for thirty years, that woman who's chancellor of Germany, and more senators, governors, and mayors than you can count."

He's an icon.

Only in America . . . Only in boxing.

Having said all that; an alternative view of King might begin with the poetry of Henry Wadsworth Longfellow:

> There was a little girl
> Who had a little curl
> Right in the middle of her forehead;

When she was good
She was very good indeed
But when she was bad she was horrid.

King's detractors view him as a cross between an evil warlord and a robber baron from the late-1800s. They think that he's horrid.

Don says that he has made more money for more fighters than any promoter in history. His critics maintain that he has stolen more money from more fighters than any promoter in history. They also note the unholy alliances that he has fashioned over the years with various world sanctioning organizations and believe that his reputation for malfeasance has scared corporate sponsors away from boxing. In their view, he has hurt too many people to ever be considered good for the sport.

An in-between assessment might be that King has cleaned up his act in recent years but, overall, has done less with his enormous talent than he could and should have done to help boxing reclaim its status as a major sport.

That brings us to Don King today.

The Biblical belief in the perfectibility of man is inapplicable to the business of boxing. The sport was dirty long before King got his hands on it. Within that environment, he ruled the jungle that's professional boxing for decades. He reveled in (and propagated) the idea that he controlled the sport. But by last year, Golden Boy had established itself as boxing's lead promoter (with Top Rank a close second). HBO televised seven major pay-per-view cards in 2007. Golden Boy was involved with six of them.

One of the reasons for the decline in King's power is that, whatever tactics he employed in the past, there are others now who do things in a similar way. He might have been the pioneer who showed them how. But he's hardly the only power broker who plays hardball and cuts corners when it comes to contracts today. He's not the only person who benefits from questionable alliances with television network executives. Nor is he the only promoter to have a symbiotic relationship with the world sanctioning bodies.

The larger question with regard to King in 2008 is the extent to which he's still a significant force in the business of boxing.

"Don's greatest contributions, the good and the bad, are in the past," says Jerry Izenberg, who has covered sports for more than fifty years.

"When he goes, it won't have a major impact on boxing because he's no longer a major force."

"He's a guy who was once king and now he's just part of the court," adds Larry Merchant. "Some people find him entertaining. I remember him for what he was."

King today is regarded by some in the same vein as Butch Cassidy and the Sundance Kid; two guys who robbed banks but were loveable rogues at heart.

However, it would be a mistake to think of King's current role in boxing as being reduced to that of an entertainer. The world saw what he's still capable of doing last month, when Felix Trinidad versus Roy Jones was faltering. Ticket sales were mediocre. Insiders were fearful that the fight would engender only 300,000 pay-per-view buys. Some observers drew parallels between the promoter and his fighters, noting that all three were past their prime.

Then King put on his "Only in America" jacket and went to work. Over the course of four days, he made more appearances and granted more interviews than most presidential candidates accommodate in a week. His itinerary included press conferences, luncheons, fighter work-outs, and interviews at hockey and basketball games. There was a television satellite media tour, a radio satellite media tour, and sit-downs with myriad talk-show hosts ranging from Bill O'Reilly to Howard Stern. He worked his ass off to promote the fight. At times, he seemed like a force of nature. His personality, presence, and sheer physical bulk are such that it was easy to forget he's seventy-six years old.

Trinidad-Jones recorded 500,000 pay-per-view buys. It's unlikely that anyone other than King could have pushed the fight to that level. Like Mick Jagger, he can still produce on the big stage.

King is not an introspective man. He doesn't talk publicly about his feelings or the future; nor does he have any plans to leave boxing. "I'm more of a fighter now than I ever was," he says. "I'm like boxing itself. Boxing has been assaulted, attacked, and vilified so bad that there ain't much more you can do to it. It's remarkable that boxing is still standing. I'm like a great fighter. I won't give up."

He won't go quietly; that's for sure. When finally he departs, boxing will miss him.

So will I.

Danny Milano is one of the steady dependable people who contribute to boxing today.

Danny Milano: The Cutman

When Paulie Malignaggi steps into the ring on May 24th for his rematch against Lovemore N'dou, an integral member of Team Malignaggi will be watching intently from the corner.

Danny Milano was born in the Bronx on June 1, 1957. His father owned a small business repairing home appliances (refrigerators, dishwashers, ovens, washers, and dryers). At age twelve, Danny started working for his father. Then the family and business moved to New Jersey. When Danny Milano Sr died in 1986, his son took over the company now known as Danny's Appliance Service.

"If you work for Sears," Danny says, "you work on one kind of Sears appliance all day long. I work on five different kinds of appliances times ten different brands times fifteen or twenty different models. And there's more options to break now than when I was young. When I started, refrigerators had a thermostat and a compressor. Now you have fans, fan motors, ice-makers, sensors; so there's a lot more to know. I'm a perfectionist. If I can't be one of the best at what I do, I don't want to do it. But I think I'm good at repairing appliances and I make a living from it. Someone always has something broken."

Danny's Appliance Service is its proprietor's primary source of income, but his passion is boxing. Milano is a cutman, respected throughout the sport as a capable craftsman and stabilizing influence in the corner. Many insiders see him as a successor to the likes of Ace Marotta and Al Gavin, which isn't surprising since he grew up surrounded by old-school guys.

Milano's uncle (his mother's brother) is Al Certo, so boxing is literally in his blood. "When I was young, I spent a lot of time hanging around the gym and going to fights with Al," Danny says. "Promoting, matchmaking, managing, training; he did it all."

Certo also taught Milano to box. "I had thirteen amateur fights," Danny recalls. "I won twelve, three of them by knockout, and lost one.

The loss was on a decision, and it was the right decision. I knew I wasn't good enough to go all the way, so I got out."

When Milano was in his mid-twenties, he started working the spit-bucket in the corner for Certo's fighters. For ten years, that was all he did during fights. Then, one night toward the end of Buddy McGirt's career, Danny was in the corner with Certo and Howie Albert. "Buddy had a swelling around his eye," Danny remembers. "Howie's hip was hurting, and he told me, 'Danny, you go up and handle it.'"

Not long after that, Milano started working on cuts. "Most of what I learned came from Al and Howie," he says. "But I got tips from a lot of guys, and practice makes perfect. Some guys do cuts every six months. Right now, I do forty to fifty shows a year."

Milano's current client list includes Paulie Malignaggi, Andre Berto, Chazz Witherspoon, and Vinny Maddalone ("I get plenty of practice with Vinny"). He has also worked with Antonio Tarver, Arturo Gatti (more practice), Andrew Golota, Sharmba Mitchell, Tomasz Adamek, and Yory Boy Campas.

Before a fight, Milano loads his bucket with ice, bottles of water, an Enswell, adrenaline, Vaseline, latex gloves, swabs, gauze, and (depending on the state) avitene and thrombin. "People think we have magic potions," he says. "And obviously, we don't. I love adrenaline; that's my coagulant of choice. But the key to it all is knowing how to apply pressure."

Milano greases his fighter down in the dressing room before a fight and then again in the ring prior to the opening bell. "If there's a cut, you don't have a full minute between rounds to work on it," he says. "It takes the fighter about ten seconds to get back to the corner, and a fighter's seconds are supposed to leave the ring ten seconds before the bell that starts each round. I try to cheat five seconds at each end. The instant a round is over, I'm in the ring. I go to the fighter and start toweling the blood off his body as he's walking to the corner. By the time he's on his stool, I'm holding the cut. You have to know what you're doing. A good cutman is quick, careful, and confident. The fighter's career and physical well-being are in your hands, and every second counts."

The job is also about personal relationships.

"If a fighter gets cut, he looks to the cutman to see the reaction," Milano explains. "He might be the toughest SOB in the world; but if he's cut, maybe he loses his composure. So no matter how bad a cut is, I tell the fighter, 'Don't worry; I've got it under control.' After you've worked with a guy a couple of times, he starts to trust you. If he's cut, it bothers him less because he knows you can handle it. And over time, the ring doctors get to know you. Once they understand that you know what you're doing, they'll give you a round or two more to do your job than might otherwise be the case."

But frustration often attaches to the job.

"A lot of guys treat the cutman as an afterthought when he should be a priority," Milano says. "I can't tell you how many times I get to a show and I'm planning to work with just one fighter, and someone will see me and ask if I can work their fighter's corner that night. How do you go to a fight and not know who your cutman will be until you get there?"

And then there's the matter of money.

"I don't get rich doing this," Milano says. "I charge a minimum of fifty dollars a fight. That's against a percentage of the purse that starts at three percent and goes down to one percent as the purse increases. For a big fight, I get a flat fee. I pay for my own avitene and adrenaline, and some states require a sealed bottle for each fight; so the fifty dollars I get for a fight can disappear into a cut real quick. And I treat my four-round fighters the same way I treat the world champions I work with. They bleed the same if they're cut."

"I try to get along with everybody and treat them the way I'd like them to treat me," Milano continues. "Sometimes it works; sometimes it doesn't. Some guys are loyal and some aren't. I hear a lot of, 'Danny; when we make it, you'll make it.' Then they get to the $100,000 purses. I ask for my two percent and I hear, 'Gee, that's a lot of money.' I say, 'Wait a minute. What happened to, 'When we make it, you make it?'"

"Over the years, I've done a fair number of $5,000 fights and a couple of tens," Milano says. "But most of the time, it's fifty or a hundred dollars. What can I say? I love boxing. Saturday is the busiest day of the week for an appliance repair business. I'll close the business on a Saturday, drive to Atlantic City or Philadelphia, and get maybe two or three hundred dollars. Losing a thousand dollars to work a fight card for two or three hundred says it all. But knowing I've made a difference in a fight makes me happy."

Most of Milano's fighters appreciate his efforts. Last year, Vinny Maddalone was scheduled to fight Evander Holyfield in Corpus Christi on the night of March 17th. It was far and away the biggest fight of Vinny's career. But Maureen Shea had a four-rounder at Madison Square Garden the night before, and Danny works with Maureen. He figured he'd cover her fight, catch a 6:00 A.M. flight to Houston on Saturday, and fly from there to Corpus Christi.

But there were complications. On Saturday morning, it was snowing in New York and the major airports (JFK, LaGuardia, and Newark) were all shut down. Maddalone's people were telling him, "Don't worry; we'll get Joe Souza." And Vinny was telling them back, "Joe Souza is a good cutman, but I want Danny." Finally, the Maddalone camp arranged for a private jet to fly Milano directly from Westchester County Airport to Corpus Christi.

That problem was easy to resolve compared to a June 2006 conflict. Milano had worked with Antonio Tarver since Tarver's 2002 rematch against Eric Harding and been in his corner for every fight thereafter (three against Roy Jones, two against Glen Johnson, and one against Montell Griffin). But he'd worked with Paulie Malignaggi for every fight of Paulie's career. Then Antonio and Paulie were "double-dated" for June 10th. Tarver against Bernard Hopkins in Atlantic City and Malignaggi at Madison Square Garden against Miguel Cotto.

"I didn't know what to do," Milano remembers. "It bothered me a lot because I felt a sense of loyalty to both guys. Finally, I asked myself, 'Which one needs me more?' Paulie thought I'd go with Tarver because the money was bigger. But I decided that Paulie was in the fight of his life. He hadn't fought at that level before and he needed all the support he could get. So I went with Paulie. Antonio was angry about it. He hasn't used me since then. But no one can say I walked away from Antonio when he was down. He was on top when I made that decision."

Seconds into round one of Malignaggi-Cotto, Paulie was badly cut by an accidental clash of heads. Later, his face began to swell from a broken orbital bone. His courage kept him in the fight, but Milano's cornerwork helped.

"I think Danny is the best cutman in the business," Malignaggi says today. "And I'm not just saying that because he's mine. You got all these guys out there with reputations who don't know what they're doing, and Danny does. I know because I've been cut in three of my last four fights; and each time, Danny stopped the bleeding. How many times have you seen one of Danny's guys get stopped on a cut? It doesn't happen."

To which Milano says simply, "The fighter does his job and I do mine."

Knowledgeable fight fans are some of the best people in boxing.

Anthony Catanzaro and Chris Santos

When Paulie Malignaggi steps into the ring to face Ricky Hatton on November 22nd, two fans with unique perspectives will be at ringside. Anthony Catanzaro and Chris Santos are part owners of restaurants that are as different as the styles of the fighters they'll be watching in Las Vegas. But they share a passion for the sweet science and for Paulie.

Catanzaro was born in the Bensonhurst section of Brooklyn in 1968, one year after his parents emigrated from Sicily to the United States. "My father's side of the family was all fisherman," he says. "My father decided to stay on land and repair the boats." Anthony is fluent in English, Italian, and Spanish, but notes, "When I was growing up, the first language in our neighborhood was a Sicilian dialect of Italian. That's what I heard at home and on the streets."

"Soccer was my first passion," Catanzaro continues. "At New Utrecht High School, I was co-captain of the soccer team. When I was sixteen, I started playing semi-pro and got paid fifty dollars a game. I thought I was rich. Eventually, I made it to $150 a game, but that came with a lot injuries so I retired."

In 1993, Catanzaro began work as a sales assistant for Georgio Armani. "People like Robert DeNiro, Pat Riley, and Eric Clapton came in from time to time," he remembers. "Once, Sigourney Weaver undressed in front of me. That was a treat."

But there was a lot he didn't like about the job, including the fact that he was bored stiff. So he started working as a bartender in an Italian restaurant ("I'm a people person, so I got along well with everyone at the bar; I was a good bartender"). Then he managed a restaurant in Brooklyn.

In 2001, Anthony was offered a partnership in a pizzeria in Manhattan. He's still part-owner of Portobello's at 83 Murray Street. He and his wife (a substance-abuse therapist) live in the Dyker Heights section of Brooklyn with their six-year-old son, Joseph.

Catanzaro and Malignaggi first crossed paths in 1997, when Anthony was sparring with a soccer teammate named Filippo Giuffre at Gleason's

Gym. "We sparred three times," Anthony remembers. "We wore headgear and used 16-ounce gloves. Each time, Filippo beat the shit out of me. There were no knockdowns, but I didn't enjoy it. Three minutes can be an eternity."

"After one of our sparring sessions," Anthony continues, "Filippo and I were speaking Sicilian, and this skinny malnourished-looking kid who was skipping rope overheard us and joined the conversation. He was sixteen years old, hadn't had an amateur fight yet. He told us that someday he was going to be a champion. I said to Filippo, 'Yeah; champion of the neighborhood.' But we liked him. We gave him a ride home. And the whole way home, he didn't shut up. That was Paulie."

Malignaggi, for his part, looks back on that day and says, "I remember it well. I didn't get many rides home in those days."

A decade later, Paulie and Anthony are like family to one another. Catanzaro advises Malignaggi on business matters, helps schedule many of his media appearances, and watches his back in general. He has been to all but four of Paulie's twenty-six fights. And if a fight is anywhere in the New York metropolitan area, Anthony is there after the weigh-in with replenishment from Portobello's.

"It's hard to put into words how I feel about Paulie," Catanzaro says. "To see him progress over the past ten years from being a kid in the neighborhood to a mature world-class fighter means so much to me. The Cotto fight [which Malignaggi lost] was one of the most difficult times in my life, but I was very proud of Paulie that night. He got cut by a head butt in the first round and was dropped in the second. Then bones in his face started getting broken. A lot of guys would have said, 'I'm getting paid anyway' and called it a night. But Paulie stayed in there and won four or five rounds depending on how you scored it. And to come back from that, to beat Lovemore N'dou and become a world champion just one year later; that was a magical night for me. It was the culmination of every step run, every punch taken, every injury overcome, every word spouted. I know how much winning the championship meant to Paulie. It was a great moment in my life."

"I love fighters," Catanzaro continues. "The courage and discipline they show when their body tells them they can't survive the pain and their mind overrides that and forces them to fight on; that's amazing to me. I go to work and the worst thing that can happen to me is I get

burned making a pizza. A fighter gets in the ring, and anyone who understands boxing knows what can happen to him. There are no bums in a
boxing ring. There are unskilled fighters who shouldn't be there. But any
man who steps into a boxing ring is a better man than I am."

Chris Santos was born in Bristol, Rhode Island, in 1971. His father
was an electrician. His mother was a registered nurse, who earned a master's degree and advised hospitals on risk management.

"My father was a very good athlete at the high school level," Santos
says. "That was a source of pride for him. He had a fighting spirit as an
athlete, but he never applied it to other aspects of his life. He and my
mother were separated and, as he grew older, he became kind of a her-
mit. He was estranged from his children. He lived alone and didn't go out.
Sometimes he wouldn't even answer the phone. The last few years, I
started to reconnect with him. He died two years ago, and I live my life
as a direct result of the way he didn't. His life and death made me realize
that we don't have a lot of time. It's one of the reasons I'm driven in
everything I do and get angry when I see people squander their opportunities and talents."

Santos's introduction to the culinary industry was washing pots in a
French restaurant. He was thirteen years old. "I fell in love with the chaos
of it all," Chris recalls. "The chef was like a rock star to me. He flirted
with the pretty waitresses. People were always telling him how good the
food was. From that time on, I wanted to be either a professional fighter,
a rock star [he played drums for twenty years], or a chef. My mother won
that argument, so I went to Johnson and Wales [the largest culinary insti-
tute in the country]."

At culinary school, Santos completed a two-year associate-degree
program and a two-year program in hospitality management. Prior to that,
cooking had been a means to an end; to make money so he could buy
clothes or a car. At Johnson and Wales, he got serious about it.

Santos graduated in 1993, came to New York, and took a job at Time
Café. Ten months later, he was the executive chef. A series of positions at
other restaurants followed. As part of that journey, he met Richard Wolf
(a creator and co-owner of Tao) and Peter Kane (the owner of Happy
Landing).

In due course, Wolf and Kane opened a bar called Double Happiness
in Chinatown. "There was a retail space above the bar," Chris recalls.

"Peter and I opened a small restaurant there called Wyanoka. That was my purest food experience ever because it was so small. We served new American cuisine, and I could do everything in the kitchen myself because the restaurant had only twenty-seven seats."

Then 9/11 devastated Wyanoka's business. The restaurant closed four months later. Still, Santos had gotten enormous accolades as its chef and was a sought-after free agent. For a while, he worked as executive chef at Suba (modern Spanish cuisine). It was a successful "foodie" destination. But Chris had enjoyed being his own boss at Wyanoka and no longer had that freedom. For a while, he thought about "leaving food" altogether. Then, in 2003, he reconnected with Wolf and Kane, and the three of them asked each other, "Why haven't we opened a restaurant together?"

The Stanton Social (at 99 Stanton Street in Manhattan) followed.

Meanwhile, Santos is a boxing junkie. "The three great passions in my life," he says, "are cooking, music, and boxing. I go to every fight card in Manhattan and maybe six shows a year in Las Vegas and Atlantic City. I'm a sucker; I buy every pay-per-view fight. When I'm doing something boxing-related, even if it's just watching a fight on television, it blocks everything else out for me."

Santos also practices what he preaches. For the past ten years, he has worked out at Gleason's. "It's not boxerobics," he explains. "I train two days a week with Martin Gonzalez [who trains Edgar Santana] and twice a week with Melissa Hernandez. I train like a fighter; I spar several times a month. The past few years, I've taken boxing very seriously. Probably, I should have been a fighter. I think I would have been a good one. It makes me crazy that I'm thirty-seven years old and found that talent in me and it's too late. But I'm not about to turn pro at thirty-seven. That sort of thing doesn't work out well."

Santos and Malignaggi met five years ago at Gleason's. "I used to see him all the time in the gym," Paulie remembers. "One day, we started talking and I liked him. Chris is a big boxing fan; he knows his stuff."

Santos, for his part, says, "Like everyone else, I like knockouts. But I love the nuances and subtleties of boxing. Pernell Whitaker, Roy Jones Jr, Floyd Mayweather Jr; those guys are magic. That's one of the reasons I like watching Paulie. You better believe, I'll be in Las Vegas when he fights Ricky Hatton."

Meanwhile, Portobello's and the Stanton Social are as different as a good club fight and a glitzy main event on HBO.

Portobello's has a service counter up front, a linoleum tile floor, and formica-topped tables. It's most distinctive decorating touch is "Paulie's wall"—a montage of newspaper clippings and photos that honor Malignaggi.

The restaurant is open sixty-five hours a week (Monday through Saturday). Catanzaro works fifty to sixty of them. Sunday is his day of rest. "I would never dare to compare what I do with what a fighter does," Anthony says. "But when I leave Portobello's at night, there are times when I feel like I've been in a fight." A second Portobello's opened recently at 61 West Broadway.

The Portobello's at 83 Murray Street attracts five hundred walk-in customers each day. "We don't get many tourists," Catanzaro acknowledges. "It's the same customers day after day. Stuyvesant High School is three blocks away. That helps. And some of Paulie's fans come here on a regular basis."

"Most of our business is at the front counter," Anthony continues. "Pizza, calzone, cannoli. And we have a pretty good delivery business. On an average day, we sell fifty whole pies and another 150 pies in slices. We're the official caterers for the City of New York 311 Unit. And there are other things that come along like being the official pizzeria for the Kids Festival portion of the Tribeca Film Festival. We were also the official pizzeria for Fleet Week in 2005 and sold 400 pies a day. That was stressful. You try delivering a hundred pizzas an hour."

Portobello's also supplies the on-site food for several New York area promoters; most notably Lou DiBella's Broadway Boxing series at the Manhattan Center. For a 7:00 P.M. show, Catanzaro starts cooking at three in the afternoon and arrives at the arena around five o'clock. For a crowd of one thousand, he'll bring ten trays of food (pasta, meatballs, chicken parmesan, sausage and peppers), fifty hero breads, and a hundred cannoli.

"The fans are happy we're there," Anthony says. "It means they can eat something besides a pretzel and a dried up hot dog. If we sell out, after paying the driver and staff and giving the house its cut, we make only a couple of hundred dollars. But the exposure is good. It gets our menus and business cards out there, and sometimes we get other catering jobs from it."

The Stanton Social occupies a different region in the New York food chain. It has a trendy website (www.thestantonsocial.com) and evokes phrases like "hot spot . . . A-list celebrities . . . glitzy, trendy, and bustling." Each dish on the menu is created by Santos and composed like a traditional appetizer or entrée, but the portions are all appetizer size.

Writing in the *New York Times,* food critic Frank Bruni proclaimed, "Chris Santos has an imagination and a talent that shine. The Stanton Social is the restaurant as playlist, a compendium of highlights with no allegiance to a single source of inspiration. It doesn't dawdle anywhere or dwell on anything. It bolts to Mexico to assemble a few tacos; then zips to Japan, wok-charred edamame in its sights. It touches down in Thailand to infuse a broth below steamed clams with lemongrass; then pivots to New England to scratch an itch for lobster rolls. There are no designated appetizers or entrees and no arc to a meal. Everything should be shared. Dishes don't arrive in neatly grouped batches or at neatly timed intervals. They come steadily and continuously throughout the meal, an orgy of hors d'oeuvres."

In the restaurant business, volume equals success. Santos ticks off some numbers.

"Three thousand people eat here each week, with another fifteen hundred to two thousand coming in for drinks only. We do five hundred dinner reservations on a Saturday night. I create every dish, oversee the production of the food, and inspect every plate before it leaves the kitchen. I have forty people in the kitchen; fifteen to eighteen on each shift. There are fifty people up-front; servers, bartenders, hostesses, busboys, food runners, coat-check girls, eighteen to twenty per shift. The first guys come in at 6:00 A.M. The last ones leave at 4:00 A.M. Friday and Saturday are the busiest nights. On those nights, we serve a full menu from 5:00 P.M. to 3:00 A.M. The average plate is fourteen dollars and we do $8,500,000 in sales annually. My payroll is $42,000 a week for staff; $30,000 a week for food supplies; $20,000 for wine and liquor. There's rent, linens, and more. If we're lucky, there's a twenty percent profit margin."

Santos works at least sixty hours a week. "It used to be more," he says. "I work nights; I work weekends. I work when everyone else is out having a good time. I sleep four hours a night and don't get a lot of time off, but I'm okay with that. The whole concept of cooking for a living; you

have to be different to want to do it. The keys are creativity, passion, con-
sistency, and attention to detail. It's a crazy life. It takes a long time to get
to the big money, and most people never make it. Sort of like boxing."

Chris smiles. "There are times when it seems like everything is a boxing analogy to me. I typically work twelve-hour days. And after six hours,
I tell myself, 'Six more rounds to go.'"

Santos recently signed a television deal. A cookbook and more restaurants seem like an inevitable part of his future. This summer, he spent
eleven weeks in Las Vegas, working a hundred hours a week, helping
Richard Wolf and Marc Packer launch Lavo (a Mediterranean restaurant
in the Palazzo).

Through it all, Chris's respect for, and obsession with, the culinary arts
is clear. When asked who he would invite to the Stanton Social if he
could host any historical figure, his choice is Francois Vatel; a famed French
chef who oversaw a banquet for two hundred people held in honor of
Louis XIV in April 1671. When an expected consignment of fish was not
delivered, Vatel was so distraught at the thought of not feeding the king
properly that he went to his room, penned a suicide note ("The shame is
too much to bear"), and stabbed himself to death. Minutes later, the fish
arrived.

"I couldn't have said this when I was younger," Santos acknowledges,
"but right now, I know who I am. I know what I do, why I do it, and
where I'm going. I'm a craftsman and it means a lot to me when people
appreciate my craft. I love my life. I'm my own boss. But my end game is
about boxing. I hope to retire from the food business when I'm fifty and
do something hands-on in boxing like refereeing or judging or training a
fighter. And I know that I can't date a girl who won't go to the fights with
me."

So there you are: Anthony Catanzaro and Chris Santos; Portobello's
and the Stanton Social. Let's give the final word to noted food critic,
Paulie Malignaggi.

"Both guys are good friends to me," Paulie says. "They understand
fighters; they respect fighters. If I ate their food all the time, I'd never
make weight. The things I eat there; I wish I had three stomachs."

"The Stanton Social is more upscale and trendy," Paulie continues. "If
you wanted to impress a date, you'd bring her there before you brought

her to Portobello's. But Portobello's has a special place in my heart because of Anthony. Anthony is like a big brother to me. There are so many things he helps me with; everything from small sponsorships to making sure that I have the right kind of car insurance. He doesn't get paid; he does it out of kindness. He cares about me for myself; not just because I'm a fighter. And believe me; I appreciate it."

"Also," Paulie says in closing, "no matter how good the food is at the Stanton Social—and it's great—the pizza is better at Portobello's."

In recent years, Boxrec.com has become boxing's indispensable website.

Boxrec.com

How important is Boxrec.com?

Ask people in the boxing industry:

> • Bruce Trampler (Top Rank matchmaker): Short of actually being at a fight, they're the best source of information out there. I have my own computerized records, and I'm on Boxrec at least a dozen times a day. We take it for granted, but everyone in boxing would miss it if it was gone.
> • Cameron Dunkin (honored by the Boxing Writers Association of America as the 2007 "manager of the year"): It's an incredible tool for everyone in boxing. I use it all the time. We all do. You have to use it.
> • Carl Moretti (DiBella Entertainment vice president for boxing operations): I use it every day, many times a day, for every reason imaginable. It's the quickest cheapest easiest way to find out what I need to know.
> • Ron Scott Stevens (chairman of the New York State Athletic Commission): Fight Fax is the mandated record-keeper for athletic commissions in the United States. But Boxrec does more than supplement Fight Fax. In many respects, it surpasses Fight Fax.
> • Mike Silver (boxing historian): Boxrec.com is a dream come true. It's one of the greatest gifts to boxing fans and boxing historians in the history of the world. Years ago, you needed a whole shelf of *Ring* record books to track the records of fighters. Now anyone can do it in seconds for free. Every time I write about boxing, I want to thank them.
> • Lou DiBella (promoter): Anyone in boxing who says he doesn't use Boxrec is either a complete imbecile or lying.
> • Dan Rafael (ESPN.com boxing writer): It's great for fans. It's great for people in the industry. I use it all the time. I don't know who's behind it. But whoever he is, God bless him.

The prime mover of the above-referenced adoration is a forty-four-year-old Englishman named John Sheppard, who was born in London and moved with his family to Doncaster when he was two years old.

Doncaster was once a coal mining town. Sheppard's grandfather, uncles, father, mother, brother, and sister all worked in the coal industry. In the mid-1990s, John was a computer systems analyst for the National Coal Board. He was also friendly with Riath and Nabeel Hamed (Naseem's older brothers).

"To be honest," Sheppard acknowledges, "I didn't know who Naseem was. But Riath and Nabeel talked me into going with them to see Naseem fight Enrique Angeles [on May 6, 1995]. It was the first time I'd been to a fight, and my reaction to it was that the entire spectacle was barbaric and degrading. I sat there watching people punch each other in the head, wondering why they were doing it. It went on and on interminably for hours. I was sprayed with blood, getting more and more miserable, telling myself, 'I don't want to be here.' And then, during Naseem's fight, something clicked in my head. The subtlety of what he was doing, the genius of it all, became obvious to me. It wasn't a disgusting spectacle anymore. It was art, and I found myself cheering."

In 1999, Hamed broke with promoter Frank Warren and launched his own promotional company. Sheppard went to work for him and soon became the lynch-pin of Prince Promotions and a related company that was formed to promote fights on Sky-TV with Barry Hearn.

"We had a matchmaker who I didn't fully trust," John remembers. "I started a little data base to track all the British boxers for myself as a way of keeping tabs on him. The Internet was taking off at the time. And I asked myself, 'Why not put the data up on the Internet so everyone can use it?'

In May 2000, Sheppard rented space on a server. "It was a hobby more than anything else," he explains. "I paid for it out of my own pocket. Then I got an email from someone in America saying that he was a record-collector and wanted to help, so I gave him the password. After that, there were more emails from more collectors. Pretty soon, the people who owned the server complained that I was getting more traffic than the other six hundred sites on the server combined and that my traffic was overwhelming the server and they gave me the hook. So I bought a server and installed it at a data center in Manchester; but a year later, that was overloaded."

Boxrec.com has grown organically and exponentially since then. It's now the most heavily trafficked boxing website in the world. On a typical day, it has 50,000 visitors who view 700,000 pages. Forty percent of its traffic comes from the United States and 12 percent from the United Kingdom.

Sheppard has worked on the site fulltime since 2005 ("eight hours on some days; twenty hours on others"). "But it's hard to describe it as a job," he says, "because I love what I'm doing."

What he's doing is fashioning and sharing a data base that's unparalleled in the history of boxing.

Boxrec now has close to 1,300,000 bouts in its data base encompassing 17,000 active and 345,000 non-active fighters. Those numbers keep growing as new fights take place and old ones are recorded.

"There are roughly 150 editors," Sheppard says. "On an average day, about sixty of them contribute to the site. Nobody on the staff gets paid. It's all on a volunteer basis. Our editors are motivated by incredible passion for the sport. As best I can tell, very few of them are young. Record-collecting is an old-fashioned hobby. But the young editors we have are just as enthusiastic as the old ones."

"Where active fighters are concerned," Sheppard continues, "we assign different editors to different countries and, in some instances, regions within countries. The majority of work done on the site now is historical. The historical editors work on historical data and don't touch current data. We've exhausted the record books and obvious sources like old boxing magazines. So a lot of what the historical editors do now is combing through old newspapers, looking for local fights that have never been recorded. Our records are incomplete for many of the old fighters. But the closer we get to the current day, the more complete our records are."

The site also has data on 28,000 non-fighters (referees, judges, managers, promoters, matchmakers, and supervisors). And a boxing "encyclopedia" was added in 2005.

In addition, Boxrec rates every active fighter in each weight division, using a purely statistical formula based on the outcome of fights. An "active" fighter is one who has a fight scheduled or has fought within the previous 365 days. A fighter who announces his retirement is reclassified as "inactive." Every active fighter with one fight or more in the database is rated.

The Boxrec ratings aren't perfect. But they make a lot more sense than those of the world sanctioning bodies. And equally important, the process is open, verifiable, and not influenced by anyone's subjective opinion. The BoxRec computer re-calculates the ratings on a daily basis. A boxer earns or loses ratings points with every bout he has fought since the last calculation and with every bout added to any of his opponents' records or to their opponents' records.

Boxrec also maintains historical ratings within each weight division. But Sheppard concedes that these are mostly for entertainment purposes, since he has been unable to develop a computer program that credibly matches boxers across generational lines.

The main competition (such as it is) to Boxrec comes from Fight Fax, which is the only record-keeper whose reports are officially accepted by members of the Association of Boxing Commissions in the United States.

Every state athletic commission in America is required by law to send bout results, suspensions, and federal ID numbers to Fight Fax (as are ABC associate members in Canada). Boxrec tries to get this information. Some commissions provide it to Sheppard as a matter of course. Some send it upon request. A few refuse to send it to Boxrec even when asked.

Fight Fax, in essence, is a government-mandated monopoly. In exchange for its favored position, it provides an updated list of suspended boxers to state athletic commissions free of charge. But everyone else must pay for the list.

And more significantly, the ABC requires that promoters submit a Fight Fax record for each boxer on a proposed fight card before the card is approved by the governing athletic commission. Fight Fax charges promoters (and everyone else) nine dollars to fax up to three records.

Fight Fax's records contain less information regarding individual fighters and fights than Boxrec's offerings. But because Fight Fax enters only official commission reports in its data base, its records are believed to be more accurate.

Promoter Russell Peltz observes, "There's no such thing as perfect record-keeping. Very few things in life are one hundred percent. But I've come across some glaring errors at Boxrec, mostly in the historical records."

And Dan Rafael notes, "So many people have a hand in Boxrec that the records aren't always accurate. Ricardo Mayorga's record has been wrong for years. There's a mistake on Derrick Gainer's record too."

Sheppard is aware of the issue. "The thousand-dollar question," he says, "is how we check for accuracy. For historical data, whenever possible, we go back to local newspapers and other primary sources. For contemporary results, we exchange emails and faxes with local commissions and do back-up research for commissions we don't trust."

"Also," Sheppard adds, "unlike Fight Fax, we have an open system. The data is there for everyone to see. So if we make a mistake, particularly on a contemporary fight, the aggrieved boxer and a dozen of his fans let us know about it."

In addition, Boxrec is now tracking suspensions. If a visitor to the site goes to an individual fighter's record and clicks on a box, a report of suspensions will be emailed to him. It's not official, but it's a start. The site has also begun posting the federal ID numbers of fighters when those numbers are available to it.

And there's another feature unique to Boxrec that makes it the clear industry favorite. Anyone who views a fighter's record can also see the complete record of that fighter's opponents, his opponents' opponents, and so on down the line.

"That's invaluable," says Bob Goodman (director of boxing for Don King Productions). "When you're looking at a fighter, you don't just want to know that he's 20-and-2. You want to know who he beat to get to 20-and-2, and you want to know who he lost to. In terms of accuracy, Boxrec is getting better all the time. Even when it's not one hundred percent, you get a good picture of any fighter you're interested in. The cross-referencing is what makes the site great."

Ron Scott Stevens adds, "Boxrec isn't the official record-keeper. But you get the records of opponents and the records of the opponents' opponents. You get weights. You get the judges' scores, so you can see how close a fight was. Those are important elements in deciding whether or not the commission should allow a fight."

"And it's not just the record of the fights themselves," points out veteran matchmaker Ron Katz. "There are so many things on Boxrec that help me do my job. I can find out who manages a fighter, who promotes a fighter. I can search for fighters by location, which is important because it costs money to bring guys in for a fight."

Lou DiBella sums up for his brethren when he says, "Fight Fax might be slightly more accurate. But Boxrec is free and gives you more information. And Fight Fax isn't online. You have to email or fax or call in your request. Usually, they get back to you quickly. But sometimes you have to wait until the next day. It used to be that, if a promoter was considering thirty guys for three open slots on a fight card, he had to pay ninety dollars to Fight Fax. Now you pick your three guys on BoxRec and pay nine dollars to Fight Fax for their official records."

Fight Fax is feeling the pressure. As Dan Rafael notes, "Boxrec is cutting into Fight Fax's business. Fewer people are ordering records, and it's the primary reason why a lot of people don't buy the Fight Fax record book anymore. Why pay sixty-five dollars for a cumbersome book that's increasingly out of date from the moment you buy it when you can get the same information updated on Boxrec for free?"

Indeed, many people on the boxing scene are beginning to question why the ABC isn't more receptive to Boxrec. Or at the very least, why it doesn't require its member commissions to share data with Boxrec. Here, the thoughts of Greg Sirb (executive director of the Pennsylvania State Athletic Commission and former president of the ABC) are instructive.

"As far as I'm concerned," says Sirb, "The most important provision in the Ali Act, and certainly the one that has been the most effectively enforced, is the requirement that all results and all suspensions be reported in one place. The ABC determined that Fight Fax would be the proper clearing-house for that information. There's a certain administrative burden in sending the information to more than one record-keeper, and it's better if there's one official organization for everyone to go to."

But having said that, Sirb goes on to say, "Boxrec has been a pleasant surprise. I use it five or ten times a day. They're definitely an asset to get a feel for fighters who are coming into your jurisdiction for the first time and for a first look at everything. If Fight Fax went out of business, Boxrec would be a logical candidate to step into the void, and I'm not aware of anyone else who could do that."

Meanwhile, Boxrec.com has become the one indispensable website in boxing. Virtually everyone (from the most powerful to the most insignificant denizens of the boxing world) uses it.

Fighters check out prospective opponents on Boxrec. Television executives reference it in determining which fights to buy. Craig Hamilton (the foremost boxing memorabilia dealer in the United States) says, "I absolutely love it. Let's say I have an uncut ticket with a date and venue but no fighters' names on it. I can go to Boxrec, punch in the information I have, and see who fought on the card. Usually it's not much. But every now and then, I find out that someone who wound up in the Hall of Fame was early in his career and fought in a preliminary bout that night."

Given Boxrec's prominence in the boxing industry, it's frequently suggested to Sheppard that he turn his creation into a pay-site. At present, managers pay ten cents a day per fighter ($36.50 a year) to list their email address, telephone number, and fax number. There's also modest advertising revenue.

A pay-site could mean big dollars (or pounds sterling as the case may be). But so far, Sheppard has resisted the lure. "I've always lived within my means," he says. "I've never needed a lot of money to be happy. That's not why I started the site. That's not what it's all about. I don't want Boxrec to ever become a closed shop."

"I'm much more cynical now than I was when I first got into boxing," Sheppard acknowledges. "But I like to think that Boxrec is a driving force to improve the quality of the sport. It's an industry tool, but it also lifts the stone a bit so fans can see what's crawling around underneath and decide for themselves if a fight is worth watching."

In sum, Boxrec.com is making a significant contribution to the conduct of the sweet science today. And it has become a key player in the recording of boxing history. That merits a sincere "thank you" from the entire boxing community.

There was a sad note at year's end. On December 23rd, Dave Wolf died.

Dave Wolf: A Remembrance

I've lost a good friend. Dave Wolf died in his sleep last night.

When I say "good friend," I mean it.

I met Dave in 1984 when I was researching a book about the sport and business of boxing. Dave was managing Ray Mancini. He did it as well as any manager ever represented a fighter.

On first impression, Dave struck me as passive-aggressive and anti-social. He was also one of the smartest people I'd ever met.

We crossed paths again in 1989. I'd begun writing *Muhammad Ali: His Life and Times*. Dave had been in Joe Frazier's camp for the three Ali-Frazier fights. He came to my apartment for an interview, much of which was later incorporated in the book.

That was the extent of our relationship. We lived only eight blocks apart on the west side of Manhattan, but never saw each other on the street. Occasionally, but not often, I'd run into him at fights. Once or twice, I telephoned to ask a question about something I was writing. Dave never picked up the phone. All I'd hear was a recorded voice: "You have reached the office of David Wolf. At the sound of the tone, please leave a message."

There was no "hello" on the tape. And no promise to call back (he rarely did). So I watched from a distance as Dave continued to work his magic for Donny Lalonde (maneuvering him to a huge payday against Sugar Ray Leonard) and a handful of other fighters. In the mid-1990s, he dropped out of the boxing scene.

In October 2006, Dave telephoned me. I'd just written my annual "More Important Than Boxing" article for Secondsout, railing against the abuses of George Bush and the Republican-controlled Congress.

"I loved the article," Dave said. "I keep current by reading as much as I can about boxing. I'm loath to admit it; but in the grand scheme of things, politics is more important than boxing."

I asked if he wanted to have lunch sometime. To my surprise, he did.

Several days later, we met at a diner. Dave looked much older than I'd remembered him. It was more than the passage of time. He'd been battling leukemia and other ailments for a dozen years. We talked over lunch for two hours, mostly about boxing. The rage in him that once bubbled close to the surface had been replaced by warmth.

Thereafter, we had lunch once a week almost every week. We exchanged confidences and got to know each other well. Much of Dave's past anger, he confided, stemmed from the fact that he hadn't learned to read in a meaningful way until the age of twelve and thus had been labeled "dumb."

That made his later accomplishments as an assistant sports editor for *Life Magazine* and his authorship of *Foul* (one of the best sports books ever written) all the more remarkable. His one real professional disappointment was that the book he'd hoped to write about Joe Frazier was never completed because of issues involving editorial control.

I also learned that Dave was a creature of habit. In restaurants, he always sat facing the door. At our lunches, he always ordered an omelet. One time, Showtime boxing commentator Steve Albert joined us and we varied our routine by going to a pizzeria. "This man would like an omelet pizza," Steve advised the waitress.

There are a handful of people who can talk knowledgeably, endlessly, and in a thoroughly entertaining way about boxing. It's in their blood. They love it. Dave was one of them. Once, I was sitting with Bruce Trampler (another member of that fraternity). Dave's name came up.

"Let me tell you a story," Bruce said. He proceeded to recount what a pain in the ass Dave had been when Ray Mancini fought Alexis Arguello in Atlantic City on a Top Rank card. Arguello was the champion, so Mancini would have to enter the ring first. Dave didn't want Ray to cool off after warming up in the dressing room. So he measured the distance from Arguello's dressing room to the ring; timed how long it would take Alexis to make his ring-walk; and told Bob Arum that, if Arguello wasn't in the ring within a given number of seconds after Ray, he'd take Mancini back to the dressing room to warm up again (which, of course, would throw the television schedule into chaos).

"Dave meant it," Trampler reminisced. "And we knew he was crazy enough do it. We made sure that Arguello got to the ring ontime."

Moments later, Arum joined our conversation. "Tom and I were just talking about Dave Wolf," Trampler informed him.

"Oy!" Arum blurted out. "Let me tell you a story."

And he told me the exact same story about Mancini and Arguello.

Dave was quite pleased when I reported back to him. "I always felt that I was at a disadvantage when I negotiated with Arum," he confessed. "I couldn't shake the feeling that Bob was smarter than I was and knew more about promoter-boxer contracts than I did. So whenever Bob asked for something in a negotiation, I figured it was valuable because he wanted it. And whatever it was, I'd fight with him about it."

Dave had as full an appreciation of boxing and its traditions as any person I've known.

My lunches with him became part of the fabric of my life.

I've known for a long time that I've been blessed with an extraordinary group of friends. Dave was one of them. As I write this, tears are streaming down my face because he's gone.

Round 3
Curiosities

Most of us can only fantasize about ring glory. But fighters have had other experiences that we can readily identify with.

Fighters Remember: "My Greatest Moment in Another Sport"

Most sports fans have experienced a moment of athletic glory. It might have come in a school playground or a Little League baseball game. Maybe it was the first victory over an older sibling. Whatever, whenever, the memory is savored forever.

Professional fighters know the thrill of victory in the prize ring. But many of them also have fond memories of accomplishments in other sports. This writer asked a dozen present and former champions what their greatest moment was in a sport other than boxing. Their thoughts follow:

JOE CALZAGHE: That's easy. The happiest I've ever been in my life was when I scored my first goal ever in a league football [soccer] game. I was nine years old, playing for a team called Pentwynmawr in the under-ten league. My daddy had said he'd give me fifty pence when I scored my first goal. We were down 4–0 late in a game against a team called Cefn Forest, when I kicked at the ball from about six feet out. It sort of scrambled over the line and I went crazy. I ran down the field, waving my arms like I'd just won the World Cup. My coach called me over and said, "We're losing. What are you so happy about?" But I'd scored my first goal.

MARK BRELAND: I played Pop Warner football when I was fifteen years old. Quarterback and, believe it or not, defensive end. Both ways, almost every down. I weighed 120 pounds and was on a team called the Garrity Knights. We were playing a team from Queens in the New York City championship game. I didn't throw any touchdown passes, but we had a good offensive line and our running game was working. At the end of the game, they were on our five yardline; last play of the game. We were winning by a touchdown. They ran it to my side of the field and I shut them down. Game over. It's hard to describe how good that felt. I loved football; football was my game. I just couldn't put on enough weight to get to the next level.

ROY JONES JR: Three years ago [in 2005], I sent twelve roosters to a twelve-cock derby in Louisiana. That's when fighting was legal there. The way a twelve-cock derby works is, everybody enters twelve roosters; each rooster fights once; and the team with the best record wins. There were a hundred, maybe a hundred and fifty, teams entered. Now there's three things you got to know. First of all, you don't just send twelve birds to a twelve-cock derby. You send extra in case one gets sick or injured before-hand, but I only sent twelve. Second, this was gaff-fighting [fighting with implements that have sharp points but no cutting edge on each bird's foot]. You're not supposed to send white roosters to a gaff derby. You send red or gray. I sent eleven white roosters and one red, so people thought my birds had no chance. Third thing; I was out of the country the week before the derby, so someone else fed the roosters for me. And your birds fight better if you've fed them yourself. The derby lasted three days. And when it was over, my roosters had the best record of any birds there. Ten wins, two losses. And the two that lost, neither of them died so that was cool. I love being the underdog and winning. I love doing what I'm not supposed to be able to do. That derby was the best feeling in the world for me. And let me say one thing more. People say that cockfighting is cruel to animals. No; it's not cruel to animals. What's cruel to animals is making them live their entire life shut up in a cage where they can hardly move so they get fatter sooner for the kill. What's cruel to animals is not know-ing how to take care of them; leaving a dog in the car with the windows up when it's ninety degrees outside. That's cruel. Each time a rooster fights, that rooster could die. But if it dies, it dies doing what God intended it to do.

PAULIE MALIGNAGGI: My father was a professional soccer player who left my mother when my brother and I were young. My mother didn't let us play organized sports because she didn't want us to turn out like him, so I was never part of an organized league or team. But I was a good athlete on the playground and in the street. There's one game I still remember. I was sixteen years old, playing basketball in Dyker Park [in Brooklyn]. Me and some friends were up against some other guys. The way it worked was, you played till one team had 21 points. Anything outside the arc counted for two points; everything else was one. It was a heated game, full-court, five-on-five, both sides talking a lot of trash. And I had a hot hand. I hit shot after shot from the outside. I couldn't miss. One of the guys on the other team said, "Oh, he's just a chucker." He moved up to guard me tighter. So I stopped ten feet outside the arc and put up a jumper that went in. I made something like seven shots from outside the arc; and we won, I think it was, 21-to-16. When I started boxing, I gave up basketball. I didn't want to turn an ankle or do something else to injure myself. Now I do my roadwork running around Dyker Park. I think about that day once in a while. "He's just a chucker." I'll never forget that. But that day, I was chucking them in.

BERNARD HOPKINS: I'd have to say it was the good times I had playing street football when I was eleven, twelve years old in North Philadelphia. The games were on concrete; five guys on a side, hard two-handed touch. The field was a block long. There was broken glass on the streets. There were no referees, no rules. You didn't call pass interference. If a guy grabbed you before the ball arrived, you smashed him with an elbow and he didn't do it again. You got knocked down and pushed into cars and had the wind knocked out of you. But we were young; we didn't care. I was tall and thin, so I was a receiver. I always wanted to be [Pittsburgh Steelers wide receiver] Lynn Swann. Every touchdown pass I caught in those games was a moment of glory.

EARNIE SHAVERS: I played football at Newton Falls High School in Ohio. I was an end on offense and defensive end. I got my share of sacks, but that was before players celebrated a sack by dancing around. When you tackled the quarterback, you were just doing your job. I liked football, but the best moment for me came when I was running track. It was only the second year that Newton Falls had a track team. Anytime anyone on the team won anything, it was good. I wasn't that fast, but I was fast for my size. One meet, I came in first and broke the school record in the 440-yard run. That felt good because it was an individual achievement and also I was part of building something for the school's future. I don't know how long the record lasted. I know it was still there when I graduated that year.

KELLY PAVLIK: I played a lot of baseball when I was growing up; almost all of it as a catcher. I was good, but I pretty much knew that I didn't have what it takes to get to the major leagues. When I was fifteen, I was playing for Salem in the Pony League state all-star tournament. We ran through the tournament. I caught all of the early games. Right before the championship game, I said to the coach. "Let me pitch." He said okay. I went out, struck out six or seven guys, pitched a shut out, and hit a home run. I was on top of the world that day.

RICKY HATTON: I had a real thrill in football [soccer] when I was thirteen years old and was picked for the School of Excellence in Manchester. The way it worked was a group of twenty youngsters was chosen to train together and play as a team. And each day when we finished training, the Manchester City team was coming in. I was always a massive football fan, so it was very exciting to me. We weren't in an organized league, but we did play other teams. I wasn't the most skillful player the world has seen, but I was definitely fit. I played midfield and had a decent kick on me. I scored quite a few goals from long-range. Then, after two years, they let me go. By that time, I'd won four national titles in boxing, and it was getting harder and harder for me to fit the two training schedules together. The people who ran the school told me, "Ricky; we're impressed with what we've seen, but we haven't seen enough of you." That was the end of my football career. But several of the players who were in the School of Excellence with me went on to play for Manchester City.

JUAN DIAZ: In sixth grade, I played on the Alameda Elementary School basketball team. I was as tall as I am now; but I wasn't a good basketball player and the team didn't win many games. One time, we were playing Woodson Middle School. There were about fifty students and parents in the stands. I'd never scored a point before in a league game. The ball was passed to me. I was standing at the free throw line. I closed my eyes, threw it up, opened my eyes, and it went it. When I saw the ball go in, it was like when a magician makes something appear by magic. I only scored six or eight points the whole season. And like I said; we didn't win many games. But we won that one.

LARRY HOLMES: When I was young, I played football and I wrestled a lot. The wrestling was at a youth center in Easton. I've still got a picture of me in my wrestling uniform. I was a skinny little kid, ninety-nine pounds. It's hard to believe that I wrestled at ninety-nine pounds. My right arm weighs more than that now. We'd wrestle teams from other youth centers near Easton. I only lost a few times. Football, I played fullback and defensive tackle at Shaw Junior High School in Easton. In seventh grade [age twelve], I was good enough to make the ninth grade team. I never made it past that because I dropped out of school the next year. I wasn't the fastest one on the team, but I wasn't the slowest one either. And I was strong. They used me to run in the extra points after touchdowns. I didn't really have a moment of glory in either sport. That came for me later on in boxing. But with wrestling and football, the practices, the competition, hanging out with the other kids, I had a lot of good times.

LENNOX LEWIS: In my senior year of high school, I played power forward [for Cameron Heights High School in Ontario, Canada]. In the championship game of the McDonald's Basketball Tournament, we were down by one point and had the ball out of bounds with fifteen seconds left in the game. The coach called a play called "spread." I was the man in the middle. The idea was, the ball would be inbounded to me and I'd pass it to the best shooter on the team. But he was completely covered. So I deked left, went to the right—I had a fast first step—dribbled to the top of the key, and put up a jump shot. Swish ! We won by one point and I felt great. It isn't the sort of thing you do all the time. And I'd done something that made everybody happy; at least, everybody who was rooting for us. After the game, a very pretty girl from another high school came over to me, smiled, and said, "Hey; that was a good shot." That was the icing on the cake. There was instant chemistry between us. I smiled back. But I didn't ask for her name and telephone number, which I should have done.

SHANE MOSLEY: When I was growing up [in Pomona, California], there was a public pool in Ganesha Park near where I lived. The summer when I was eight years old, I went there every day. I watched people going off the diving board, and I decided I wanted to do a one-and-a-half forward somersault. I was the type of kid who would set a goal for himself and then do everything I could to accomplish it. With the one-and-a-half forward somersault, I tried and I tried and I just couldn't do it. So I kept trying. No one taught me how. I learned by watching other people. Finally, near the end of the summer, I did it. That felt so good. It didn't matter whether or not anyone else saw it. I did it for myself. And then, being me, I started trying to do a double forward somersault.

*2008, like its predecessors, brought its share of miscellaneous insights, and
humor.*

Fistic Nuggets

Speaking at a campaign rally on Valentine's Day in Ohio, Democratic
presidential candidate Hillary Clinton held up a pair of boxing gloves and
likened herself to middleweight champion Kelly Pavlik. Pavlik is one of
Ohio's favorite sons and was scheduled to do battle against Jermain Taylor
on February 16th. Given the fact that Taylor is from Little Rock and
Senator Clinton was once first lady of Arkansas, the act struck some as
disloyal. But such is politics.

Not to be outdone, Janet Huckabee (wife of former Arkansas governor and current Republican presidential aspirant Mike Huckabee)
donned a pair of boxing gloves and posed for photographers while pre-
tending to work-out on a weight-lifting machine. Later, Ms. Huckabee
outdid Senator Clinton by actually attending Pavlik-Taylor II and rooting for Jermain.

The political maneuvering brought to mind the hours before Taylor's
December 3, 2005, rematch against Bernard Hopkins. Early in evening,
Marc Ratner (then executive director of the Nevada State Athletic Com-
mission) entered Jermain's dressing room and told trainer Pat Burns, "The
Governor of Arkansas (Mike Huckabee) will be coming in before the
fight to see Jermain."

"If the Governor is coming, get his ass in here now," Burns instructed.
"I want no distractions later on."

Five minutes later, Ratner returned with Mike and Janet Huckabee.
Jermain rose to greet them.

"We're so proud of you," the governor said. He and his wife posed for
a photo with Jermain.

"Now how do I say this as politely as I can?" Burns interjected.

"I know," Governor Huckabee responded. "Get the hell out of here."

"Yes, sir. That's right."

Looking back on the moment, how does Burns feel about his actions?

"I'm glad I did it," he says. "Someone has to keep these politicians in line. Besides, if Mike Huckabee becomes president of the United States, it will make for a good story."

It's a pretty good story now.

★　★　★

The legal committee of the Association of Boxing Commissions addressed a matter of note during its most recent (December 2007) monthly conference call. It's memorialized in the meeting minutes under the heading, "Sex with ring girl as compensation to an MMA victor."

More specifically, it was brought to the attention of the ABC that a mixed martial arts promotional group in Florida is purportedly holding events entitled "Bang the Champ" with the winner being entitled to engage in sexual intercourse with the roundcard girl of his choice. The ABC's investigation of the matter has been hampered by the fact that the promotional group's website is "adult themed" and thus (according to the minutes of the ABC legal committee) "inappropriate for access via a government-owned computer."

The ABC minutes further state, "It is presumed that such activity is being conducted underground and is not licensed or regulated by a boxing or athletic commission. In such instance, local law enforcement should be contacted toward the end of putting an end to such unsanctioned and unregulated activity. It is doubtful that any state or tribal regulation expressly addresses matters such as prohibiting sex acts as the quid pro quo for a fighter's participation in a bout. However, a generic regulatory provision (e.g. not in the best interests of MMA) may be applicable. Further, if sex with the ring girl is deemed to be the fighters' compensation, such activity may constitute prostitution or the solicitation of the same."

Hey, guys! Have you considered the possibility that the fights don't exist and this is just a scam to promote a pornographic website?

★　★　★

Let's start with the less desirable side of the coin. There are some very bad jobs in boxing.

Being an "opponent" is the hardest job imaginable in the sweet science.

Working for promoter Lou DiBella is rough at times, although Seth Abraham (who was president of Time Warner Sports when Lou was making fights at HBO) observes, "If you think working for Lou is hard, imagine what it was like to be Lou's boss."

Isadore Bolton is Don King's valet. There's job security because no one else wants the job. Isadore works irregular hours and is called upon to jump on planes to far-away places at the drop of a hat.

Andy Olson, Steve Brener, Ed Keenan, and a few others are responsible for credentialing the media at big fights. Every person they deal with is screaming that he (or she) is entitled to a ringside seat.

And how about the unfortunate souls who serve as Mike Tyson's accountant, Gary Shaw's tailor, and ticket-scalpers for an Artie Pelullo fight.

Still, a handful of people in boxing have great truly jobs. In no particular order, some of them are:

Michael Buffer: The pay is great. When Buffer intones, "Let's get ready to rumble," thousands in attendance and millions watching around the world have a Pavlovian response. And when a closely-contested fight goes to the judges' scorecards, these same millions hold their collective breath, hanging on his every word. As Michael himself said recently, "It beats working for a living."

Harold Lederman: Harold has a great seat for boxing's showcase events and television exposure to boot. He's a fanatical fan and everyman as a sports icon. "I love it," he says. "It's a lot of fun, but I'm still working at Duane Reade [as a pharmacist] because I don't get paid like Jim and Larry."

Ross Greenburg: Ross might say, "Are you nuts? You can't believe the headaches I have in this job." But by virtue of his position as president of HBO Sports, Greenburg is the most powerful person in boxing and thus in position to do the most good. Also, the perks are great.

Tomas Mendoza: Tomas is the balding guy with a red mustache often seen on television, waving the flag of a fighter's country as he leads the fighter to the ring. Sharing the ring-walk is a rush. And since Mendoza is waving the flag, the crowd is cheering for him too.

John Bailey: As chairman of the Nevada State Athletic Commission, Bailey has considerable power and the ability to influence the sport and business of boxing for better or worse. It's a part-time job. And under the rules and regulations of the NSAC (which violate the Muhammad Ali Boxing Reform Act), he gets six free tickets for every fight.

LeRoy Neiman: LeRoy sits at ringside and sketches. Then he sells his work for hundreds of thousands of dollars. But there's a catch. Most boxing insiders think they could perform the other great jobs on this list. But to do what LeRoy does, one needs unique talent.

Rope-Splitters: These are the guys who sit next to roundcard girls and have the arduous task of separating the ring ropes so the women can enter the ring between rounds. Enough said.

High-profile ring judges: Judges have the three best seats in the house. They have a say in the outcome of historic fights. And the pay is great (up to $7,500 for a mega-fight).

Me: I've sat on the sofa in my apartment with Muhammad Ali watching tapes of "The Rumble in the Jungle" and "The Thrilla in Manila." I've been in the dressing room with fighters like Evander Holyfield, Roy Jones, Bernard Hopkins, James Toney, Jermain Taylor, Ricky Hatton, and Kelly Pavlik before a big fight. I write what I want to write. I sit at ringside. And people pay me to do this.

★   ★   ★

Charles Barkley once opined, "You know the world is going crazy when the best rapper is a white guy and the best golfer is a black guy." One can only begin to imagine where Sir Charles would put Barack Obama in that equation.

Now boxing has something to add to the dialogue. At present, according to virtually all consensus rankings, the best heavyweight (Wladimir Klitschko), light-heavyweight (Joe Calzaghe), and middleweight (Kelly Pavlik) are white. The last time something similar to that happened was in 1935, when those three divisions were ruled by James Braddock (heavyweight), Bob Olin (light-heavyweight), and Marcel Thil (middleweight).

Charles Barkley might also note that the first three players chosen in this year's NFL draft (Jake Long, Chris Long, and Matt Ryan) were white. The last time that happened was 1975.

★   ★   ★

Every now and then, I get put in my place. On October 18, 2008, I was in Kelly Pavlik's dressing room as cutman Miguel Diaz readied the tools of his trade.

"I got water, ice, Q-tips, gauze . . ."

The list went on. But there was no mention of an Enswell.

"Do you have an Enswell?" I queried.

"Mr. Hauser," Miguel countered, summoning up of all the righteous indignation that he could muster. "Do you have paper and a pen with you?"

★   ★   ★

Last year, Mikkel Kessler lost his WBA and WBC super-middleweight titles in a unification bout against Joe Calzaghe. Now Kessler has his WBA belt back, courtesy of some questionable maneuvering outside the ring and a twelfth-round stoppage of Dimitri Sartison in it.

Mikkel has admirable boxing skills. But he's better known in some circles for his tattoos. Much of his body looks like Mike Tyson's cheek.

"The first tattoo was when I was fourteen," Kessler explains. "It was small on my arm; just my name, Kessler. I could not show it to my daddy because I thought he would kill me. Then he saw a tape of an amateur fight that I won, and the tattoo was there. He didn't kill me, but he said it was ugly."

"When I became eighteen and could decide for myself," Kessler says, "I had many more tattoos. I like them, and my daddy still thinks they're ugly."

★   ★   ★

What is life like as a boxing promoter? Don Elbaum offers a clue.

Elbaum promoted a night of boxing in Sweden earlier this month and telephoned a manager to ask if one of his fighters would appear on the card. The opponent, purse, and travel expenses were discussed. Then the manager told Elbaum, "I'll have to think about it. What country is Sweden in?"

★ ★ ★

Some words of wisdom from cut man Danny Milano: "Between rounds, if you're working on a cut, you don't want the fighter to move his head. And chances are, he got cut in the first place because he wasn't moving his head. Go figure."

★ ★ ★

More on Don Elbaum—

How old is he? Elbaum won't say. But as a reference point, the man once known as boxing's "boy promoter" was in Korea before it became a tourist destination.

"I'm dating this dynamite woman," Elbaum confided recently. "The only problem is, she keeps asking me how old I am."

And the answer?

"I told her, 'I'm forty, but I look like crap.'"

★ ★ ★

THIRTY THINGS YOU'LL NEVER READ ON A BOXING WEBSITE

(1) It was a hard-fought battle with lots of controversy, but promoter Gary Shaw accepted his fighter's loss gracefully.

(2) The WBA said that, in calculating the sanctioning fee, it had inadvertently overcharged the champion. But it discovered the error on its own and was voluntarily refunding the excess payment.

(3) "Ross Greenburg sure knew what he was doing when he decided to replace Larry Merchant with Max Kellerman," a source at HBO said.

(4) Harold; you'll have to speak louder. I can't hear you.

(5) Before the 220-pound mugger could say a word, Jim Gray decked him with a single punch and stomped on his head.

(6) Tell the production coordinator to move Al Haymon to the side. He's hogging the camera.

(7) Officials at Canastota said there was a typographical error in the press release that stated Jose Sulaiman had been indicted into the Boxing Hall of Fame.

(8) Everyone in the office is dying to know when Wladimir Klitschko will fight Ruslan Chagaev.

(9) Golden Boy is growing increasingly frustrated by its inability to get dates on HBO.

(10) "Just salad for me," James Toney told the waitress.

(11) "How should I know?" Dan Rafael grumbled. "I haven't seen a tape of either guy."

(12) Vasquez and Marquez in Snoozefest.

(13) We're so pleased to have you back as a judge at the Miss Black America Pageant, Mr. Tyson.

(14) Alfonso Gomez KOs Miguel Cotto in 2.

(15) "Go for it," Richard Schaefer told Oscar. "I think that a Maori tattoo on the side of your face would be great for your image."

(16) Merry Christmas from the entire Duva family.

(17) First I was Cassius Clay. Then I was Muhammad Ali. Now I'm changing my name to Irving Goldberg.

(18) A failed medical test KO'd this week's title fight in Arkansas.

(19) Don King and I shook hands on it, so I'm not worried.

(20) Separated at birth: Harold Lederman and Michael Buffer.

(21) Eliot Spitzer leaned over to Bill Richardson and whispered, "The roundcard girl with the tattoo beneath her naval is kind of cute."

(22) And the #1 best-selling book this week: "Where the Bones are Buried" by Bob Arum.

(23) Even though it was grossly unfair and resulted in the loss of two television dates, Lou DiBella reacted calmly to the development.

(24) Bernard Hopkins Mellows Out

(25) "Shave my head like Michael Jordan," Don King told the barber.

(26) It's another Cedric Kushner success story.

(27) Wow! Vinny Maddalone slipped that punch nicely.

(28) I never knew his name was Dave Itskowitch. I thought it was Dave Fromloudibellasoffice.

(29) Here's a nice photo of Gary Shaw in fishnets.

(30) This article was edited and fact-checked for accuracy by . . .

★   ★   ★

Now that Spring 2008 is over, Emanuel Steward is reflecting on what he believes is the cruelest month of the year.

April starts with April Fools Day. At the midway point, the IRS comes calling. Over the years, April has been particularly cruel to Steward.

On April 12, 2008, Kermit Cintron (who Emanuel trains and manages) lost his IBF welterweight title when he was knocked out by Antonio Margarito. "But that's not the half of it," Steward moans. "Tommy Hearns was knocked out by Marvin Hagler in April. Lennox Lewis was knocked out by Hasim Rahman in April. Wladimir Klitschko was knocked out by

Lamon Brewster in April. Naseem Hamed lost to Marco Antonio Barrera in April. Even Hilmer Kenty lost his title to Sean O'Grady in April."

"It goes on and on," Steward says. "I got to leave April alone."

★   ★   ★

PAULIE MALIGNAGGI'S "TOP TEN REASONS WHY I WON'T WEAR HAIR EXTENSIONS INTO THE RING WHEN I FIGHT RICKY HATTON"

(10) It's really stupid.

(9) It's really stupid.

(8) They didn't look good.

(7) Right now, my hair isn't long enough to extend.

(6) It called attention to the fact that my hairline is receding.

(5) Ricky Hatton will make some crack about it and everyone will laugh at me.

(4) Danny Milano gives lousy haircuts during the middle of a fight.

(3) People compared my hair with Don King's. And anything that puts my name in the same sentence as Don King's is bad.

(2) Lou DiBella says he'll break my neck if I do it again. And he means it.

(1) I want to be able to see what I'm doing so I can knock Ricky Hatton out.

★   ★   ★

Just when I think that I've put all of my memories of Muhammad Ali on paper, something new filters through my mind. The most recent recollection to surface concerns a moment in an airport years ago.

I was waiting with Ali to board a plane while the customary throng stood around him. Handshakes, kisses, and autographs were in demand. One of the people in line was a young boy with a piece of paper in his hand. When he reached Ali, Muhammad asked, "How old are you?"

"Four."

"What's your name?"

"Mommy says I shouldn't tell my name to strangers."

*At the end of the day, Floyd Mayweather Jr versus Big Show was enter-
tainment. No more; no less.*

Floyd Mayweather Jr versus Big Show

As most of the sports world knows by now, Floyd Mayweather Jr
will battle Big Show in the featured event on WWE's March 30, 2008,
WrestleMania XXIV card in Orlando.

"It's entertainment," Mayweather told the media at the February 25
kick-off press conference in Los Angeles. "You have a chance to just be
you and do what you want to do." Floyd was also pleased to report that,
"Wrestling takes care of business right on the spot. There's no waiting
three, four, five months. Quick results, quick money. Big money, too."

Few people believe that Mayweather will actually receive the
$20,000,000 figure that has been bandied about. But he will be well-
compensated.

As for the tale of the tape, Floyd is 5-foot-8, 150 pounds. Big Show,
at least in theory, is seven feet tall and weighs 430 pounds. Here it should
be noted that, five years ago, he was listed by the WWE as being 7-feet-
2-inches tall and weighing 500 pounds. Obviously, professional wrestling
has taken a heavy toll on Mr. Show.

In 1976, Chuck Wepner was thrown from the ring by "Andre The
Giant" in a similar boxer-wrestler confrontation. Wepner knows a bit
about entertainment. His 1975 match-up against Muhammad Ali served
as the basis for Sylvester Stallone's *Rocky*. What does Chuck think of
WrestleMania XXIV?

"If it was on the level, Big Show would squash him," Wepner opines.
"In fact, that's what should happen. Floyd is a great fighter. But as a person, I don't think much of him. Big Show should pick him up, body-slam
him, fall on him, and squash him like a bug."

Not likely. Nor should we expect to see Al Haymon (Mayweather's
publicity-shy adviser) in the ring before the fight, wearing a sequined
leisure-suit and trash-talking to incite the crowd.

So how will it be scripted?

"Very carefully," says Cedric Kushner. "Otherwise, Big Show might fall on Floyd by accident and his proposed rematch against Oscar De La Hoya will be off."

"Whatever it is, it won't be subtle," adds Jerry Izenberg.

Myriad other theories abound. One fair maiden in the boxing community suggests that the roundcard girls could stomp Floyd unconscious with stiletto-heeled boots.

An attorney with experience in the industry predicts, "There won't be a fight. The WBC will go to court and get an injunction against it because Big Show is wrestling against a WBC champion but neither guy will pay a WBC sanctioning fee."

Another observer suggests, "Let Joe Cortez referee it, and Floyd won't have any problems."

The most ambitious scenario comes from Sam Simon (co-creator of *The Simpsons* and the man who guided Lamon Brewster to the WBO heavyweight crown). Sam's script is as follows: "Big Show enters with his trainer, Floyd Mayweather, Sr. Then Floyd Jr comes out and the crowd gasps. Thanks to WWE steroids and human growth hormone, he, too, is now seven feet tall and 430 pounds. In the early going, Floyd looks good thanks to his previous experience in another choreographed embarrassment, *Dancing with the Stars*. Then a melee erupts. Mike Tyson and Lawrence Taylor storm the ring followed by Pete Rose, the ghost of Joe Louis, and several of Michael Vick's dogs. Order is restored and Floyd is declared the winner. But another fight breaks out between Floyd and Vince McMahon, when Floyd gets his paycheck and sees that it's nowhere near $20,000,000. Floyd then announces his retirement; apologizes for his materialism and gangster image; and sings a version of John Lennon's *Imagine* so beautiful that it makes everyone cry. For the first time in history, the audience for a Floyd Mayweather pay-per-view event feels that it got its money's worth."

Other scenarios come from:

Showtime boxing commentator Steve Albert: "I think that Floyd will draw from the legendary Killer Kowalski and go to the claw hold. You can't go wrong by using the claw hold. When I was a kid and wrestled with my brothers, it worked every time. That is, it worked until my brother Al punched me in the nose and I stopped doing it."

IBF junior-welterweight champion Paulie Malignaggi: "First, you have to have Roger Mayweather working Floyd's corner. Then you do some unexpected things like have Big Show box and Floyd wrestle. At the end, Roger can come into the ring and try to hit Big Show in the head with a chair, but miss and knock Floyd unconscious."

Contender producer Jeff Wald: "Floyd kicks him in the testicles in the first five seconds and everyone goes home."

HBO boxing analyst Larry Merchant: "Big Show should throw Mayweather into the upper deck like he was shot out of a circus cannon because this is nothing but a glorified circus. Or maybe he can do to him what Muhammad Ali pledged to do to Sonny Liston, and turn Floyd into a human satellite."

Promoter Don Elbaum: "Who gives a [bleep]. I am so not into this. It means nothing to me. It turns me off completely. As far as I'm concerned, Floyd deserves the last three figures of the $20,000,000."

HBO's unofficial ringside judge Harold Lederman: "Big Show should lie down on his rear end on the ring canvas and kick at Floyd's legs for forty-five minutes the way Antonio Inoki did with Muhammad Ali."

Former top-ten heavyweight Lou Savarese: "All I know is, Mayweather has to get body-slammed at least once. And at some point in the fight, Floyd should scoot between Big Show's legs."

HBO Sports president Ross Greenburg: "Floyd throws a wad of bills in Big Show's face and the fight is stopped on a paper cut."

Dr. Margaret Goodman: "Big Show can one-up Floyd's appearance on *Dancing with the Stars* by doing the tango on his way to the ring."

And then there are the thoughts of one of boxing's greatest champions, the legendary Larry Holmes. "Big Show is serious about this," Holmes says. "There isn't any script. I'm worried for Floyd. Big Show is going to pick him up and throw him around like a rag doll. He might break Floyd's neck. You know me; if something is fake, I tell it. But this is for real."

(AND A WEEK LATER)

A few thoughts on the press conference that was held in New York for WrestleMania XXIV.

The press conference was called for noon and began at noon, thus distinguishing itself from virtually every boxing press conference ever held. "Shock" and "dismay" best describe the reaction of the boxing writers in attendance, who learned on arrival that no food would be served.

It was confusing to figure out which titles were at stake and who would be fighting who because the number of combatants per match ranged from two to twenty-four and the encounters bore labels like "WWE Championship Match," "Ladder Match," "Career-Threatening Match," and "BunnyMania Lumberjack Match." Be that as it may; WrestleMania was described in glowing terms as "the event that the Super Bowl, World Series, Academy Awards, and Grammy Awards aspire to be."

After introductory remarks by Jonathan Coachman, Vince McMahon, and Shane McMahon, three wrestlers named Triple H, Randy Orton, and John Cena explained to the audience what they were planning to do to each other in a "Triple Threat Match."

Then two women who were said to have posed recently for *Playboy* spoke. One of the women had studs in her lips and looked like the sort of girl you'd bring home to your mother if you wanted your mother to have a heart attack.

The high point in the proceedings came when Floyd Mayweather Jr and Paul Wight (a/k/a Big Show) stepped onstage. The crowd took to Mayweather like boxing fans in San Juan embrace Bernard Hopkins. Floyd tried to win them over by throwing some hundred dollar bills in their direction (the resulting chaos was a negligence lawyer's dream). That led Big Show to observe, "Only an insecure punk goes around throwing money in other people's face." Mr. Show also proclaimed, "It's gonna be bad weather for Mayweather. I'm gonna cloud up and rain all over you."

The press conference ended at 12:50. Afterward, Wight met with a small group of reporters. He's well-spoken and articulate in one-on-one conversation with a decidedly pleasant manner.

Wight bemoaned the fact that, when he's playing the role of the "bad guy" in WWE matches, "Little kids come up and give me the finger in front of their parents. And I'm looking at the parents, wondering, 'What's wrong with you. Your kid is going around giving people the finger, and you think it's cute. Teach them some manners.'"

He also criticized United States involvement in Iraq and said that the money spent on the war could be put to better use providing education and health care for American citizens.

Elect this man to Congress.

The parallels between boxing and politics are obvious.

An Open Letter to Hillary Clinton

Dear Senator Clinton,

I know you're disappointed at the way things worked out with your presidential campaign. But all is not lost. There's a good chance that you can still be president of something.

Bernard Fernandez (current president of the Boxing Writers Association of America) says that he has no interest in another term. In fact, he has declared in Shermanesque fashion, "If nominated, I will not run; and if elected, I will not serve."

That leaves a vacuum. To be honest; almost no one wants to be BWAA president because the job entails organizing the annual awards dinner, which is a time-consuming pain in the ass. That's where you could come in.

Two days before the February 16th rematch between Kelly Pavlik and Jermain Taylor, you were campaigning in Ohio and held up a pair of boxing gloves. I saw it that night on *ESPN SportsCenter.* Jermain is from Arkansas. And if I recall correctly, you were first lady of the Ozark State for twelve years. But the Arkansas primary was over; the Ohio primary was coming up; and Pavlik is from Ohio. So there you were, rallying the troops for Kelly.

Anyway, while you were waving a pair of boxing gloves in the air, I said to myself, "This woman belongs in boxing."

There are a lot of similarities between boxing and politics. John Schulian once wrote, "Nobody said boxing is polite. The only standard it ever had is that lying and succeeding often go hand in hand."

Barney Nagler crafted the words, "Boxing is a craft in which double-dealing and malfeasance are considered tools of the trade."

And then there are the thoughts of promoter Robert Waterman, who was asked if one of his fighters was loyal to him and responded, "He is today."

Does that remind you of certain super-delegates?

Boxing, like politics, is mired in a perpetual civil war. The most disheartening thing about both endeavors is that outrageous conduct occurs in full view and no one in a position of authority does anything about it.

If you think that the federal government wastes money, you'll be fascinated by the license fees that HBO pays for some of its fights. If you think that Karl Rove is a master of spin, you should have heard Golden Boy CEO Richard Schaefer extol the competitive virtues of some of his recent undercards. And you can learn a thing or two about fundraising by watching WBC president Jose Sulaiman collect sanctioning fees.

Like politics, boxing is addictive. One of the anomalies about each is the number of people who tell you that they hate the business and it's a miserable blankety-blank business; but they love being in the business anyway.

Like a true politician, Sugar Ray Leonard once said, "I always try to smile at the right time."

And listening to you talk for the past year about the great state of wherever you happened to be campaigning at the moment, I couldn't help but think that you sounded like a boxing promoter praising "the great chairman of the great state athletic commission" of wherever his fight was.

If you think that the in-fighting in politics is ugly, wait until you see what goes on with the world sanctioning body ratings committees and competition for network television dates.

If you think that the Republicans have been saying ugly things about you and Bill, check out what Ricardo Mayorga and Fernando Vargas said about each other.

Filibusters in the Senate? Listen to Bernard Hopkins.

As far as the Boxing Writers Association of America is concerned; as a rule, the BWAA requires that all new applicants show a substantial body of work for admission. You might not qualify under those guidelines. But I'm on the membership committee with Dan Rafael, Steve Farhood, Tim Graham, Tom Gerbasi, and Doug Fischer. I can't promise anything; but you might catch a break.

If you get to be a member, the sky's the limit. Apart from becoming BWAA president, you might win a Barney Award for good writing. And think big. With a boxing background, you conceivably could convince the

Democratic National Committee to declare that, as the winner of the New York primary, you should be the mandatory challenger to John McCain.

And one more thought. How do I say this politely? As your campaign progressed, I noticed that your pants-suits started to look a bit tight. If you'd like, I can give you Mackie Shilstone's telephone number. Mackie worked wonders as a physical conditioner with Bernard Hopkins and Roy Jones. Alternatively, Gary Shaw can tell you where he buys his track suits.

In fairness, I should warn you that BWAA presidents are unfairly criticized from time to time. Bob Arum was upset because Floyd Mayweather Jr edged out Kelly Pavlik in balloting for 2007 "Fighter of the Year" honors. Thereafter, Bob questioned the manner in which Bernard Fernandez conducted the election. But given what the "Hillary haters" have said about you, it shouldn't bother you much if Arum implies a teenie weenie bit that your integrity is at issue.

Also, Bob is a loyal Democrat. Earlier this year, he was asked if his political leanings were liberal. And he responded, "Of course I'm a liberal. Don't I look intelligent?" You're more likely to have trouble with Don King than with Bob.

Speaking of Don; he's the only person I know who can conduct an entire press conference in a Santa Claus suit and make it work. He did that at the kick-off press conference for Roy Jones versus Felix Trinidad. One of the joys inherent in becoming a boxing writer is that you'll meet people like Don, Richie Giachetti, Norman Stone, and James Toney. As for some of the others; I won't even try to explain Lou DiBella to you, other than to say that his heart is bigger than his mouth. Don Elbaum is a treat. And I'll be curious to know what you think about Shelly Finkel.

Anyway, let me know if you're interested in becoming a BWAA member. I can be reached by email at thauser@rcn.com.

More from the political arena.

The Vice Presidential Sweepstakes

Most people don't know it, but Republican Party insiders say that Sarah Palin was the "safe" choice as John McCain's running mate. Some McCain strategists opposed her selection on grounds that America isn't ready for a vice president who names her children "Track, Bristol, Willow, Piper, and Trig." And there was a school of thought that someone who's a heartbeat away from the presidency should be able to do more than recite sound bites on national security and major economic issues. But in the end, the half-baked half-term Alaska governor was a safer pick than the alternatives.

Over the years, McCain has been a vocal advocate for the creation of a federal boxing commission. That put him in close contact with a number of people in the boxing community, and he hoped to choose one of them as his running mate.

McCain's first choice for the vice presidential nomination was Bernard Hopkins. Part of McCain's appeal on the campaign trail is that he was a prisoner of war for five years. He feels a strong bond with Hopkins as a consequence of Bernard having endured a similar experience in Graterford State Penitentiary. Also, Hopkins is a fiery debater who would have stood up to Joe Biden in the October 2 vice-presidential debate. Alas; in the end, Team McCain felt that Hopkins is too old and that his presence on the ticket would highlight the issue of McCain's age.

Next, McCain turned to Oscar De La Hoya in the belief that he'd bring Hispanic voters into the fold. But Oscar said he'd only accept the nomination if the Democrats nominated Manny Pacquiao or Dennis Kucinich as his vice presidential opponent.

Lou DiBella was McCain's third choice on the theory that Americans would like an anti-establishment candidate who went around the country ranting, "Politics is a blankety-blank business [with the blanks filled in]." But DiBella couldn't sit still long enough to complete the vetting process.

Shelly Finkel was disqualified on grounds that he looks too much like Dick Cheney.

WBC president Jose Sulaiman was on the short list because of McCain's admiration for Sulaiman's fundraising ability. Naysayers pointed out that Jose is a Mexican citizen and thus not eligible for the vice presidency under the Constitution of the United States. That didn't bother Republican leaders, who have shredded the Constitution in recent years. But as with Hopkins, the age issue did Sulaiman in.

Evander Holyfield was favored by those who wanted McCain to strengthen his appeal to evangelical Christians. Those same advisors likened Evander's heroic pursuit of the heavyweight championship to McCain's longtime support of George Bush's economic policies and suggested the slogan, "McCain-Holyfield: Why face reality?"

Bob Arum was also under serious consideration. McCain operatives considered the slogan, "Yesterday, we were lying; today, we're telling the truth." But after conducting several focus groups, they changed that to "McCain-Arum: Trust Us." Arum was a close runner-up to Sarah Palin.

Before the choice of Palin was finalized, bumper stickers and banners were also prepared for the following tickets:

> John McCain and Dan Goossen:
> "America's checkbook is in safe hands"
>
> John McCain and Floyd Mayweather Sr:
> "Republicans: We're the party of family values"
>
> John McCain and Cedric Kushner:
> "The Republican Party: One success story after another"
>
> John McCain and Mike Tyson:
> "Sound financial management for America"

And then there was Don King, who has homes in the swing states of Florida and Ohio. Ultimately, King was passed over because he's too closely identified with George Bush. That's too bad. Imagine the banners and bumper stickers—"McCain-King: Only in America"

And a bit more political satire.

Sarah Palin Talks Boxing

Sarah Palin has avoided open-ended interviews with the media since her nomi-
nation at the Republican National Convention last month. But she was willing
to sit down for an extended conversation with Thomas Hauser on the subject of
boxing on the condition that an unedited transcript of the interview appear on
Secondsout.com.

TH: I'd like to welcome you to Secondsout.

Sarah Palin: Thank you. Once, I was a roundcard girl at a toughman contest in Alaska, so I know something about boxing.

TH: What appeals to you about the sport?

Sarah Palin: One of the reasons I like boxing so much is that it's filled
with mavericks. I mean, Lou DiBella and Norman Stone are the
original mavericks. When it comes to mavericks, John McCain and I
love 'em.

TH: Who else in boxing do you like?

Sarah Palin: I love the fat one who makes all those hamburgers. Bless his
heart. Grill, baby, grill.

TH: You've attacked Roy Jones for being a fan of cock-fighting, yet you're
a hunting enthusiast. Is there any contradiction there?

Sarah Palin: Not at all. With cock-fighting, you're making animals fight.
And when I hunt caribou, there's no fighting. I just sneak up from
behind with a high-powered rifle that has a telescopic sight and shoot
them, so it's different.

TH: What would a McCain-Palin administration do to help the American
worker in today's economy?

Sarah Palin: Well, first you have to identify the cause of today's economic
crisis. A small group of executives who work in New York at HBO
and aren't properly supervised got into wild spending and made bad
decisions that destroyed ratings. And when ratings at HBO went
down, all of boxing suffered and that pulled down the entire American
economy. Some people I know complain that HBO and Showtime

are part of a Jewish conspiracy. But I think that Jewish people should have all the rights that other people have including the right to work at television networks and the right to marry. Some of my friends don't feel the same way about Jews that I do. I mean, they think Jews should have the right to marry each other as long as they're not gay, but they don't like them. But all of my friends love Israel. Everyone in Alaska loves Israel, except there's a guy named Aftab who runs a newsstand near the capitol building in Juneau who's Muslim, and I don't think Aftab likes Israel very much. Anyway, John McCain will fix all that and get the economy moving again.

TH: Senator McCain has introduced legislation to establish a federal boxing commission. Would that be part of the cure?

Sarah Palin: I'll have to get back to you on that. A couple of years ago, John McCain started getting a lot of campaign contributions from patriotic Americans who run casinos in Las Vegas. He hasn't talked much about a federal boxing commission since then. But there's another thing we could do to help the economy that has to do with boxing. John McCain and I are considering taking all of Bernard Hopkins's money away from him and using it to fund the bailout. Bernard wouldn't like it, but tough times require sacrifice.

TH: Is there anything that you don't like about John McCain?

Sarah Palin: Well, sometimes he looks at me in a kind of creepy way that reminds me of Gert Frobe in *Goldfinger*. And at the convention, right after my acceptance speech, he put his arm around me and I could tell he was feeling the back of my bra. I ask myself sometimes—probably, you shouldn't write this—whether John is one of those guys who goes on the Internet to look at those phony naked pictures of me. Probably not, because he doesn't know how to use a computer.

TH: I think that's right.

Sarah Palin: Some of those pictures make me mad. I've had five kids so my breasts sag a bit. But I don't look anything like what people are doing with PhotoShop. That photo of me wearing fishnets and boxing gloves isn't real.

TH: There have been complaints recently that some of your attacks on Barack Obama are going too far. Do you have any comment on that?

Sarah Palin: I'm patterning my campaign speeches on Ricardo Mayorga's press conferences. That's just one of the things I've learned from boxing.

TH: What else have you learned?

Sarah Palin: John McCain and I have been talking to the world sanctioning bodies and some of the state athletic commissions about judges
for the election. Eight years ago, the Supreme Court did a good job
for us. This year, we might need the judges who had Joel Casamayor
ahead of Jose Armando Santa Cruz. By the way; I want all the voters
in Florida to know that Oscar De La Hoya is my favorite fighter from
Cuba.

TH: Are there things that you don't like about boxing in general?

Sarah Palin: I hate it when a fighter's corner throws in the towel. John
McCain and I would never waive the white flag of surrender like
that. When Richard Schaefer and Bob Arum sit down and negotiate
with each other, that's negotiating with the enemy. John McCain and
I would never do that. And I also want to say; America has the greatest boxers in the world. It makes me mad when liberal boxing writers attack the American heavyweights. Being a hockey mom, I feel
very strongly about that.

TH: Any final thoughts?

Sarah Palin: I just want to thank you for letting me talk directly to all the
boxing fans at Secondsout.com without everything I say being filtered by the liberal media. And I also want to say that you seem like
a nice guy. After talking with Ross Greenburg last week, I thought
you'd have blood dripping from your mouth and horns and stuff like
that.

Round 4

Issues and Answers

*Throughout 2008, HBO continued to be the most powerful player in
boxing.*

24/7 and *Countdown:* Docudrama
or Infomercial ?

The line between programming and marketing in sports is often
blurred. Two HBO offerings—*24/7* and *Countdown*—exemplify this cir-
cumstance.

24/7 is the four-part "reality-TV" series that preceded the De La
Hoya–Mayweather and Mayweather-Hatton fights on HBO-PPV last
year (2007). *Countdown* is a half-hour special that has been televised by
HBO prior to fourteen fight cards during the past three years.

24/7 and *Countdown* have legitimate entertainment value. They're an
audience attraction in and of themselves. But there's an issue as to whether
their primary purpose is programming or marketing.

Mark Taffet (HBO's senior vice president, sports operations and pay-
per-view) says, "HBO practices separation of church and state between
marketing and programming. Both of our *24/7* series were the result of
independent programming decisions. Their purpose was not to boost pay-
per-view buys."

But there's no doubt that *24/7* engenders pay-per-view buys. Indeed,
based on the success of De La Hoya–Mayweather (2,400,000 buys) and
Mayweather-Hatton (850,000), it's obvious that *24/7* is a promotional
juggernaut. And more significantly, in considering whether *24/7* is programming or/and marketing, it should be noted that each series cost
$1,400,000 to produce. And prior to Mayweather-Hatton, Taffet acknowl-
edged, "There are contingencies that could lead to the promoter under-
writing certain production costs."

Why would a promoter underwrite production costs if *24/7* wasn't
a marketing tool?

Here, the thoughts of Richard Sandomir (who writes about the relationship between television and sports for the *New York Times*) are instructive. "I think the *24/7* shows are well-done enough to be viewed as

documentaries," Sandomir says. "If you take away the fight, the episodes would still be pretty good. But at the same time, *24/7* is a commercial lure for viewers and serves an infomercial purpose. It's not three guys trying to sell a carpet-cleaner, but the final impact is to sell a pay-per-view fight. In that sense, *24/7* is as good an infomercial as you're going to get."

If HBO is sincere in its claim that *24/7* is programming for the benefit of its subscribers rather than a well-packaged infomercial, it will produce a *24/7* series for a *World Championship Boxing* fight. After all, good drama doesn't have to be about superstars. HBO's most successful program ever was a series about a small-time crime family in New Jersey. Fighters like Kassim Ouma have personalities and back-stories that are just as compelling as those of Oscar De La Hoya, Ricky Hatton, and Floyd Mayweather Jr.

Don't hold your breath.

Meanwhile, HBO's *Countdown* shows also straddle the line between regular programming and infomercial. There were five *Countdown* shows in 2007 (Pacquiao-Barrera II, Hopkins-Wright, Taylor-Pavlik, Barrera-Marquez, and Cotto-Mosley); six in 2006 (Pacquiao-Morales III, Baldomir-Mayweather, De La Hoya–Mayorga, Tarver-Hopkins, Taylor-Wright, and Mosley-Vargas II); and three in 2005 (Gatti-Mayweather, Tarver-Jones III, and Taylor-Hopkins II).

All but two of the fourteen (Taylor-Pavlik and Taylor-Wright) were for pay-per-view cards. And keep in mind; at the time of those two Taylor fights, HBO was trying to develop Jermain as a pay-per-view attraction.

Looking ahead; HBO's first two *Countdown* shows in 2008 will be for Trinidad-Jones and Pavlik-Taylor II (both pay-per-view events). That ties fourteen of the sixteen *Countdown* shows to pay-per-view.

And most significantly, in the two instances when a *Countdown* fight was shown live on *HBO World Championship Boxing* (the network's regular subscription service), HBO paid the production cost (which runs in the neighborhood of $100,000). But when *Countdown* is devoted to a pay-per-view fight, the cost is generally paid by the promoter. This strongly suggests that the purpose of most *Countdown* shows is to market pay-per-view.

In response, HBO might say, "Hey, wait a minute. We don't specifically market pay-per-view telecasts in our *24/7* and *Countdown* shows because we don't cite the date, time, and suggested retail price." But that might be because the network has contracts with film studios that preclude it from televising commercials at any time for any product.

Nor can HBO cite tape-delay telecasts of pay-per-view fights in arguing credibly that *24/7* and *Countdown* are promotion for regular HBO programming. There's an embargo on announcing that the tape-delay will be seen on HBO until after a pay-per-view telecast has aired.

In sum; when HBO televises a *24/7* or *Countdown* show prior to a pay-per-view event, the message is, "We have a great show. It will cost you 'X' dollars to watch it." That's an infomercial.

Almost anything that pushes boxing into the public consciousness is good for the sport. In that sense, *24/7* and *Countdown* are good for boxing. But two red flags are visible on the horizon.

The first danger involves the integrity of HBO's programming. To a degree, all documentaries are distortions of reality. If nothing else, a good documentary-maker cuts out the boring parts. And some sports leagues, as well as many individual teams, often have influence over program content (including which announcers cover their sport). But HBO has long prided itself on adhering to a particularly high journalistic standard. And when a boxing promoter underwrites the cost of HBO programming, it compromises the editorial independence of that programming. The subjects of *Real Sports* and *Costas Now* don't share production costs with HBO.

And more importantly, *24/7* and *Countdown* have been key elements in HBO's increasing emphasis on pay-per-view to the detriment of *HBO World Championship Boxing* and *Boxing After Dark*.

2007 was the year that HBO fine-tuned its pay-per-view machine. At the close of the year, the network trumpeted the fact that it was the highest-performing year in HBO-PPV history, with 4.8 million buys engendering more than $255 million in revenue.

That meant 2007 was a good year for fans who could afford to pay up to $54.95 for a pay-per-view fight. It was a good year for high-rollers who were comped by the casinos for big fights. And it was a good year for boxing writers who got to sit ringside for those fights.

But 2007 wasn't such a good year for HBO subscribers, who pay a monthly fee for programming that includes *HBO World Championship*

Boxing and *Boxing After Dark*. There were only two shows on *HBO World Championship Boxing* during the final twenty-four weeks of 2007. And there will be two HBO-PPV cards in 2008 before the first *HBO World Championship Boxing* telecast of the year (a February 23rd match-up of dubious merit between Wladimir Klitschko and Sultan Ibragimov).

One year ago, HBO Sports president Ross Greenburg called the expansion of pay-per-view "the biggest economic issue in boxing," and said, "I can't tell you that pay-per-view helps the sport because it doesn't. It hurts the sport because it narrows our audience."

But there are times now when HBO Sports seems to be a marketing arm for HBO-PPV. The tail is wagging the dog. And the trend is accelerating.

HBO has three marquee fights in the first three months of 2008: Jones-Trinidad (January 19), Pavlik-Taylor II (February 16), and Pacquiao-Marquez II (March 15). Each one will be on pay-per-view.

And let's not forget; Time Warner (HBO's parent company) profits from pay-per-view through its ownership of Time Warner Cable (one of the largest cable systems in the country) and its equity interest in In Demand (the conduit through which most cable-TV pay-per-view telecasts flow to cable system operators).

So let's give credit where credit is due. *24/7* and *Countdown* are entertaining and well-produced. But they're also marketing tools for pay-per-view.

Does the Academy of Television Arts and Sciences give Emmy Awards for infomercials?

This might have been the most important article I wrote in 2008.

HBO: 2008

On January 22, 1988, former champion Larry Holmes challenged Mike Tyson for the heavyweight championship of the world. That night, a staggering 53 percent of all homes with HBO tuned in to the fight. By way of comparison, only 35 percent of homes equipped with HBO had watched Barbra Streisand's historic HBO concert two years earlier.

Fast-forward to May 3, 2008. Oscar De La Hoya (boxing's reigning commercial superstar) fought on "free" HBO for the first time in seven years. The telecast averaged a meager 4.0 rating that rose to 4.7 percent during the fight.

HBO Sports was once synonymous with THE BIG EVENT. If a fight was on HBO, it was presumed to be "must watching" for fans. That's no longer the case. HBO didn't cause the decline of American heavyweights or cut off the flow of potential stars coming out of the Olympics. But in recent years, a series of decisions have diminished the HBO brand. The situation is now at a point where, even when a fight is well worth watching, many fans don't tune in.

HBO is still the most powerful force in boxing. It has the power to impact heavily upon the sport. There are things that HBO does better than anyone else in the business. Some very talented people work at HBO Sports.

But HBO boxing today is in danger of becoming a tired old heavyweight. The era when it was the "heart and soul of boxing" is gone. And the criticism of HBO Sports has gone mainstream. It's no longer only a handful of Internet writers who are concerned.

Dozens of people in the boxing industry were interviewed for this article. Some spoke on condition of anonymity. Others agreed to talk on the record. HBO Sports president Ross Greenburg, senior vice president for programming Kery Davis, and senior vice president for sports operations and pay-per-view Mark Taffet met jointly with this writer to discuss some of the issues involved. I thank everyone who shared their thoughts with me for this article. This is HBO: 2008 as I understand it to be.

On April 25, 2007, Bernard Fernandez of the *Philadelphia Daily News* wrote, "If you're an HBO fighter these days, chances are, the pay is excellent and the opposition soft."

Fernandez's comment came after HBO Sports president Ross Greenburg made what Steve Kim of Maxboxing.com called Greenburg's "annual Groundhog Day speech." Earlier in the year, Ross had said, "We intend to dig our feet in a little more on mismatches and not give in to promoters, managers, and fighters who don't want to take a risk."

But mismatches still plague HBO. On April 12, 2008, the network televised Miguel Cotto versus Alfonso Gomez as half of a doubleheader on *HBO World Championship Boxing.* Cotto entered the ring a 12-to-1 favorite. Blow-by-blow commentator Jim Lampley labeled the bout "a full-scale annihilation." Dan Rafael of ESPN.com wrote. "Cotto was never remotely challenged by Gomez." Nor was there a chance that he would be.

Three weeks later, Oscar De La Hoya was an 18-to-1 favorite over Stevie Forbes. The fight was contested at 150 pounds, although Forbes is a junior-welterweight, whose best days were in the super-featherweight division. Before the bout, Tim Dahlberg of the Associated Press wrote, "Forbes knows his role in this farce. His job is to make De La Hoya feel like a champion again. Forbes was carefully selected for the purpose of building De La Hoya up so that he and potential future ticket buyers might forget his recent struggles in the ring."

On June 7th, *HBO World Championship Boxing* will televise Kelly Pavlik against Gary Lockett; a fight in which Pavlik is a 15-to-1 favorite.

Mismatches didn't originate with the current leadership of HBO Sports. There have always been mismatches in boxing and on HBO. But making a good fight isn't rocket science. There's no reason that HBO can't do it more often.

Sources say that the current annual budget for HBO Sports is approximately $75,000,000. That doesn't include the salaries of fulltime employees, who are listed on a different budget line. It does include salaries for "talent" (such as Jim Lampley, Larry Merchant, and Bryant Gumbel), license fees, production costs, and marketing. Approximately $60,000,000 of that $75,000,000 total is spent on boxing. By way of comparison, Showtime's annual boxing budget is slightly more than $20,000,000.

The primary problem with boxing at HBO today is that money is often unwisely spent. The network can cherry-pick the fights it wants. But too often, it picks rotten cherries. It holds the line on license fees for some fights with some promoters and then wildly overpays for others. "It's not in my best interests to say this, so don't use my name," one prominent promoter says. "But everybody in the industry knows they could buy more for less."

Current economic demands by fighters and promoters are based in large measure on expectations raised by past numbers. There was a time when HBO paid more than the going market rate for fights to lure them away from ABC, CBS, and NBC as part of an overall strategy to increase its subscriber base. That might have made sense in past decades. It doesn't now. HBO has been bidding against itself and overpaying on license fees for years.

There were raised eyebrows when the network paid a $7,000,000 license fee for De La Hoya–Forbes. $2,000,000 of that total came from the HBO Sports budget and $5,000,000 was a special corporate grant. HBO spent another $2,000,000 off-network to promote the fight and incurred production costs in the mid-six-figures. There was extensive on-air promotion as well.

Ross Greenburg says, "We weren't disappointed in the ratings for May 3rd [De la Hoya–Forbes]." Mark Taffet adds, "The nature of television viewership has changed. It's not just the live viewership that counts. The composite ratings are important. As long as viewers are consuming HBO programming, whether it's live or on a rebroadcast or on On-Demand; they're watching our product."

Also, there were subscription acquisition programs in conjunction with De La Hoya–Forbes that might make the telecast more successful.

But the fact remains that HBO spent close to $10,000,000 on licensing, marketing, and production for De La Hoya–Forbes. And the telecast generated the lowest points-per-dollar rating ever for a fight on HBO. ESPN analyst Teddy Atlas called it "the most money ever paid for a sparring session in the history of boxing."

Bob Arum (who knows a thing or two about a thing or two) understands HBO's position with regard to De La Hoya–Forbes. "Oscar has been the marquee name in boxing for years," says Arum. "I can justify Oscar against Stevie Forbes, which was a horrible fight, as a rational business decision." But Arum goes on to state, "It's absolutely crazy the way HBO squanders money on some fights."

HBO's dealings with Ricky Hatton are a case in point. Sources say that, in 2006, the network signed a three-fight deal that led to a $2,850,000 license fee for Hatton's fight against Luis Collazo; $2,850,000 for Hatton against Juan Urango; and $3,000,000 for Hatton against Jose Luis Castillo.

By contrast, Versus paid a license fee in the low six figures (very low) for its May 24, 2008, doubleheader featuring Hatton against Juan Lazcano and Paulie Malignaggi against Lovemore N'dou.

"It's one thing to be out-negotiated by King or Arum," says an industry insider. "HBO was outwitted by Artie Pelullo [Hatton's U.S. promoter at the time the three-fight deal was signed]."

There's something very wrong with the economic model at HBO Sports when the network pays a $2,850,000 license fee for Hatton-Urango and Versus pays roughly 5 percent of that amount for a doubleheader pairing Hatton-Lazcano with Malignaggi-N'dou.

To repeat: There's something very wrong with the economic model at HBO Sports when the network pays a $2,850,000 license fee for Hatton-Urango and Versus pays roughly 5 percent of that amount for a doubleheader pairing Hatton-Lazcano with Malignaggi-N'dou.

"HBO has all of the power; and the guys there don't seem to get it," says one veteran of the television wars. "They have no real competition, and they keep paying these insane license fees. If the most that Showtime will pay for a fight is $2,000,000, why does HBO pay $4,000,000?"

Showtime paid a total of $4,200,000 for all three Vasquez-Marquez encounters. HBO frequently pays an amount in that neighborhood for one fight.

There's also an issue with regard to the lack of correlation between the license fees that HBO pays and the ratings engendered by the fights that it televises. The correlation doesn't have to be dollar-for-dollar, but there should be some rational relationship. As Greenburg notes, "Hopefully, the higher the license fee, the higher the rating."

But that's often not the case. HBO paid a $3,000,000 license fee for Joe Calzaghe against Mikkel Kessler (plus another seven figures for marketing and production). The fight garnered a 2.8 rating (the lowest prime-time *HBO World Championship Boxing* rating ever). HBO then paid a $6,500,000 license fee for Calzaghe versus Bernard Hopkins, which averaged a disappointing 3.9 for the show.

To put these numbers in perspective, HBO also did a 3.9 rating for Jermain Taylor against Kassim Ouma, but paid $3,500,000. And it paid $6,500,000 for Taylor against Winky Wright, but that fight did a 5.9 rating.

Not all of HBO's ratings issues are attributable to poor programming decisions. But some of them are. As Seth Abraham (former president of Time Warner Sports and the original architect of HBO's boxing program) observes, "There was a conscious effort to pump new life into *HBO World Championship Boxing* this year, but they did it with questionable fights."

HBO Sports won't solve its problems with regard to boxing until it learns to allocate its financial resources more intelligently. Meanwhile, one member of the network's production team states, "When your audience comes to expect tune-up fights and replays of week-old pay-per-view bouts, ratings will drop. Given the amount of money that we spend on boxing, the return is abysmal."

Part of the problem is that HBO is no longer building fighters the way it once did because it tries to televise the biggest names; not the best fighters and fights. "If you want good apples," says one industry veteran, "you have to prune the tree from time to time. These guys just keep picking off all the low-hanging apples. That might be good for short-term gain, but it hinders the development of new stars."

Sports thrive as a business and on the playing field by matching the best against the best. If HBO were running college football—or so the theory goes—it would put Notre Dame in the bowl championship series finale every year.

In that regard, HBO Sports seems to be increasingly rooted in the past. *Sports of the 20th Century* and *Legendary Nights* are about the past. The two big-budget fights for *HBO World Championship Boxing* so far this year were largely about the past. Within the span of two weeks, the network paid $13,500,000 in license fees and more than $4,000,000 in marketing and production costs for Hopkins-Calzaghe and De La Hoya–Forbes. Most likely, the three guys in those fights who matter will be gone in a year.

"Hopkins–Calzaghe and De La Hoya–Forbes were an investment in the future of Golden Boy, not the future of HBO," says one disgruntled promoter. "Right now, HBO is jumping through hoops for [Golden Boy CEO] Richard Schaefer and Oscar."

That leads to another issue. Anytime a promoter seems to secure a favored position vis-à-vis a network, there are complaints from rivals. That's built into the fabric of boxing. In recent years two suppliers of talent have been said to have an inside track at HBO.

The first is Al Haymon. Haymon came out of the music business, where he made his mark promoting and marketing national tours for superstars like Whitney Houston, Janet Jackson, M. C. Hammer, and Boyz II Men. He also has longtime links to boxing. His brother, Bobby Haymon, was a welterweight, who fought from 1969 through 1978 and amassed a 20-8-1 career record with eight knockouts. In the last fight of his career, Bobby was stopped in three rounds by a young prospect named Sugar Ray Leonard.

Al Haymon is smooth and smart. He's a private man and avoids media exposure as if it were the plague. "The best way to deal with Al Haymon," says someone who has, "is, don't try to figure him out."

Haymon represents elite fighters as an advisor-manager, generally in exchange for a percentage of their purses. For example, his initial contract with Lamon Brewster (who left manager Sam Simon in 2005 after becoming a world champion) called for Alan Haymon Development Inc. to get 7 percent of the first $2,000,000 of any Brewster purse and 5 percent thereafter.

In recent years, Haymon's fighters have benefited from a large number of dates on HBO. Often, they've received substantial license fees for going in soft. Other times (as was the case with Brewster in his 2007 fight against Wladimir Klitschko), they've been the opponent. There have also been complaints that HBO allows Haymon (a manager) to function as a promoter.

"No one pays to watch Al Haymon on television," says an attorney active on the boxing scene. "I just don't get it. Al Haymon is a question, and no one I talk with seems to have an answer."

"I don't know how it happens," adds Don King. "But there's things going on with Al Haymon and HBO that aren't right. Someone should do a striptease show and expose that act."

Bob Arum refers to Haymon as "Mr. Macchiavelli" (no laughing, please) and speculates, "Initially, Haymon got his juice from [former Time Warner CEO] Richard Parsons. Now it comes from Ross."

Greenburg rejects any suggestion of favoritism toward Haymon with the comment, "Sugar Ray Leonard fought Bruce Finch in 1982. It was a crappy fight, and Al Haymon didn't have either guy."

Whatever the reality of the situation, the complaining about Haymon's perceived influence at HBO has been muted this year. Once, the grumbling was that HBO stood for "Haymon Boxing Organization." Now the complaint is that HBO stands for "Headed By Oscar."

Other active champions have had their own promotional companies. But what they did was largely limited to maximizing earnings from their own fights by cutting out the third-party promoter.

Golden Boy is different. From day one, it had a far more ambitious agenda than its predecessors. That agenda has been brilliantly implemented by Richard Schaefer, who has made the transition seamlessly from successful banker to successful boxing promoter.

Golden Boy is doing what *The Contender* tried unsuccessfully to do several years ago. It is on the verge of becoming the dominant promoter in boxing. The boxing business is like chess. The more pieces a player controls, the more leverage that player has. Schaefer has played his pieces flawlessly vis-à-vis HBO, accumulating more firepower at every turn.

Golden Boy's original "big four" fighters are showing their age. Oscar De La Hoya has lost three of his last six fights; Bernard Hopkins, three of five. Shane Mosley was beaten in his most recent outing, and Marco Antonio Barrera has lost his last two. But there were seven major pay-per-view shows on HBO last year. Golden Boy had a piece of six of them. And there are widespread complaints from Golden Boy's promotional rivals that HBO now gives different financial support and dates to Golden Boy for specific fights and fighters than it gives to other promoters and, by its conduct, is steering fighters to Golden Boy.

HBO, this line of reasoning goes, has been a principal factor in turning Golden Boy into a promotional giant.

"There's an agenda at HBO to give Golden Boy every advantage," says one promoter. "They take stuff from Golden Boy that they wouldn't take from anyone else."

Bob Arum, who is willing to go on the record, maintains, "We're not on a level playing field. Foreign fighters without American promoters get steered to Golden Boy. Golden Boy gets dates without fights. There are times when it seems like they have carte blanche to put whatever fights they want on HBO."

"There's a methodology to making a fighter popular," says an industry insider who has done business with HBO for two decades. "You have to build a fighter. And right now, HBO is refusing to work with anyone except Golden Boy and Al Haymon, and maybe the Klitschkos, to do that."

"Paulie Malignaggi is a poster boy for what I'm talking about," the same person continues. "Lou DiBella [Malignaggi's promoter] isn't entitled to everything he wants. But Paulie is good-looking; Paulie can talk. Better yet, he can fight. And look at the way HBO has treated Paulie. That wouldn't have happened if Paulie had been with Golden Boy or Al Haymon. Look at the way they've treated Paulie compared to Librado Andrade, Paul Williams, and Andre Berto [three of Haymon's fighters]."

Malignaggi's two *Boxing After Dark* appearances in 2007, at a fraction of the cost, drew higher ratings than Joe Calzaghe versus Mikkel Kessler and the live telecast of both Wladimir Klitschko fights.

Meanwhile, DiBella points with great dismay to the May 3rd telecast of Oscar De La Hoya against Stevie Forbes on HBO. At the close of that telecast, HBO showed highlight clips of two young fighters who'd been on the undercard (Danny Jacobs and Danny Garcia). Contrary to what was publicly announced, Jacobs had not signed with Golden Boy. DiBella (who, like Jacobs, is based in New York) is actively pursuing the fighter. He considered the clips to be one of many efforts by HBO to steer a prime prospect to Golden Boy; or at the very least, tilt the playing field a bit.

"They wouldn't have done that for any promoter but Golden Boy," DiBella grumbled.

As a rebuttal to DiBella's complaint, HBO prepared a list of ten instances during the past three years when brief excerpts from a preliminary bout were shown on an HBO telecast. But in each of those instances, the fighter in question was much further along in his career than Jacobs or Garcia (each of whom had only five pro fights). For example, HBO showed a brief clip of Mikkel Kessler versus Marcus Beyer on its Calzaghe-Bika telecast. But Kessler was 38–0 and the unified WBC–WBA 168-pound champion.

Bob Arum complained loudly when HBO said that it had no plans to produce a half-hour *Countdown* show in advance of the upcoming pay-per-view battle between Miguel Cotto and Antonio Margarito. *Countdown* shows are a key marketing tool, and Arum voiced his displeasure at a press conference in New York, declaring, "Everyone knows they'd be doing a show if it was a Golden Boy fight."

The following day, HBO reversed its position and announced that it would, in fact, produce *Countdown to Cotto-Margarito.* But one source with knowledge of the inner workings at the network says, "If Arum hadn't publicly humiliated them and if some of the people around Ross weren't getting worried about all the complaints in the industry about special treatment for Golden Boy, there wouldn't be a *Countdown* show for Cotto-Margarito. Think about how absurd that is. You're talking about a fight that everyone thinks will be one of the best fights of the year."

But the most disturbing news for Golden Boy's competitors comes in the form of reports that HBO is on the verge of signing a longterm output deal with Golden Boy. Both Greenburg and Schaefer acknowledge that such a deal is in the works. A source says that it could be for as long as five years, although Schaefer says that, most likely, the term will be shorter.

Output deals whereby a network commits to buying a given number of fights for a given number of dates aren't new in boxing. Over the years, Arum has had them with numerous networks; most notably one that made him the exclusive provider of fights for ESPN. Don King once had a similar deal with Showtime.

The proposed HBO–Golden Boy deal would be non-exclusive for both parties. Schaefer explains the logic behind it, saying, "Golden Boy has a lot of fighters; we're going to have more fighters; and it's important to have dates to keep them busy. HBO wants the best content that it can buy for its subscribers. All we're doing is asking them to make a deal with us to provide content the same way they make deals for content with movie studios and other suppliers."

But the proposed deal is, by definition, for fights and fighters unknown. It would undercut HBO's leverage in future negotiations with Golden

Boy because the promoter would already have certain dates, which in and of itself is a major negotiating point.

Greenburg justifies the proposed longterm Golden Boy deal on grounds that "Golden Boy has the good young fighters."

"Not so," say others. "Golden Boy is getting the good young fighters because it's getting preferential treatment from HBO."

Greenburg says, "There's no advantage given to Golden Boy here. None. We expect to do a lot of business with them in the future because they've given us plenty of quality over the years. But it's ridiculous to say that we'd sacrifice the quality of HBO boxing by giving too much power to one promoter or enter into an agreement that would interfere with the ability of other promoters to bring their best fighters to HBO."

But Arum responds, "It makes no sense at all for HBO to enter into a five-year deal with anyone, and that includes Top Rank. To protect themselves from whom? It smells bad. HBO has the power. It's not a start-up network that's just getting into boxing. It doesn't have to do that sort of thing. The hierarchy at HBO should take a long look at some of the things that Ross has been doing with Golden Boy lately and ask themselves why."

Meanwhile, Seth Abraham adds some thoughts of his own, opining, "It's hard to believe that HBO would commit to buying a specified number of fights from Golden Boy for a specified number of dollars over a [longterm] period. I don't see how Ross could get that through [HBO CEO] Bill Nelson. Teddy Brenner once said, 'Fights make fights.' How could you know what fights and fighters you're buying?"

"Oscar is the Golden Boy for a reason," Lou DiBella says, summing up his feelings on the situation. "He earned it, and there are legitimate advantages that come with it. If HBO wants to pay a huge license fee for one of Oscar's fights, fine. But open competition among promoters on a level playing field is good for boxing and good for HBO. Don't give special treatment across the board to Golden Boy in a way that undermines every other promoter in the business."

Why the tilt to Golden Boy; if such a tilt in fact exists?

"Ross doesn't like boxing people," says one insider at HBO. "And Ross dislikes most promoters. I think that, subconsciously or otherwise, he's using Golden Boy to stick it up their ass."

That's considered by some to be a paranoid view. But a more ominous note is sounded by a promoter, who says, "At some point, if this
keeps up, a bunch of us are going to get together and say, 'We have nothing to lose. Let's go to the Justice Department or file a lawsuit ourselves.'
I used to think that you couldn't file a lawsuit against HBO unless you
were planning to leave the industry. Now I'm not so sure."

Richard Schaefer thinks that's garbage. He's aware that there's unhap-
piness regarding the success of Golden Boy. And there have been threats.
He got a call not long ago from someone who told him, "You'd better
check your brakes."

"What sickens me," says Schaefer, "is the continuous attacks on HBO
from some of the promoters and managers and other people in boxing. If
HBO wasn't there, they'd all be out of business. It's jealousy. That's all it is;
jealousy. These people should go out and build something of their own.
But whatever they do, stop crying about it. And stop criticizing HBO. The
people at HBO are good people. Think where boxing would be without
HBO. All the other promoters who are crying and complaining that boxing is a terrible business would be better served if they refocused their
energy on their own companies and tried to make their own companies
better."

"This claim of preferential treatment at HBO is ridiculous," Schaefer
continues. "Look at what Golden Boy has done with sponsors. Everyone
in the business was complaining, 'Oh, this is terrible; boxing can't get
sponsors.' So we went out and got sponsors. No one else is getting sponsors for boxing like we are. That's not just good for Golden Boy; it's good
for boxing. Manchester United gets better players and better television
contracts and better deals all around because it's better than its competitors. When Bob Arum had Oscar, look at how many dates he had with
HBO. Gary Shaw gets a lot of dates from Showtime. Showtime even
acquired a stake in his martial arts business. Do you hear me crying about
it? The other promoters should stop complaining, step up, and do what
we've done. Boxing is a global sport, and it's a big world with a lot of television networks."

Then, somewhat ominously for his competitors, Schaefer declares,
"People still don't get it. They think we'll lose our leverage when Oscar
stops fighting, but it ain't gonna happen. They're underestimating us. I love

that. Wake up and smell the roses. I'm just warming up. There's much more in store. We're building a fully integrated business for the sport of boxing like no one has ever done before. It takes creativity. It takes thinking outside the box. If other promoters don't have the business background and financial backing to do what Golden Boy is doing, that's not my problem. The people who are crying haven't seen anything yet. You saw in Manchester the kind of event that Golden Boy will be promoting all over the world. There were 56,000 people in a stadium for a fight [between Ricky Hatton and Juan Lazcano]. That's the future. Golden Boy is a global brand now. Maybe we'll change the name to Global Boy."

Meanwhile, there's another factor that's impacting adversely on the product that HBO delivers to its subscribers: the accelerating trend toward putting fights on pay-per-view.

The first significant pay-per-view fight on HBO was Evander Holyfield versus George Foreman in 1991. Thereafter, the vehicle was sparingly used. The network televised a total of twenty-five pay-per-view cards in the 1990s; an average of less than three per year. Its only pay-per-view card in 1998 was the rematch between Oscar De La Hoya and Julio Cesar Chavez. There were four pay-per-view cards in 1999 (Holyfield-Lewis I and II, De La Hoya–Trinidad, and De La Hoya–Quartey).

Seth Abraham left HBO in autumn 2000. Since then, the number of HBO pay-per-view shows has grown, peaking at ten in 2006. That total includes only shows that are produced, distributed, and fully staffed by HBO, not niche shows. Indeed, it might be that Greenburg's primary legacy as president of HBO Sports (as opposed to his tenure as executive producer) will be the shift of significant fights from *HBO World Championship Boxing* to pay-per-view.

HBO's subscribers are now conditioned to think, "If it's not on pay-per-view, it can't be that good." Also, having big and small pay-per-view shows is confusing with regard to the branding of HBO.

Ironically, the issue crystallized for some observers with the telecast of a fight on "regular" HBO. After De La Hoya–Forbes, Bob Raissman of the *New York Daily News* wrote, "That was some infomercial, disguised as an Oscar De La Hoya–Steve Forbes 'fight.' This 'fight' was nothing more than the official start of PPV sales for De La Hoya–Mayweather II."

Greenburg takes a contrary view, countering, "Was the broken bone in Oscar's eye-socket an infomercial?"

Either way, the largest license fee that HBO Sports has paid in years wasn't a "gift" from De La Hoya to his adoring fans. It was in large measure an investment in Oscar's next pay-per-view venture.

Publicly, Greenburg bemoans the flight of boxing to pay-per-view. "I can't tell you that pay-per-view helps the sport because it doesn't," he said last year. "It hurts the sport because it narrows our audience, but it's a fact of life. Every time we try to make an *HBO World Championship Boxing* fight, we're up against mythical pay-per-view numbers. The promoters and fighters insist on pay-per-view because that's where their greatest profits lie. It's a big problem."

More recently, Greenburg added, "The sport would benefit from more *HBO World Championship Boxing* fights and fewer pay-per-view events. But we can't turn back the clock and shut the cash register off. If we don't do the pay-per-view shows, someone else will. Why should we create business for someone else?"

But the reality is that, by its conduct, HBO has enabled the flight to pay-per-view. If it wanted to, the network could take steps to reverse the trend. There's no countervailing power to HBO in boxing today. If a promoter wants to maximize pay-per-view buys on a fight, he goes to HBO.

If HBO refuses to put a fight on pay-per-view, where does the promoter go? Bob Arum has had success on his own with small "Latin Fury" cards on pay-per-view. But when Top Rank tried to promote major pay-per-view shows without the help of HBO (e.g. Cotto-Malignaggi and Pacquiao-Solis), the number of buys was disappointing.

Pay-per-view doesn't translate into an automatic revenue flow. ESPN experimented with pay-per-view boxing several years ago, and the results were so bad that the experiment was cut short. Last November, Showtime did poorly with Fernando Vargas against Ricardo Mayorga.

HBO's biggest competition (and its only real competition right now) is HBO-PPV. It would be very easy for HBO to say to promoters, "Pay-per-view undermines the commitment we've made to deliver the best content possible to our loyal paying subscribers, so we're going to cut back on pay-per-view in the future."

Network executives could also tell promoters, "We're not going to promo your pay-per-view fight on our regular boxing telecasts. There will be no promotional *Countdown* show. We won't guarantee a given number of buys in the form of an advance against pay-per-view revenue. And by the way; we can't guarantee that we won't counterprogram you [as HBO frequently does with Showtime's first-of-the-month telecasts]."

Then sit back and watch how quickly mid-level pay-per-view shows return to *HBO World Championship Boxing*. There would be nowhere else for them to go.

HBO shouldn't be afraid of losing fighters to other networks. It lost separate bouts involving Miguel Cotto and Antonio Margarito to Showtime for a one-time telecast in December 2006. But Cotto and Margarito are fighting each other on July 26, 2008, and it won't be on Showtime. HBO can outbid Showtime and everyone else for anything it wants.

Here, it should be noted that Mark Taffet (HBO's pay-per-view guru) is very smart; so we'll assume he's figured out that it's HBO promotion that drives pay-per-view buys.

HBO Sports has to ask itself whether it's in the subscription television business or the pay-per-view business. The fly in the ointment is that, despite protestations to the contrary, it might prefer the latter.

Greenburg says, "The flight to pay-per-view is bad for HBO."

It's certainly bad for HBO's subscribers. But it might be good for HBO's parent company, Time Warner.

When a fight is on HBO-PPV, instead of spending money in the form of a license fee, HBO is taking in money from its subscribers and others. What sort of profit does HBO make from pay-per-view? We keep hearing, "It isn't as much as you think it is." But there is a profit for HBO Sports, and there's a far greater profit for Time Warner.

When a fight is on pay-per-view, more than fifty cents of every dollar in pay-per-view revenue goes to the cable or satellite company that provides the signal to consumers and the "clearing houses" through which pay-per-view telecasts are sold to cable and satellite system operators.

Time Warner Cable is the second-largest cable operator in the United States with more than 13,000,000 basic video subscribers. Moreover, roughly 90 percent of the homes in the United States that are addressable by cable for pay-per-view telecasts are "cleared" by a company called In-Demand. In Demand is owned by Comcast, Cox Communications, and Time Warner.

Financial gain comes in many ways.

Meanwhile, HBO is dominating and changing the character of an industry. Its power is being used, either by plan or acquiescence, to drive boxing to pay-per-view. The public is hurt because it can no longer see big fights on regular subscription cable.

In that regard, one prominent promoter notes, "Boxing is growing more and more robust all over the world. And in the United States, HBO wants to control everything, either by televising it on pay-per-view or minimizing it to the thirty million homes that have HBO."

The above issues are not frivolous. And they're playing out against a belief that some (not all) of the people who run HBO Sports are disengaged from boxing.

Here, a look at the relationship between Seth Abraham and Lou DiBella (who served as a senior vice president under Abraham at HBO) is instructive.

"Lou was a television executive," Abraham says. "But Lou spent his days and nights inside the boxing business. He lived in that world and he understood it as well as anyone I know. Once I understood and admitted to myself that Lou knew more about boxing than I did, I became a much better boss and Lou was able to become much more effective than he'd been before."

No one in senior management at HBO Sports today lives in the boxing world. "For some of these guys," says one HBO employee, "the hotel they stay in is more important than what they show."

The week of a big fight offers a unique opportunity to mix with a cross-section of people in the boxing industry and learn. When Jermain Taylor defended his title against Kelly Pavlik in Atlantic City last year, the host hotels were Bally's and Caesars. The HBO brass stayed at the Borgata. When Joe Calzaghe and Mikkel Kessler fought in Cardiff, the host hotel was the Cardiff Hilton. The top-ranking HBO official on site stayed at St. David's Hotel. That takes them out of the mainstream of what's going on.

"Mark Taffet is usually available in the media center during the week of a pay-per-view fight," says one observer of the boxing scene. "The rest of them rarely are. When the lead programmer stays at a different hotel from the fight center, goes golfing instead of being in the media center, and shows up for the fight at the same time as the high rollers; that's a problem."

"They stumble from blunder to blunder, patting themselves on the back," says an industry insider who often sits across the negotiating table from HBO Sports executives. "They alienate people right and left; and they're so powerful that people have to smile and accept it."

The July 7, 2007, rematch between Wladimir Klitschko and Lamon Brewster is an example of what can go wrong when people in power are out of touch with the universe they control. It was a matter of record (for those who cared to look at the record) that Brewster hadn't fought in fifteen months, hadn't won a fight since 2005, and had undergone eye surgery three times. Against Klitschko, he wasn't in shape, lost every minute of the fight, and was spared further damage when his trainer (Buddy McGirt) called a halt to the proceedings after six rounds. After the fight, it was announced that Lamon had re-injured his left eye. Later, there were reports that the eye had been re-injured during training.

HBO's subscribers weren't particularly interested in Klitschko-Brewster. The fight scored a 1.7 live rating and 2.3 for the evening replay.

More significantly, at the time Brewster fought Klitschko on HBO, Lamon was on medical suspension in the United States as a consequence of his eye problems.

Ross Greenburg says, "We didn't know at the time that Brewster was on medical suspension when he fought Klitschko."

Why not? Isn't that among the things that Ross and his staff are paid to know?

Greenburg made his mark at HBO as a producer. The many Emmy Awards on display in his office attest to his talent in that regard. Ross pioneered the use of punch-stats, which were introduced to the world during HBO's 1985 telecast of the rematch between Ray Mancini and Livingstone Bramble. He also created the production templates that have been used for boxing on HBO for decades. "They're very precise," says one producer. "And the attention to detail is impressive."

But the production values for HBO's boxing telecasts are growing stale. When asked to list recent innovations, Rick Bernstein (who succeeded Greenburg as executive producer) cited high-definition TV; having both hand-held cameras at ringside in super-slo-mo; and X-mo replays (slower and more defined than super-slo-mo). These are all technological innovations. Bernstein also noted that HBO has added a one-minute countdown clock to the screen between rounds and is experimenting on *Boxing After Dark* with showing punch-stats on the screen during rounds.

And on the editorial end? After all; the short-lived "Ask Harold" does not qualify as a successful production innovation.

The answer is that the primary production innovations relating to boxing on HBO in recent years have been the network's *Countdown* and *24/7* shows. Both of those shows have helped drive the trend toward putting major fights on pay-per-view.

Where fight production is concerned, HBO also has an unresolved problem relating to its lead-analyst slot. The members of HBO's announcing team serve as its representatives to the boxing community. They are also essential to branding in the collective mind of subscribers. Two years ago, over the objection of virtually everyone on his staff, Greenburg put in motion a series of events designed to replace Larry Merchant with Max Kellerman. HBO is now in a situation where lead-analyst duties are divided between them.

Greenburg professes to be delighted with the way things are working out. "Max's performance has been very strong," Ross says. "I'm getting a lot of good reaction from a lot of people about him. He has a vast historical understanding of the fight game and gives us deep penetrating analysis."

Most people in boxing disagree with that assessment. Kellerman has many talents. Analyzing a fight as it unfolds in front of him isn't one of them. Even if one accepts the view that HBO had to begin laying the groundwork for someone to succeed Larry Merchant, Max isn't the guy.

Kellerman is a provocateur, not an analyst. The "vast historical understanding of the fight game" that Greenburg trumpets hasn't been particularly helpful. The last time it surfaced was during a March 22, 2008, *Boxing After Dark* telecast, when Max likened Michael Katsidis to Rocky Marciano (although Max conceded that Katsidis had yet to prove himself on Marciano's level as a fighter). That word of caution became obvious when Joel Casamayor knocked Katsidis out in the tenth round.

With proper training, Max conceivably could evolve into a good blow-by-blow announcer. He has the right kind of voice and could probably learn to describe the action as it unfolds in front of him (although he'd have to accept the fact that the blow-by-blow role is not a platform for opinion).

If HBO wanted to try a serious production innovation, it could unleash Max as a hard-edged field reporter during fights to ask tough questions and impart information on various issues in boxing. Let him ask the Klitschkos and other fighters about the use of performance enhancing drugs and the role of steroids in boxing today. Max once said that "seven out of the ten top heavyweights are on the juice." There are people who agree with him. That remark deserves serious follow-up one way or the other.

Then, to fill the lead-analyst chair once Merchant is gone, HBO should think outside the box. Michael Buffer knows a lot about the sport and business of boxing. His role as a ring announcer requires neutrality. In a different capacity, he'd surprise a lot of viewers. Boxing historian Craig Hamilton (Michael Grant's former adviser) is verbally gifted and remarkably knowledgeable about all aspects of the sweet science.

And how about a new ad campaign? Talk to aging boxing fans today and there's a familiar refrain: "My love of boxing began when I was a kid and watched the *Gillette Friday Night Fights* on television with my father." It would be good for HBO and good for boxing if the message went out, "Watch a fight on HBO with your son and daughter."

But whatever comes next, it will unfold in a financial environment that's different from the one that existed in the past. A new economic era is dawning at HBO. The company has three "co-presidents" with different areas of responsibility: Richard Plepler (programming), Eric Kessler (sales and marketing), and Harold Akselrad (legal, new business, and administration). They report directly to chairman and CEO Bill Nelson.

Nelson is demanding a high level of financial accountability at HBO. Every element of every budget is being examined. He's not a big fan of boxing.

For a long time, HBO Sports has been so powerful and had so much money to spend that it has never been held accountable within the boxing industry. Now, there's a demand for accountability within HBO.

In a May 12, 2008, interview, Greenburg said, "There's no push at all to cut costs. We're spending more now than we did a year ago on boxing."

But multiple sources say that there is a budget crunch at HBO Sports. The point person in the effort is said to be Barbara Thomas (senior vice president and chief financial officer), who oversees the day-to-day budget numbers and is widely respected throughout HBO.

The same sources say that *Inside the NFL* was cut for budgetary reasons and that *Costas Now* could follow suit when its host's contract expires despite the exemplary nature of Bob Costas's work.

"But it doesn't stop there," says a member of the HBO production team. "They're looking at three- and four-figure expenses that they never thought twice about before. They're planning to leave both Merchant and Kellerman home when they do [the June 28th telecast of] Pacquiao-Diaz to save airfare and three nights at the hotel."

The average *HBO World Championship Boxing* and HBO pay-per-view telecast incurs roughly $400,000 in production costs. For *Boxing After Dark,* the number is closer to $250,000. These numbers are being scrutinized to bring them more in line with Showtime's lower production costs. Some of the differential relates to production values that are important to HBO and should be maintained. But some of the differential relates to expenses that can be trimmed.

"The guys in charge nickel-and-dime the low-end people on the production team," says a current HBO employee. "But they spend thousands of dollars more than they need to spend for travel expenses and other perks for themselves. They act like it's their birthright to stay at the Four Seasons."

"Look at the number of people in the Showtime sports department and the number of people at HBO Sports," adds Bob Arum. "HBO spends more money on unnecessary salaries than you can imagine. There are so many places where they have two people doing the same job. Half of the people at HBO Sports could disappear tomorrow and they wouldn't be missed."

But the biggest waste at HBO Sports is in the license fees it pays for content. And the core issue involving these fees is the allocation of resources in furtherance of a strategy that's weakening HBO's boxing franchise and diminishing the product that it delivers to subscribers.

The next step for senior management at HBO (after demanding that HBO Sports adhere to a lower bottom line on spending) should be to seriously examine how boxing programming decisions are made. The corporate culture at HBO runs counter to an HBO chief executive officer dictating programming to the sports department. But when programming fails, a close look at the reasons why is in order.

Greenburg is expected to remain in command at HBO Sports for the foreseeable future. He hasn't been entirely happy at HBO and has tested the waters periodically to see if there's an attractive opening elsewhere. His old contract expired at the end of December 2007. Two issues deadlocked negotiations on a new one.

First, Ross wanted a salary commensurate with what Seth Abraham was paid in his last years at the network. HBO offered to guarantee a portion of that amount with the rest dependent on meeting certain performance benchmarks.

There was also an issue with regard to a clause in Greenburg's previous employment contract that allowed him to produce films for companies other than HBO and be compensated by those companies for his work. Pursuant to that clause, Ross served as executive producer on *Miracle* (a 2004 film that told the inspiring story of the 1980 United States Olympic hockey team). *Miracle* was a Disney film. At the time, Disney was in competition with New Line Cinema (part of the Time Warner empire).

This isn't just a perk. It's a mega-perk. In his most recent contract negotiation, Greenburg reportedly asked for the right to present programming of any kind that HBO doesn't want to anyone else in the industry (including competing television networks).

There's nothing illegal about the contract clause in question. One shouldn't blame Greenburg for taking advantage of an opportunity that was given to him. Several years ago, Abraham was asked about the clause and said, "If HBO felt this was necessary to keep a very talented employee and that the challenge would keep Ross fresh and focused, it was appropriate."

But this is a different time. And there are those who feel that Time Warner shareholders have a right to demand Greenburg's full attention.

Hours before this article was posted, a source reported that Greenburg had signed a four-year contract extension with HBO.

None of the thoughts contained in "HBO: 2008" have been written with a personal agenda in mind. They're a summary of where this writer understands HBO's boxing program to be at the present time.

It's easy to criticize. Finding solutions is harder. With that in mind, I've sought solutions from knowledgeable people in the boxing industry. Two suggested strategies stand out.

The first strategy comes from Bob Arum, who knows how to build fighters and has given HBO as much, if not more, good product over the decades than any other promoter.

"If I was running HBO," says Arum. "I'd get out of the pay-per-view business. Maybe I'd do two huge per-per-view shows a year. Other than that, I wouldn't touch it. I wouldn't produce; I wouldn't distribute; I wouldn't have Jim Lampley at ringside for pay-per-view fights. Right now, it's idiotic. Every time HBO-PPV is involved, you know they're going to show the delay a week later. For what? You don't make new fans for boxing by making people wait a week to see a fight. You make new fans by showing people an exciting fight as it happens. Watching a fight a week afterwards takes away the drama of the sport. It's like waiting a week to watch the World Series on television Who wants to do that?"

"If I was in charge of boxing at HBO," Arum continues, "the core of my programming would be twelve big shows a year. If they want to do *Boxing After Dark,* fine. But the key would be twelve big shows a year. Go back to being the network that puts on great fights that everyone wants to see and everyone talks about. If you use that formula, there's no reason why fights like Cotto-Margarito, Pacquiao-Marquez, and Pavlik-Taylor II can't be on regular HBO. Their budget for license fees is big enough; particularly if you cut waste and factor in all the money they'd save on salaries and production costs. That's how to make people enthusiastic about HBO like they used to be and how to make new fans for boxing."

HBO's plans for the future should be predicated on getting the biggest and best fights possible on *HBO World Championship Boxing.* As for *Boxing After Dark,* Seth Abraham suggests, "HBO should go to Golden Boy, Bob Arum, Don King, Frank Warren, Lou DiBella, Main Events, and a few other promoters and tell them, 'Give me a proposal for your best young fighters. We'll match these guys up, put them in tough. At the end of two years, we'll have some new stars.'"

The Arum and Abraham plans can work. But they'll only work if the matches are approved by people who are grounded in boxing and know what they're looking at. And they'll only work if HBO firmly adheres to the policy, "We will only consider proposals for competitive compelling fights. If you propose something less than that, the dates will go to someone else."

Big fights don't happen today without television. For that reason, HBO still enjoys a commanding position in boxing. But like a once great championship team that his slipped, HBO Sports has to re-evaluate what it's doing and rebuild. More of the same won't work.

As 2008 progressed, Bob Arum became a standard-bearer for those in opposition to HBO.

Bob Arum and HBO

The July 26, 2008, battle between Miguel Cotto and Antonio Margarito unfolded against a backdrop of the never-ending struggle for television dates and control of boxing. Behind the scenes, tempers were flaring; tensions were rising; and an out-of-the-ring confrontation was raging between Bob Arum and HBO.

HBO Sports has struggled the past few years. Most recently, the July 12th *World Championship Boxing* telecast of the fight between Wladimir Klitschko and Tony Thompson did a 1.4 afternoon rating and 1.9 for the replay that night. Those were Klitschko's lowest ratings ever and the first time a same-day HBO *World Championship Boxing* prime-time telecast slipped below 2.0. Adding to HBO's woes, just prior to that, the June 7th pairing of Kelly Pavlik and Gary Lockett engendered a rating of 2.0.

HBO is the banker of boxing. Its deep pockets allow it to dictate much of what happens in the sport. HBO Sports president Ross Greenburg has the final say in deciding which fights HBO buys. That goes a long way toward determining the course of the industry and which promoters thrive.

There have been complaints that Greenburg plays favorites among promoters. In mid-July, these allegations peaked amidst a flurry of activity that saw HBO's dates for autumn 2008 change more rapidly than the pairing of Johns and Janes in a bordello.

HBO had planned to televise Shane Mosley against Ricardo Mayorga (a Golden Boy promotion) on pay-per-view on October 11th. Then Showtime revealed its intention to televise Chad Dawson against Antonio Tarver on the same night and pair it with a same-day tape-delay of Samuel Peter versus Vitali Klitschko.

At that point, HBO (which habitually counterprograms Showtime's first-day-of-the-month telecasts) became sensitized to the dangers of counterprogramming. A remarkable stream of events followed.

Peter is co-promoted by Dino Duva and Don King. Klitschko is promoted by K2 Promotions. An agreement between the two camps calls for Duva Boxing to be the lead promoter on Peter-Klitschko in association with Don King Productions and K2. HBO had repeatedly said that it had no interest in televising the fight. Thus, Duva made an agreement with Showtime to televise Peter-Klitschko for a license fee of $600,000. Both Duva and Showtime boxing tsar Ken Hershman say that the deal was verbally approved by Shelly Finkel (who has a close working relationship with Golden Boy and is also an advisor to Klitschko). Then Golden Boy CEO Richard Schaefer grew concerned that the Showtime doubleheader would undermine pay-per-view buys for Mosley-Mayorga.

On July 12th, Finkel told Duva that HBO had reversed course and was now interested in making an offer for Peter-Klitschko. In response, Duva sent Finkel an email that read in part, "I cannot agree to your suggestion that we solicit an offer from them. As you are aware, we have an agreement with Showtime already. You and I both made personal commitments to Ken Hershman to broadcast the fight on a tape delay on specific terms. As you also know, HBO had always advised both of us that they weren't interested in the fight. I'm not sure what caused their sudden change of heart which, by the way, only came after talk in the business that we made a deal with Showtime. Something isn't right with this. Regardless, it is my strong belief that we have a deal with Showtime and cannot violate that."

On July 14th, according to Duva, Finkel told him that Duva Boxing couldn't proceed with Peter-Klitschko on Showtime because Duva had a legal obligation to maximize revenue from the fight and HBO was now ready to make an offer that exceeded Showtime's.

On July 15th, Schaefer called Duva and told him that Don King (who promotes Mayorga) had promised Golden Boy that Peter-Klitschko would not take place on Showtime on October 11th in competition with Mosley-Mayorga. Duva immediately emailed King, saying "I don't believe [Schaefer]" and asked King to "make sure that there is no understanding between you and him on this matter."

On July 16th, Schaefer faxed a letter to King that read in part, "I just wanted to confirm our numerous conversations and mutual understanding relating to the Sam Peter vs. Vitali Klitschko fight. You have expressly warranted to me that, as the co-promoter of Sam Peter, you will not compete against the PPV event scheduled for October 11, 2008, between Mosley and Mayorga. You have clearly stated that you will not sign off on a possible October 11th event between Peter and Klitschko if it is held on Showtime. Or to put it in your words, 'Under no circumstances will I compete against myself.' You have as well stated to me that, as the co-promoter of Sam Peter, you have never agreed to any Showtime deal and that any representations by Dino Duva are not valid without your approval. By the way, your representation is consistent with what Shelly Finkel has represented to me on behalf of the Klitschko side."

That same day, King sent a return fax to Schaefer with copies to Duva, Hershman, and Ross Greenburg. In relevant part, King's letter read, "Dear Richard, I must say that you have misstated the case. While I do not intend to 'compete against myself,' I first and foremost do not intend to act against my partner." In the same letter, King represented that he had spoken with Greenburg on July 15th and communicated the King-Duva position to him.

HBO sports senior vice president for programming Kery Davis says that HBO never made an offer for Peter-Klitschko; that the offer came from Golden Boy. But Duva has a distinctly different impression.

"Finkel and Richard Schaefer kept calling me about the fight," Duva says. "Finally, at their suggestion, I called Kery and he made an offer of $850,000. I specifically asked him, 'Is this a definite offer?' And Kery said, 'Yes.' Kery was saying to me, 'This is a fight that should be on HBO. Come on; we want to build up to a rematch between Samuel and Wladimir.' I told him, 'Look; you guys told me point-blank that you weren't interested in the fight. Now I have a deal with Showtime; and all of a sudden, you're interested. Where were you before?'"

One source says that, when Duva told Davis that he had given his word to Showtime, Kery responded, "Fuck Showtime. This is a better offer."

"I don't remember those exact words," Duva says. "But that was the sentiment Kery expressed. It wasn't pretty."

On July 17th, in an effort to avoid a Mosley-Mayorga pay-per-view disaster, HBO began discussions to move Mosley-Mayorga to *HBO World Championship Boxing* on September 27th (a date that had been held for Kelly Pavlik). Arum had been trying to make Pavlik against Paul Williams for that date. Sources say that HBO had offered $3,500,000 for the fight.

That left the parties $300,000 apart; a gap that Arum was confident could be bridged.

"I think Kery Davis tried in good faith to make Pavlik-Williams happen," Arum says. "And I think Dan Goossen [Williams's promoter of record] negotiated with me in good faith. But at the end of the day, Williams didn't want the fight."

Meanwhile, sources say that, unbeknownst to Arum, during the week of July 14th, Greenburg had told Schaefer (acting on behalf of Winky Wright) to make a deal for a fight between Wright and Williams for a $2,500,000 license fee. Wright claims that he agreed to the fight and had a binding agreement for a seven-figure purse. Then HBO changed its position and, on July 16th, attorney Judd Burstein (acting on Wright's behalf) sent a letter to HBO's legal department, threatening to sue the network for breach of contract. In settlement of Winky's claim, HBO has reportedly agreed to put him on an *HBO World Championship Boxing* card in early 2009.

During the same time frame, HBO kept turning down opponents other than Williams (such as Marco Antonio Rubio and Joe Greene) who Arum suggested for Pavlik. Arum told his fighter that he was willing to promote an independent pay-per-view show headed by Pavlik-Rubio with Julio Cesar Chavez Jr on the undercard. But that would have required Kelly to take a cut in pay, which he didn't want to do.

Arum recounts what happened next: "Richard Schaefer had asked me a long time ago if Kelly would fight Hopkins. Kelly said he would, but at 168 pounds, not 170. Then all this nonsense started with HBO turning down opponents and Paul Williams refusing the fight and we had no place to go with Kelly other than Hopkins if Kelly's income level was going to be preserved. So I called Schaefer. I was the one who initiated the new discussions. We made the fight at 170 pounds for pay-per-view on October 18th with a fifty-fifty split between the two camps. I don't like a lot of the things that are going on now between HBO and Golden Boy. But my experience working with Schaefer on big promotions has been good. Once a deal is in place, there are very few disagreements or problems, so I expect it will be a successful promotion."

Moving Pavlik to October 18th freed up September 27th for Mosley-Mayorga. That led to criticism from a rival promoter who complained, "HBO wouldn't have done this for anyone but Golden Boy. Why bail out

Golden Boy? Ross should have let Mosley-Mayorga fail as a pay-per-view venture. That would have restored some semblance of sanity to the industry and reminded everyone that pay-per-view isn't a bottomless pot of gold."

Another promoter noted that September 27th is part of a free HBO preview weekend and said, "Something like that should be used to showcase young fighters with a future. Mosley-Mayorga isn't a good fight to begin with and it's about the past. Why spend all that money [a license fee believed to be in the neighborhood of $3,000,000] on the past?"

Also, it now appears as though HBO will pair Mosley-Mayorga with Andre Berto against Stevie Forbes. Mosley should be fighting Berto. That would be a good fight. Instead, boxing fans will be subjected to more insulting erratic behavior from Mayorga coupled with another one-sided HBO bout between a quality fighter and an opponent provided by *The Contender* (e.g. Calzaghe-Manfredo, Cotto-Gomez, De La Hoya–Forbes, and Berto-Bravo).

Regardless; Arum was satisfied with the deal for Pavlik-Hopkins. "We made the best of a difficult situation," he says.

Then another problem arose.

On May 25th, Roy Jones and John Wirt met in England with Joe Calzaghe and his attorney to discuss a Jones-Calzaghe match-up. Wirt, also an attorney, runs Square Ring (Jones's promotional company). Enzo Calzaghe (Joe's father and trainer) was not at the meeting because he has several fighters under contract to Joe's former promoter, Frank Warren. Warren claims that he still has promotional rights to Joe, and Enzo is believed to be sympathetic to the promoter's position.

At the close of the meeting, a contract was signed that called for Square Ring to promote a Jones-Calzaghe fight with a fifty-fifty split between the two camps after the deduction of direct promotional expenses. Wirt pitched the fight to Ross Greenburg, but HBO declined to bid on it because of a claim by Don King that he had promotional rights to Jones. Then, during the week of June 23rd, King stepped aside in exchange for Jones agreeing to not pursue money that King owed him in conjunction with his January 19th fight against Felix Trinidad at Madison Square Garden.

With King out of the picture, Jones, Wirt, Calzaghe, and Gareth Williams (who had become Calzaghe's new attorney) journeyed to New

York for a meeting at HBO. On July 2nd, they sat down with Kery Davis, Mark Taffet (senior vice president for sports operations and pay-per-view), Barbara Thomas (senior vice president and chief financial officer) and Peter Mozarsky (an attorney in HBO's legal department). The following day, Greenburg joined them.

Sources at HBO and elsewhere say that a deal for HBO to televise Jones-Calzaghe on pay-per-view was finalized at the July 3rd meeting. The fight would take place on September 20th at Madison Square Garden or the Thomas and Mack Center in Las Vegas. HBO vetoed London and Cardiff as possible sites but, in return, agreed to produce a *24/7* series to promote the fight.

At the July 2nd and July 3rd meetings, Gareth Williams (who also represents Ricky Hatton and has had extensive dealings with Golden Boy) said that he wanted Golden Boy to be involved with the promotion to protect Calzaghe's interests. Jones said that Golden Boy could act as Joe's adviser, but that neither Richard Schaefer nor Oscar could hold themselves out as a co-promoter of the fight and that Golden Boy could not have any event signage.

Meanwhile, Frank Warren had sued Calzaghe in England for breach of contract. The lawsuit seeks money damages, not an injunction. But in addition to filing legal papers, Warren sent threatening letters to HBO, Madison Square Garden (which was close to finalizing a deal for the fight), and others who were potentially involved with the promotion. HBO asked Calzaghe for a promise of indemnification regarding any legal action that Warren might take against it. Calzaghe refused. Then, on, July 22nd, Wirt announced he'd been told by Gareth Williams that Calzaghe had injured his wrist two days earlier hitting a heavy bag. Also on July 22nd, the Jones camp issued a statement in Roy's name stating that HBO and Madison Square Garden were working with him to reschedule the fight for November 8th.

At that point, the feces hit the propeller. Todd DuBoef, president of Top Rank (Arum's promotional company) picks up the saga.

"After Manny Pacquiao fought David Diaz [on June 21st]," DuBoef explains, "HBO sent us a proposal for a Pacquiao pay-per-view fight on November 15th. I checked with In Demand and Direct-TV [which clear pay-per-view events for the industry] and learned that UFC was planning a show for November 15th. So I put a hold on November 8th and

November 15th. Then I called Taffet and said, 'There's no point in going against UFC. I want November 8th.' Taffet told me, 'We have a *World Championship Boxing* show on November 8th [Jermain Taylor against a then-unnamed opponent]. Let me get back to you.'

Well and good.

But then, according to DuBoef, "The next thing I know, Mark has called In Demand and Direct-TV and told them that HBO is going with Jones-Calzaghe on November 8th. I called Mark to ask what was going on, and he told me that Top Rank could do its own show on November 8th; that the industry could carry two pay-per-view events on the same night the way it did in 2006 when HBO televised Hopkins-Tarver on pay-per-view and we did Cotto-Malignaggi."

"That's nuts," DuBoef continues. "Why would HBO want to put Jones-Calzaghe and Manny Pacquiao against each other? That's not good for boxing. And why couldn't someone at HBO pick up the phone and tell us that they were doing Jones-Calzaghe on November 8th?"

"They're small thinkers," DuBoef says of HBO. "They're trying to keep the boxing world small so they can control it."

Arum is more pointed in his comments. He had planned to promote a fight involving the winner of Cotto-Margarito on November 1st and a Pacquiao fight on November 8th. HBO now has Jermain Taylor against Jeff Lacy scheduled for November 15th and Ricky Hatton versus Paulie Malignaggi slated for November 22nd. That's followed by Thanksgiving weekend and Oscar De La Hoya's farewell bout on December 6th, leaving boxing's dance card full toward the end of the year.

"With everything we were planning for Pavlik, Pacquiao, and the winner of Cotto-Margarito," Arum says, "I never contemplated losing the November 8th date. We cleared it with In Demand and Direct-TV. HBO knew what we were doing. Representations were made. And then, all of a sudden, without anybody telling us, HBO takes the date away. Nothing like that ever happened before. There was a time when people in boxing said, 'You can't trust what promoters say.' Now you can't trust what HBO says. It's not my fault that Ross got himself into a bind for November."

Arum is a fascinating figure. Former Time Warner Sports president Seth Abraham (the architect of HBO's boxing program) says that fighters and strategies provided by the promoter contributed significantly to the network's early success. Later, Arum was instrumental in building Showtime Boxing as a counterbalance to HBO. For years, he was ESPN's sole supplier of fights. More recently, he put Versus in the boxing business.

Arum is now seventy-six years old and has enough money to retire the national debt of a small country. But he still plays the boxing game successfully and hard.

In recent years, Arum and Greenburg have been at odds. Their feud went public in 2006, when the promoter criticized HBO for refusing to offer a date to Kelly Pavlik and proclaimed, "There's a perception with boxing network guys that, if you're a white guy, you can't fight. They judge by color."

In response, Greenburg called Arum's comments "a disgraceful and undignified remark by a disturbed man."

That exchange resonated on July 4th of this year when the *Grand Rapids Press* quoted Floyd Mayweather Jr as saying that HBO's announcing team was "racist" and singled out Jim Lampley for criticism. In response, Greenburg issued a far more measured statement that read, "Floyd is a tremendous athlete who gave his all to the sport. We have nothing but admiration for what he accomplished in the ring. His remarks regarding HBO broadcasters and executives are unfortunate and we could not disagree more. We will not engage in a debate. We are very disappointed in hearing about this. We wish him well in retirement."

The difference in content and tone between the two Greenburg statements was not lost on observers. "Res ipsa loquitur," Arum said in his best Latin legalese. "The facts speak for themselves. A real general defends his troops as wholeheartedly as he defends himself."

During Cotto-Margarito fight week, Arum sat for two long interviews to detail his relationship with Greenburg and HBO. "I don't blame Richard Schaefer for what happened with the November 8th date," the promoter said. "There's a conspiracy theory that HBO took November 8th away from me to put Manny Pacquiao in a position where he has to fight Oscar, but I don't believe that. I think it's just Ross being a moron."

Then Arum went into high gear. Among the thoughts he offered were:

> • "HBO still does some things right. It deserves credit for lighting a fire under De La Hoya–Mayweather and helping to make it the event that it was. But Ross thinks that, if HBO does one or two really big pay-per-view shows a year, he's doing his job. That's not how you build a boxing program. You build a boxing program month after month,

one fight at a time, the way HBO used to do it when people who understood boxing were running the show. Right now, most of the fights are horrible; the ratings are horrible. And things will get worse before they get better because the guy with the juice acts based on ignorance and his own personal feelings rather than what's good for the sport and HBO."

• "Anybody who knows anything about boxing knows that Cotto-Margarito is going to be a great fight. Could something bad happen where it gets stopped early because of a cut from a head-butt? Of course. But absent something like that, everybody in boxing except Ross Greenburg knows that it's going to be a great fight. It's the kind of fight that HBO should get behind to build a fan base for the sport and for HBO boxing. Fights like this are building blocks. Fights like this make fight fans. HBO could have bought this fight for *World Championship Boxing* for $6,000,000, which is less than they've paid for some of their fights this year. But no one at HBO expressed any interest in it. In fact, not only was there no interest in putting Cotto-Margarito on regular HBO; I had to embarrass them through the media to get them to do a *Countdown* show for it. A *Countdown* show for this fight is a no-brainer unless you're dealing with someone who doesn't have a brain."

• "You need a boxing guy to run boxing at HBO; not a bunch of TV guys who think they know boxing. The biggest problem with Ross, far worse than his personal animosity toward me and one or two other promoters, is his lack of knowledge and lack of interest in boxing. Ross has no idea who the fighters are. If they hadn't drafted Kelly Pavlik as cannon fodder for Edison Miranda, Kelly still wouldn't be on HBO."

• "When HBO was HBO, Seth Abraham did the overall planning and Lou DiBella was the expert when it came to knowledge of boxing. Other than Taffet, no one does any intelligent planning at HBO anymore, and Taffet's planning is all about pay-per-view."

• "Ross was a good producer, but that doesn't qualify him to be the head of a major department at a major premium network. I'm sorry to say it, but Ross is ill-equipped for the job and he's certainly ill-equipped to run HBO's boxing program. If someone has no understanding of boxing and no love for the sport, he gets hooked on names he's heard of, even if those names belong to fighters who are way past their prime or could never fight to begin with. That's why you see so many horrible fights and so many of the same tired old faces on HBO. The only reason HBO is televising Mosley-Mayorga is that Ross has heard of both guys. Make up a quiz about boxing, and give it to all the executives who've been involved in buying fights for the television networks over the past ten years. I guarantee you; Ross would come in last."

• "There's no adult supervision at HBO as far as boxing is concerned. And that's a shame because HBO could be so good for boxing if the guy in charge knew what he was doing."

• "Ross has stopped speaking to me altogether. He won't take telephone calls from me anymore because he's mad that I've criticized him. I've called him five or six times in the past few weeks, and he won't return my calls. That's not how a responsible television executive behaves. It's worse than unprofessional. It's fucking moronic. I'm supplying Manny Pacquiao, Kelly Pavlik, Miguel Cotto, Antonio Margarito. None of them are tied to HBO, which means they can bolt at any time. Ross might despise me. But doesn't he have an obligation as the head of HBO Sports to talk with me? Don King and I were mortal enemies at times, but we always talked. Seth Abraham was pissed off at me more times than I can count, but we always talked. Even when Seth and I were fighting, he'd pick up the phone and call to say 'congratulations' after a great fight."

Ross Greenburg declined to be interviewed with regard to his rift with Arum. Instead, an HBO spokesperson sent a response that read in part, "We've grown weary of Bob Arum's tirades against HBO Sports. They are foolish, unproductive, and marginal in accuracy. Bob's mission is to create leverage. We are not going to play his game."

HBO is correct is saying that Arum's remarks should be viewed through the prism of self-interest. But give Arum credit. He's willing to go on the record. A lot of promoters in boxing today are saying the same things that he is, but only on condition of anonymity.

"It's like the old Soviet Union," Arum observes. "If you spoke out against mismanagement or abuses of power, you were punished. Promoters today are afraid that, if they speak out about what's going on at HBO, Ross will retaliate and they won't get the one date a year they hope he'll give them. I don't give a damn. At my age and in my position, I'm able to speak out. So I do."

Also, as Todd DuBoef notes, "Pissing on the number-one boxing buyer in the world doesn't create leverage. Bob is simply telling the truth as he sees it."

As the year progressed, I had occasion to append several "notes" regard-ing HBO to my column on Secondsout.

HBO Notes

Artie Pelullo promotes Verno Phillips (42–10, 21 KOs), who lifted the IBF junior-middleweight crown from Cory Spinks earlier this year. Phillips is thirty-eight years old and nearing the end of his ring career. Pelullo's task is to get him a good pay-day, preferably in a fight that Verno can win.

Ireland's John Duddy is boxing's latest matinee idol. Fighting out of New York, he has fashioned a 25-and-0 record in the middleweight divi-sion and is ranked in the top-ten by all four world sanctioning bodies. Given his new training regimen, Duddy can make 154 pounds with rela-tive ease.

Last month (June 2008), Pelullo approached HBO with a proposal for what could have been a doubleheader featuring a Phillips-Duddy cham-pionship fight to be held this fall. The fighters were willing to fight on a date chosen by HBO at a location chosen by HBO (the most logical site being New York, Belfast, or Dublin).

On June 26, 2008, HBO informed Pelullo that it wasn't interested in the fight.

That was poor decision-making. Verno Phillips isn't an elite fighter and his best days are behind him. But he was good enough to dethrone Cory Spinks, who went the distance in a split-decision loss to Jermain Taylor in a 160-pound title fight that was televised by HBO.

John Duddy is undefeated and extraordinarily marketable. He has a passionate following and his fights are high drama.

Phillips-Duddy, if it happens, is likely to be a competitive compelling action fight for a legitimate world title. It's precisely the type of fight that HBO should be televising on *Boxing After Dark*.

But there are implications here that go far beyond Phillips-Duddy.

Pelullo says that, when Kery Davis (HBO Sports senior vice president for programming) rejected the fight, he told Pelullo, "We don't have any dates available. Why don't you call Richard Schaefer at Golden Boy. Maybe they can put it on one of their shows."

"I'll pass," Pelullo responded.

"It could lead to Duddy against De La Hoya."

"I'm building my own fighters; not someone else's."

Pelullo's report of his conversation with Davis reinforces the fear that HBO is over-committed to Golden Boy to the detriment of its own boxing programming and that the playing field is tilted in favor of one promoter.

Davis declined to be interviewed on the subject of HBO's decision to not bid on Phillips-Duddy. On July 2, 2008, after the request for an interview was declined, Pelullo received a telephone call from Luis Barragan (the director of programming for HBO Sports). Pelullo says that Barragan, who reports to Davis, asked if the promoter had talked with this writer and what the substance of the conversation was. Then, after saying, "Kery wouldn't talk to Hauser," Barragan told Pelullo, "Gary Shaw has a date with us this fall and the main event fell out. Maybe he could promote it."

"Why would I give my fight to Gary Shaw?" Pelullo queried.

This is an example of why it's bad policy for HBO to give dates to promoters without fights firmly attached to settle potential legal claims against it (which is believed to be how Shaw got two dates on *Boxing After Dark*).

There's also concern that boxing in general is in trouble at HBO. The network paid a $2,750,000 license fee for Kelly Pavlik versus Gary Lockett, which aired on June 7, 2008, and engendered a disappointing 2.0 rating. To put that number in perspective, until this year, 2.8 was the lowest prime-time *HBO World Championship Boxing* rating ever for a live telecast. Now ratings below that level are common.

If HBO keeps doing 2.0 ratings for *World Championship Boxing,* the next step might be for those in command above HBO Sports president Ross Greenburg to reconsider whether boxing belongs on the network in prime time.

Meanwhile, HBO's June 28, 2008, pay-per-view telecast of Manny Pacquiao versus David Diaz was unusual in that the network left both Larry Merchant and Max Kellerman home and covered the show with a "two-man booth" (Jim Lampley and Emanuel Steward) plus Harold Lederman. The stated reason for this was to cut costs.

At first glance, that doesn't make sense. The only additional costs incurred as a consequence of Merchant or Kellerman being on site would have been airfare and hotel (a drop in the bucket by HBO standards). A more likely explanation is that HBO is exploring the possibility of going with a two-man booth on a permanent basis when the Merchant and Kellerman contracts expire.

Greenburg has made it clear by his conduct that he has limited enthusiasm for Merchant continuing with HBO Pay-Per-View and HBO *World Championship Boxing*. And the Pacquiao-Diaz telecast supported the view that Lampley is fully capable of dissecting controversies and interviewing fighters without help from Max.

Given what HBO pays for talent, a two-man booth would save the network more than $500,000 a year. But that number is far less than HBO could save on license fees with more judicious buying.

★   ★   ★

HBO's woes continue. That's not just the opinion of a boxing writer. It's HBO's subscribers talking. The ratings for the cable giant's boxing telecasts are starting to look like the declining stock price of a mismanaged financial institution.

The powers that be at HBO thought they had a winner when they paired Juan Diaz versus Michael Katsidis and Rocky Juarez against Jorge Barrios on their September 6, 2008, *Boxing After Dark* telecast. Instead, the show engendering a 1.7 rating. That was one of the lowest ratings ever for a live prime-time HBO boxing telecast.

Next came HBO's September 27th *World Championship Boxing* card featuring Shane Mosley (an 8-to-1 favorite) against Ricardo Mayorga and Andre Berto (7-to-1) versus Stevie Forbes. That constituted an almost $4,000,000 bailout (the license fee paid for the two fights by HBO) of what was to have been an October 11th pay-per-view card headed by Mosley-Mayorga.

Regarding Mosley-Mayorga, Michael Swann wrote online for CBS Sports, "Ricardo Mayorga has about as much chance of beating Sugar

Shane Mosley as 82-year-old Cloris Leachman has of winning *Dancing with the Stars.*"

As for Berto-Forbes, Larry Merchant acknowledged at the start of the telecast, "This is a young gun going up against a penknife." The best that Jim Lampley could say about the encounter was that it would be "an interesting sort of litmus test."

Apparently, Berto-Forbes wasn't very interesting to HBO Sports president Ross Greenburg, who could be seen on camera throughout the bout looking away from the ring to talk with people sitting beside and behind him. The telecast engendered a meager 2.5 rating ($1,600,000 per ratings point) despite having the premiere showing of *Chris Rock: Kill the Messenger* as a lead-in.

One week later, HBO's October 4th *Boxing After Dark* telecast offered up three more mismatches. In the opening bout, Sergio Martinez (a 6-to-1 favorite) outlanded Alex Bunema 212 to 31 before the fight was stopped at the end of eight rounds. Then Alfredo Angulo won every round against Andrey Tsurkan (outlanding him 400 to 143) before scoring a tenth-round stoppage. In the finale, Yuriorkis Gamboa (a 10-to-1 favorite) faced off against Marcos Ramirez. That one lasted until the 1:41 mark of round two. There was never a time when the outcome of any of the three fights was in doubt. In fact, the favorite would have won every round out of twenty rounds fought if referee Jerry Cantu hadn't blown a call in the first round of Gamboa-Ramirez and incorrectly called a knockdown after an elbow to the jaw sent Gamboa to the canvas.

Then came the really bad news. HBO learned that its October 4th telecast had engendered a 1.1 rating. That's the absolute worst rating ever for a live prime-time HBO boxing telecast.

Unfortunately, more mismatches lie ahead on "regular" HBO. On November 15th, Jermain Taylor will enter the ring a 5-to-1 favorite over Jeff Lacy. The November 22nd match-up between Ricky Hatton and Paulie Malignaggi shapes up as a competitive fight. But there's concern that, on November 29th, HBO will pair Paul Williams and Chris Arreola in non-competitive bouts.

To repeat what I've written time and time again: boxing fans want to see good COMPETITIVE fights.

HBO Sports was once the heart and soul of boxing. But the network is losing its audience and the respect of the industry as a whole as a consequence of presenting so many mismatches on *HBO World Championship Boxing* and *Boxing After Dark*.

The ratings show that HBO boxing is broken. A change in programming philosophy is necessary to fix it.

In a national election year, the drive to legalize mixed martial arts offered a case study in state politics.

New York State and the Legalization of Mixed Martial Arts

To its critics, mixed martial arts is ugly and grotesque. John McCain has railed against it on the floor of the United States Senate, calling it "human cockfighting."

To its fans, mixed martial arts is exciting entertainment and a legitimate sport.

Now MMA is at a crucial point in its evolution as a business. It's currently sanctioned in thirty-five states plus the District of Columbia. The most important jurisdiction not yet in the mix is New York, which has a statute that specifically bans mixed martial arts competition. To overturn that ban, the state assembly and state senate must pass new legislation and the governor must sign it.

A bill currently pending in the New York State legislature would legalize "combative sports" in addition to boxing and place these sports under the auspices of the New York State Athletic Commission. Right now, the action outside the octagon is as rough-and-tumble as the action in it.

The prime mover in the drive to legalize MMA in New York is Zuffa LLC (the company that controls UFC, more formally known as the Ultimate Fighting Championship). Marc Ratner, who served for fourteen years as executive director of the Nevada State Athletic Commission, is UFC's vice president for regulatory and governmental affairs. "We're the lead driver," Ratner says. "The other organizations are just drafting on us."

In November 2007, Zuffa hired Brown, McMahon & Weinraub (an Albany lobbying firm) for a monthly retainer of $10,000. It also hired Global Strategy Group (a media-relations political consulting firm used by then-governor Eliot Spitzer). Subsequently, Zuffa made generous contributions to Democratic and Republican campaign causes in New York.

This spring, Assemblyman Steve Englebright sponsored a bill in the New York State Assembly to legalize MMA. Martin Goldin sponsored a similar bill in the State Senate. Everything seemed on track for passage. Then the democratic process intervened.

On June 11, 2008, the state assembly committee on Tourism, Arts, and Sports Development met for what was expected to be a routine vote to send the bill to the entire assembly. But a second-term lawmaker named Bob Reilly had different thoughts.

Reilly, whose district includes Albany and Saratoga counties, evokes images of James Stewart in *Mr. Smith Goes to Washington.* He's a teacher at heart, having coached track and field for twenty-six years; seventeen of them at Siena College in upstate New York. Speaking against the legalization of MMA, Reilly told his fellow committee members, "We ban cockfighting and dog fighting. Should we allow humans to enter a cage to knee, kick, and punch each other?"

Reilly's impassioned plea carried the day. The bill to legalize MMA was defeated in committee. But like Arnold Schwarzenegger in *The Terminator,* it will be back.

Proponents of MMA point to the popularity of the sport and its potential to raise revenue, both in commerce and tax dollars, for the State of New York.

Jerry Izenberg, the dean of American sportswriters, is unimpressed. "In order to be an MMA champion," Izenberg says, "you need every skill that's outlawed on the planet. The very things we pride ourselves on not doing, these people elevate to an art form. I wouldn't even try to dignify it."

Don King adds to the debate with the observation, "UFC ain't nothing new. They started with ultimate fighting and then they civilized it and made it into boxing. All UFC is doing is taking two hundred years of rules and throwing them out the window."

Meanwhile, Bob Reilly finds himself in an unlikely position. "I consider myself the accidental opposition," he said last week. "When I came to the committee meeting, I only intended to voice my personal opposition to the measure. But when I swayed enough people on the committee to vote against it, I became the point person in opposition."

Reilly accepts the role of boxing in today's society, although he's troubled by the damage that the sport inflicts on participants. Mixed martial arts, in his view, goes too far.

"I'm opposed to the proposed legislation because of the brutality of the sport," he says. "The people who are drawn to mixed martial arts are attracted by the brutality of it, which goes above and beyond what you see in boxing. It seems to me beyond logic that we in the state legislature would consistently pass laws against physical abuse and physical intimidation, everything from domestic abuse to bullying in schools, and then allow this stuff. We should not be encouraging the glorification of this kind of violence."

As for the monetary issues, Reilly maintains, "The argument about mixed martial arts raising revenue for the state is typical. But our economy shouldn't be dependent on that sort of stuff." And he notes that the real "money" issue surrounding the legalization of MMA might be the financial resources that have been brought to bear in support of the proposed legislation.

"The battle here is difficult," Reilly says, "because we're up against a tremendous amount of money that's available for lobbying as a consequence of the money that mixed martial arts would generate for those who are hiring the lobbyists. Money is the driving force behind this. You see the influence of the lobbyists in the fact that, under the proposed legislation, New York would only get a tax of three percent of the revenue generated and whatever we get would be capped at $150,000 for each event. Rhode Island gets five percent."

Reilly also believes that Ron Scott Stevens was removed as chairman of the New York State Athletic Commission because he failed to embrace the campaign to legalize mixed martial arts.

On July 23, 2008, Stevens was notified by Secretary of State Lorraine Cortes-Vazquez that he was being replaced at the end of the week. Two days later, Governor David Paterson announced that Melvina Lathan (a vocal proponent of MMA) would chair the commission.

Thereafter, Dan Rafael of ESPN.com wrote, "Stevens got the boot for no apparent reason, unless you count the fact that he would not openly support the sanctioning of mixed martial arts in New York, where it is outlawed but facing serious lobbying pressure from UFC officials."

Reilly concurs, saying, "It's clear to me that this new person was put in her position because of her support for legalizing mixed martial arts. Can I prove that? No. But if I see something that walks like a duck and it's quacking, I call it a duck."

One of the issues that the New York State Athletic Commission will confront if MMA is legalized is that the commission doesn't presently have the personnel to effectively regulate the sport. Meanwhile, the biggest problem that those against the legalization of MMA face is that no powerful interests are actively opposing the proposed legislation. The bill has passed under the radar of news organizations like the *New York Times,* which might influence the debate if its editorial board were aware of it. The American Medical Association has been largely silent.

Indeed, Reilly notes, "This came to our committee without forewarning. It was under the radar and almost slipped through without serious discussion and debate. There was a vote. The measure was defeated in committee. And immediately after the vote, the lobbyists started working their phones again."

The bill to legalize MMA will be reconsidered when the New York State legislature reconvenes after the fall elections. Ratner says, "Our representatives have continued to stay in touch with the appropriate government officials to make sure they understand the reasons why the law should be changed. I feel very bullish that MMA will be approved in New York."

Reilly is afraid that might be right. "I've gotten a lot of email from fans of mixed martial arts," he says. "Obviously, they're against the position I've taken. But when I talk with the people in my district, they don't like the idea of legalizing this form of brutality. The problem is, no one is mobilizing the general public on this issue, and I fear that some members of the Assembly and Senate who oppose the bill on principle will fold on this."

"That would be a shame," the assemblyman says in closing. "I'm sure that some of the people who participate in mixed martial arts are good people. But in terms of what they do in this barbaric sport, they shouldn't be held up as role models. It would send a terrible message to the people of the State of New York and particularly to our children."

As a contrast to "Fistic Nuggets," these "Notes" were on the serious side.

Fistic Notes

There's an image of a fighter in trouble that has stayed in my mind,

On March 6, 2008, Curtis Stevens was in the ring against journeyman Thomas Reid in an eight-round undercard bout at the Manhattan Center in New York.

Stevens is a twenty-three-year-old super-middleweight from the Brownsville section of Brooklyn with an 18–2 record and 13 knockouts. He was once a hot prospect. In July 2006, he suffered a premature-stoppage loss at the hands of Marcos Primera. But he beat Primera in a rematch, reeled off three more victories, and seemed headed for bigger and better things. Then he lost a unanimous decision to Andre Dirrell on an HBO *Boxing After Dark* telecast. That took away his luster.

Stevens-Reid was Curtis's first fight since losing to Dirrell; a hiatus from the ring of almost nine months.

In round two, Reid staggered Stevens with a solid right hand; then whacked him again with a follow-up right. Curtis crumpled to the canvas; struggled to rise, and crumpled again. The blow knocked everything out of him but his consciousness. Most fighters don't get up when they're hit like that.

With Herculean effort, Stevens rose to his haunches. There was a vacant look in his eyes, as though he was too dazed to be dizzy. Slowly, he willed his body higher. Then he stood like a man with a 200-pound weight on his back. The bell rang before Reid could resume his attack.

In the sixty seconds between rounds, Stevens's head cleared a bit. The referee and ring doctor let the fight continue. Curtis knocked Reid out in the eighth round.

One can question Stevens's chin. Thomas Reid is forty years old and has lost five fights in a row. It has been four years and 13 fights since Reid knocked anyone out. But no one can question Curtis's heart. Climbing off the canvas and coming back to win like he did is the hardest thing to

do in sports. On March 6th, Curtis Stevens earned full respect as a professional fighter.

* * *

Each year, the International Boxing Hall of Fame in Canastota
inducts twelve new members. The problem is, with each passing year, the
list of inductees gets more and more curious. Some of this year's honorees
(such as Larry Holmes) are obvious choices. But others (e.g. Mogens
Palle) have raised eyebrows.

Hall of Fame inductees fit within one of five categories (1) pioneers
(boxers whose last contest was prior to 1893); (2) old-timers (boxers
whose last contest was between 1893 and 1942); (3) moderns (boxers
who have been retired for five or more years and whose last contest was
no earlier than 1943); (4) observers (members of the media); and (5) other
non-participants who have made a contribution to the sport.

How are they elected?

Hall of Fame executive director Ed Brophy says that pioneers are
voted upon by 21 electors with each year's top finisher being inducted.
Old-timers are voted upon by 54 electors with the top three finishers
enshrined. Moderns are considered by 200 voters (including members of
the Boxing Writers Association of America) with the top three vote-
recipients selected. 56 electors chose two observers. Three other non-
participants are designated for immortality by 57 electors.

However, the process is marked by an unfortunate lack of transparency and the absence of accountability.

The electors are chosen jointly by Brophy and a three-person screening committee. These same four people decide which names go on the
ballot. The screening committee for 2007 was comprised of former *Boxing
Digest* editor Herb Goldman, historian Hank Kaplan (now deceased), and
boxing agent Don Majeski.

The public is not told who the electors are. Most of the electors don't
know either. Nor are the electors told what the final vote totals are. Brophy
says simply that the votes are tabulated by a CPA named Dorothy Sember.

This is not a process that inspires confidence.

* * *

In the long history of the Olympics, only three New Yorkers have won gold medals in boxing.

Frankie DiGenaro was the first. Born in the Bronx in 1901, he captured a gold medal in the 112-pound division at the 1920 Antwerp Games. Later, he fought professionally under the name Frankie Genaro and won both the National Boxing Association and International Boxing Union flyweight crowns.

Floyd Patterson was born in North Carolina, grew up in Brooklyn, and won Olympic gold as a middleweight (165 pounds) at the 1952 Helsinki games. Four years later, he claimed the heavyweight throne vacated by Rocky Marciano with a fifth-round knockout of Archie Moore.

Mark Breland, now forty-five, was the third (and last) boxer from New York City to win an Olympic gold medal. Born and raised in the Bedford-Stuyvesant section of Brooklyn, he accomplished the feat in the welterweight division at the 1984 Los Angeles Games.

Going into the Olympics, Breland was one of the most-celebrated amateurs in boxing history, He won an unprecedented five New York Golden Gloves Championships (1980–84), the United States Amateur Championship (1982), and the World Amateur Championships (1982). His amateur record after the Olympics was an extraordinary 110 victories against a single defeat.

"The Olympics were hard for me," Breland recalls. "I was the top-rated welterweight in the world, so everyone was gunning for me. The first fight I had, I won but I only looked so-so. Second fight, same thing. At that point, I was kind of depressed. But then it all came together for me, and I won the rest of my fights more impressively."

"The best moment for me," Breland says, "was when I was on the medal stand. When they played the anthem, I knew it was over. People had been saying since 1982 that I couldn't lose. That's a lot of pressure for a kid. All the pressure to look good and win took a lot of the fun out of the Olympics for me."

But now Breland looks back on that long-ago time and acknowledges, "Right now, I have to say, the Olympic gold medal means more to me than my professional championships. Championships come and go, but they can never take an Olympic gold medal away from you."

★ ★ ★

More on Mark Breland—

In the past, I've recounted the recollections of various boxing person-alities regarding the first professional fight they ever saw. Breland has a special memory of his own.

"I grew up in the Tompkins Projects in Bed-Stuy [the Bedford-Stuyvesant section of Brooklyn]," Breland recalls. "There was a man named Elijah Best, who lived on the same floor as my family. When I was seven, he bought me some boxing gloves and taught me a few fundamentals about how to box. Then he took me to Madison Square Garden to see the first fight between Muhammad Ali and Joe Frazier [on March 8, 1971]. It was just the two of us. We were way up in the cheap seats. I was like, 'Wow!' The excitement, the drama. Ali was sticking, moving, dancing. But Frazier kept coming, throwing punches. He knocked Ali down in the last round and won."

Thereafter, Best introduced Breland to George Washington, who trained him from that point on.

"In 1980," Mark says, continuing the saga, "I fought at 139 pounds in the novice division of the Golden Gloves. Those were the days when the finals of the Gloves were in the main arena at the Garden. You'd come out of the tunnel and go to the ring. The lights would be out. Then they'd call your name and the spotlight would go right on you. The moment that happened, my mind flashed back to Ali-Frazier. I said to myself, 'If I never box again, I've made it. I'm standing here, getting ready to fight, right where Ali and Joe Frazier fought.'"

★ ★ ★

Like a lot of writers, I get emails from readers on a regular basis. Some of them are particularly thought-provoking. Thus, I pass along the thoughts of Benjamin Barrientes (a playwright and boxing fan who lives in San Antonio).

Benjamin was considering courage and wrote, "I was very impressed by Israel Vasquez when he stopped his participation in the first Vasquez-Marquez fight. This was an amazing move given the cultural yoke of 'machismo' that is cultivated in some circles. Many fighters have taken unnecessary punishment because of their concept of 'machismo.' Vasquez lived to fight another day and reclaimed his title by beating Rafael Marquez twice. Forging a 'Nuevo Machismo' is not going to be easy. But the demands of the fight game need to be examined."

Let the debate begin.

★ ★ ★

When fans buy tickets for an intelligently run sporting event, they're told what time the competition will start. But that's rarely the case in boxing, where the starting time for the first fight on most cards is shrouded in mystery. Indeed, there are times (such as the Joe Calzaghe versus Roy Jones card at Madison Square Garden) when the first fight starts before the doors have been opened to the paying public.

Can you imagine buying tickets for an NBA basketball game and not being allowed into the arena until after the start of the first quarter?

I didn't think so.

★ ★ ★

With boxing fans bemoaning the state of the heavyweight division, it's worth remembering that things weren't much better a hundred years ago.

James J. Jeffries relinquished the heavyweight crown when he retired in 1905. Later that year, Marvin Hart beat Jack Root for the vacant throne. Hart, in turn, lost to the lightly-regarded 5-foot-7-inch Tommy Burns. As 1908 began, Burns was heavyweight champion of the world.

Jeffries was a great fighter. He'd been undefeated when he gave up his title and suffered the only loss of his career in an ill-advised comeback fight against Jack Johnson in 1910. He's largely forgotten today, except as an appendage to Papa Jack, and that's a shame.

In the spirit of remembrance, here are a trio of insights from Jeffries:

- [On the family life of a professional fighter]: "Marriage and boxing don't go together."
- [Explaining why he was retiring as an undefeated champion in 1905]: "I've got all the money I want. There's nobody to fight me. To

hell with this business and the championship too. What's the championship? A lot of yaps run after me to pound me on the back. They don't give a damn about me. I'm nobody; they're yelling for the champ. Well, I'm sick of it."

• [On his seventy-fifth birthday, reflecting back on his loss to Jack Johnson]: "We can't fight nature. Youth tells in the long run. I don't know if I could have beaten him at my best, but it would have been a better fight."

★ ★ ★

One of the joys in covering a big fight is that I never know what "extras" fight night will bring. On October 18, 2008, I was in the press room at Boardwalk Hall in Atlantic City readying for Kelly Pavlik versus Bernard Hopkins when Joe Frazier came in.

There was a time when Frazier regarded me as an adversary. I was Muhammad Ali's biographer and thus "Ali's man." But in recent years, Joe and I have developed a friendship of our own.

Joe and I sat at a table in the press room and talked for an hour. "How the heavyweights got the way they are now, I couldn't tell you," he lamented. "But it's sad. There's one world. How can there be four heavyweight champions of the world? When I fought, people wouldn't put up with two heavyweight champions. There was me and Jimmy Ellis; so we fought and there was one. Then Ali came back and we fought and there was one. Boxing is the best sport in the world and they messed it up."

Joe talked fondly of George Foreman. "Big George beat up on me two times," he said. "Someday, I'm gonna walk over to him, kiss him on the cheek, slip to the side, and hit him with the hook . . . Not really," he added. "George is a good man. He came from a place that's just as hard as the place I came from. And he could fight."

Then Joe uttered a thought that isn't often heard from him. "Muhammad could fight too."

I thought back to Hugh McIlvanney's words: "Mentioning nobility in connection with boxing is chancy, but exposure to men like Joe Frazier encourages such boldness."

Now Joe was rooted in the past. "That night at Madison Square Garden," he reminisced, "fifteenth round when I put Ali down. A fight like that. I stood where no one else ever stood."

The conversation segued to Joe's childhood. "I grew up fast," he recalled. "I became a man early, so there wasn't much time for games. But I played a little baseball around the time I was twelve, thirteen years old. My position was catcher. I was always afraid the ball would tip off the bat, come up fast, and hit me in the face. I liked the hitting part of the game more."

And we talked about the music we'd listened to when we were young. Elvis Presley, Little Richard, the Motown revolution.

"Don't forget Fats Domino," Joe offered. And he began to sing.

"I found my thrill . . . on Blueberry Hill . . ."

I joined in.

"On Blueberry Hill . . . when I found you . . ."

And on it went through "the wind in the willow," "love's sweet melody," and "all of those vows we made" that "were never to be."

In everyone's life, there are moments that have no meaning to the world at large but are special to the person who experienced them. I'll always smile when I think back on sitting with Joe Frazier and singing *Blueberry Hill*.

The inspiration for this article came from watching an underdog with a 1-and-2 record knock a 2-and-0 favorite woozy.

One–Punch Magic

It's a feeling that most people never experience in their lifetime; the feeling of landing a punch that separates an opponent from his senses and leaves him lying unconscious on the ring canvas.

A distant parallel might be the harmonic feeling of swinging a baseball bat and—CRACK—The ball hits the sweet part of the bat and rockets out over the fence in deep left-centerfield.

A perfect punch is a work of art. In its highest form, it's Rocky Marciano, behind on the judges' scorecards, crushing Jersey Joe Walcott with a brutal right hand to seize the heavyweight throne. It's Sugar Ray Robinson reclaiming the middleweight crown with a single left hook to the jaw of Gene Fullmer.

In recent months, I've talked with world champions and club fighters, veterans and novices, and asked them to describe what it feels like to land a perfect knock-out punch. Their thoughts, joined together, follow:

★   ★   ★

A lot of punches land solid in a fight. But the leverage isn't quite right or you're a fraction of an inch off target. This time, everything was right. Perfect leverage; perfect timing; perfect placement. I felt my knuckles land flush at the moment of impact.

BOOM !

It was like a jolt of electricity running up my arm all the way to my shoulder.

It's a sin to land and wait for a receipt. So instinctively, I drew my arm back the way I've been taught and started to slide into position for the next move. Then I realized I didn't need it.

He went down. And before he hit the canvas, I knew he wasn't getting up.

The crowd was going crazy. The roar was so loud, it was a little scary.

I'd gotten a bit tired as the fight went on. Now I felt as though I could go twenty more rounds if I had to.

I felt joy, jubilation. There was relief that it was over. The tension had been building in me since I signed the contract; but I'd won, so now that weight was off my shoulders.

Then I thought about the other guy. It was like, "Let him be okay. Let him get up."

After a while, he did. That was good.

In the dressing room afterward, my body felt different. I felt like Superman and my muscles were made of steel. I could beat any man alive. It was the sweetest feeling in the world, like falling in love for the first time. I was in heaven.

It wasn't until I was in bed that night that I started to decompress. Then I took everything apart, every move, every split-second, and played them over and over again in my mind. I didn't stop until I fell asleep. And then I went through it all over again in my dreams.

I still remember how it felt. It still goes through my mind from time to time.

There's an ongoing struggle to provide the best medical care possible for fighters. Too often, it's a losing battle.

Medical Issues and Boxing

The March 15th rematch between Manny Pacquiao and Juan Manuel Marquez was a great fight, but a question lingers in its aftermath.

Marquez suffered two cuts during the fight. The first (a small cut beside his right eyebrow) was insignificant. The second (a horrible gaping wound on his right eyelid) was sustained in round nine and was so deep that it filleted open. Thereafter, Nacho Beristan (Marquez's trainer) could be seen on television packing what appeared to be a long yellow string soaked in an undetermined liquid solution into the wound, covering the cut with Vaseline, and sending Marquez out for the next round with the string still inside the wound. This appeared to happen after both the ninth and eleventh rounds. But the ring physician assigned to Marquez's corner appeared not to notice. Or maybe he noticed and just didn't care. The HBO telecast was inconclusive regarding what happened after round ten.

On March 31st, Keith Kizer (executive director of the Nevada State Athletic Commission) said he'd been told that the string had been soaked in epinephrine (a legal coagulant) and that it had been removed from the laceration before Marquez left his corner for each round.

Kizer subsequently learned that the packing had been left in the cut, but said, "Our primary concern is the safety of the fighter. There's no rule against leaving something like that in a cut, so it's at the discretion of the ring doctor whether or not to allow it."

Michael Schwartz takes a contrary view. Schwartz is president of the American Association of Professional Ringside Physicians and is widely recognized as a first-rate ring doctor. When apprised of the NSAC's position, Schwartz maintained, "That's ridiculous. It's totally absurd. It shocks me. Anytime there's a foreign object in the eye, you're increasing the danger to the fighter. If a cut is bad enough to warrant doing something like that, the ring doctor should stop the fight."

The treatment of Marquez's cut involves a serious medical issue.

The Nevada Annotated Code does not specifically state that it's illegal to place a foreign object inside a cut and leave it there during a round. But a little common sense is in order.

Can a cornerman legally put a butterfly bandage on a cut between rounds?

Can a cornerman legally suture a cut between rounds?

Can a cornerman legally leave packing in a fighter's nose and send him out for the next round?

What if a string packed into a laceration dangles out during a round and gets into the fighter's eye?

Come on, guys! The referee requires a fighter's corner to wipe extra Vaseline off a cut. And you're telling the world that it's all right for a fighter to come out with a foreign object packed into a laceration?

The core problem here is that the Nevada State Athletic Commission has a policy of refusing to admit that it ever makes a mistake. That might be good "spin politics." But it's lousy regulation because, without correction, bad decisions become standard practice.

It's precisely because Nevada is a leader that the NSAC should call a halt to the ludicrous practice of allowing foreign objects to be packed into lacerations between rounds. The appropriate response now would be to say, "We missed it when it happened in Pacquiao-Marquez II. It shouldn't have been allowed to happen then, and we won't allow it to happen again in the future."

★   ★   ★

Last month (March 2009), a press release was circulated throughout the boxing community. Its headline (in solid capital letters with an exclamation point) read, "THANK YOU, JOSE SULAIMAN and the WBC!" A sub-headline informed readers, "WBC Meets Members' Needs with Health Care Plan."

Not exactly.

The plan provides for the partial payment of medical expenses incurred in conjunction with illnesses, accidents, and other medical conditions. But it will NOT cover conditions related to boxing. That's a huge hole in the coverage.

If a fighter needs medical care for a broken jaw, detached retina, or other condition suffered as a consequence of the sweet science, he's on his own. That's like a health care plan for members of the military that doesn't cover combat-related injuries.

How will one determine if a condition is related to boxing? After all, there are gray areas. That determination will be made in the first instance by a claims examiner hired by the plan provider.

So let's put the WBC-endorsed plan in perspective.

Glenn Davidow is an insurance broker. His job is to procure policies that groups (or individuals) need when they seek insurance. Davidow was approached by Jill Diamond of World Boxing Cares about the possibility of health care insurance for boxers. He took the issue to the Consolidated Workers Association (CWA), which agreed to underwrite the plan.

CWA is not an insurance company. It's a corporation that offers life-style benefits such as discounted vacation packages and pre-paid legal fees to small employers, church groups, trade associations, and the like. In this case, CWA is offering a health care plan. Because of various state and federal laws, the offering is technically not "insurance."

Plan participants will pay dues (not "premiums") to CWA. Brad Wessler of Claims & Benefits Management Inc. (CBM) is the administrator hired by CWA. He will collect the plan dues and adjudicate claims for benefits.

The one-page press release (which modestly referred to the WBC eight times) states that the plan is open to "the entire boxing community." That, apparently, is not the case.

Davidow says that, most likely, the plan will be limited to people licensed by a government athletic commission and their families. Wessler says, "We're not talking about a clearly defined membership group. I don't think a final determination has been made yet as to who will be eligible to participate."

Either way; the rationale for limiting the plan to "the boxing community" is essentially a marketing tool. Keep in mind; as far as CWA is concerned, this is a for-profit venture (like selling discounted vacation packages). The WBC endorsement is significant primarily for marketing purposes. The program could be run just as easily with the endorsement of the Association of Boxing Commissions or another world sanctioning organization.

There will be three coverage plans, each of which will offer a different level of benefits. Depending on the plan chosen, individual rates are expected to run from $97 to $195 per month with family rates ranging from $143 to $445 monthly. These rates have been set by actuaries based on the expected demographics of the insured group. A similar package could be put together for a lower-risk group (such as certified public accountants and their families), in which case either the premiums would be less or the benefits would be greater.

Because CWA is doing this to make money (nothing wrong with that), the benefits paid to plan participants will be limited (as they are under most insurance policies). That includes limits on the amount paid for each procedure, each doctor's visit, and hospital stays of varying duration.

Health-care providers will be allowed to charge more than the benefit amount, and most of them will. By way of example, it's unlikely that the benefits paid will come close to covering the full cost of hospitalization. Plan participants will be responsible for paying the unreimbursed portion of all health care costs. But Wessler says that, if a participant uses an in-network provider, the co-payment that he (or she) is responsible for will often be less than would otherwise be the case because CWA has negotiated with in-network providers for reduced rates.

With certain narrow exceptions, pre-existing conditions will not be covered for the first twelve months of a person's participation in the plan.

The powers that be hope to launch the plan on June 1, 2008; shortly after it is presented at the North American Boxing Federation convention in Tuscon.

Let's see if anyone affiliated with the WBC winds up in a preferred position to sell the insurance.

Boxing, more than any other sport, is kept alive on the pages of books.

Notes from the Literary Front

John L. Sullivan's last fight (other than exhibitions) was in 1892. James J. Corbett retired from the ring in 1903. Bob Fitzsimmons followed a decade later. It's safe to say that no one alive today saw them ply their trade. And with the passage of time, less and less is remembered about them.

A thirty-five-year-old Iowa attorney named Adam J. Pollack wants to fill that void and restore the patina that once affixed to boxing's early gloved heavyweight champions. In pursuit of that goal, he has authored biographies of Sullivan, Corbett, and Fitzsimmons. James J. Jeffries is due in early 2009.

Pollack is a graduate of the University of Iowa School of Law. He spent several years as a prosecutor in Iowa City with the Johnson County Attorney's Office and now practices law as a criminal defense attorney ("a lot of drunk driving cases," he says). He has a boxing background, having won the Iowa Golden Gloves in the 139-pound division when he was in law school. "But it was nothing to brag about," he acknowledges. "I always had a better brain than body. I understood the sport well, but didn't have the physical ability. I'm a better writer and coach than I was a fighter."

As a coach, Pollack has seen two of his fighters advance to the quarter-finals of the men's National Golden Gloves. That's not bad considering the limited talent pool in Iowa. And then there's Emily Klinefelter, who Adam has coached since the day she walked into the gym.

Emily, now twenty-four, was valedictorian of her class at City High School in Iowa City. As an amateur, she won three U.S. Championships, four PAL National Championships, four Ringside World Championships, and two National Golden Gloves Championships. She also captured gold medals at the 2004 Women's World Invitational Tournament in Taiwan (110 pounds) and the 2006 Pan American Games in Argentina (119 pounds).

Kleinfelter is currently managed by Cameron Dunkin and married to Pollack. She made her pro debut with a four-round triumph in Reno in early 2008.

Where his writing is concerned, Pollack explains, "My original idea was to write one book that covered all the heavyweight champions from Sullivan on. I had so many unanswered questions about these guys, and the books that had been written weren't as thorough as I would have liked. Then I started researching and realized that the right way to do it would be a book on each champion. I'm committed in my own mind to at least three more books: James Jeffries, Marvin Hart, and Tommy Burns. After that, if it stops being fun, I'll stop."

"I want to take people back as though they were reading the daily newspaper reports, which is all that most boxing fans had in those days," Pollack continues. "And I want people to know what it was like for the fighters in their time. I'm not doing it for the money. Writing every detail about obscure fights that took place a hundred years ago doesn't sell a lot of books. I put thousands of hours into each volume and don't get back minimum wage. But I make enough from my law practice to pay the bills. It's a nice life. I'm happy."

The heart of Pollack's research is his reliance upon primary sources. He reads thousands of contemporary newspaper and magazine articles for each book. "Fortunately," he says, "the University of Iowa has a good library and a good loan program. But it costs me a fortune to photocopy the microfilm."

The Fitzsimmons book has the same strengths and weaknesses as Pollack's two previous efforts. It's exhaustively researched. There's drama in the author's telling of the brutal beating that Fitzsimmons administered to The Nonpariel Jack Dempsey in their world middleweight championship encounter. The build-up to Fitzsimmons versus James Corbett for the heavyweight crown is even more compelling. And there's a very good account of Fitzsimmons's loss by disqualification to Tom Sharkey in a fight that appeared to have been fixed with the primary villain being referee Wyatt Earp. At times, the writing is repetitious. But a reader who sticks with it will come away with a sense of time, place, and Fitzsimmons's greatness. And more significantly, the book is a treasure trove of documentation gathered together in one place.

Take, for example, the account of Corbett-Fitzsimmons written by T. T. Williams in the March 18, 1897, *New York Journal*. Fitzsimmons took a horrible beating early in the fight, but rallied to knock Corbett out in the fourteenth round.

"I saw a face that will haunt me until time has defaced it from my memory," Williams wrote. "There was no savagery in it, and some intelligence. There was a leer and a grin and a look of patient suffering and dogged courage. It was the face of a brave man fighting an uphill fight with lip torn and bleeding, nostrils plugged with coagulated blood, ears swollen, eyes half-closed and blinking in the sunlight, with every line and muscle drawn to an angle of suffering. Fitzsimmons's face was not cruel nor passionate. It was clear; and never once did he lose his hope of success, his watchfulness over his opponent, his waiting for an opening. It was one face from the time that first blood was claimed and allowed in the fifth round till the victory was in his hands."

Boxing fans should be grateful that Adam Pollack is writing these books. He's performing a real service in furtherance of the preservation of boxing history.

★   ★   ★

My Life and Battles (Praeger Publishers) is an edited translation of articles by Jack Johnson that were published in France when Johnson was at the peak of his glory. Three years later (in 1914), an abridged version of the articles was published (also in France) in book form.

Translator Christopher Rivers acknowledges, "The memoir is not an entirely factually accurate account of the events of Johnson's life and career." Nonetheless, he calls it "a fascinating piece of self-mythologizing that provides substantial insights into how Johnson perceived himself and wished to be perceived by others."

Geoffrey Ward (author of *Unforgivable Blackness: The Rise and Fall of Jack Johnson*), is in accord. He writes in a foreword, "The [manuscript] presents a portrait of Johnson as he himself wished to be portrayed. No man ever tended his own legend more assiduously than Jack Johnson did. And 'legend' is the operative word. His autobiographical writings are filled with exaggerations, embellishments, and outright inventions."

Regardless, the book is an interesting slice of boxing history.

The same can be said of Clay Moyle's biography, *Sam Langford: Boxing's Greatest Uncrowned Champion* (Bennett & Hastings).

In a career that saw hundreds of recorded fights from 1902 through 1925, Langford fought men like Joe Gans (who he defeated at age seventeen), Stanley Ketchel (they drew in a six-round non-title bout), and Jack Johnson (Langford lost a 15-round decision before Johnson became champion).

Barrel-chested and only 5-feet-7-inches tall, Langford was at his best as a middleweight. But the exigencies of boxing dictated that he fight heavyweights Joe Jeannette (on 14 occasions), Sam McVea (13), and Harry Wills (16)—a total of 43 times.

"He was a real professional," Wills said when their wars were done. "The kind of fighter you'd like to be but know that, no matter how hard you try, you'll never make it. When Sam hit you in the body, you'd kind of look around half-expecting to see his glove sticking out of your back. When he hit you on the chin, you didn't think at all until they brought you back to life. When he knocked me out in New Orleans, I thought I'd been killed."

Because of the color barrier, Langford never had the opportunity to etch his name in history alongside those of boxing's other gloved champions. But John L. Sullivan, who had drawn the color line during his own reign, declared in 1909, "Sam Langford is the world's best. He can whip them all right now, one after the other."

Jack Johnson opined, "Sam Langford was the toughest little son of a bitch that ever lived." Once Johnson became champion, he refused to fight Langford again.

And Jack Dempsey conceded in his autobiography, "The hell I feared no man. There was one man I wouldn't fight because I knew he would flatten me. I was afraid of Sam Langford."

Moyle's writing is cliché-ridden at times ("Sam Edgar Langford entered the world fists clenched on March 4, 1886") and far from lyrical. But the book fleshes out Langford's ring record. A few of his fights (most notably the battles against Gans and Ketchel) are nicely told. There's horror in the recounting of Langford continuing to fight while blind in one eye and suffering from a cataract in the other. And there's a moving retelling of the unsuccessful effort to restore Langford's eyesight as well as the poverty that enveloped him as he grew older.

At book's end, one has to agree with Moyle's conclusion, "There was certainly no other boxer during this period who deserved a chance to fight for a world championship more than Sam Langford."

It's a shame he never got the chance.

★ ★ ★

There's a tendency to look askance at "self-published" books. In today's computer age, anyone with a checkbook can be published. But every now and then, a self-published offering is worth the read.

Sorcery at Caesars by Steve Marantz (Inkwater Press) is about Sugar Ray Leonard, Marvelous Marvin Hagler, and their 1987 megafight, which, in Marantz's words, gave Leonard "bragging rights to an era."

The book was published pursuant to a "hybrid" arrangement. The publisher absorbed more of the costs than it normally does. But there was no advance and Marantz paid some of the expenses.

"I couldn't get a traditional publisher interested in this," Marantz says. "It's a dated story; I'm an unknown writer. But writing the book was a rewarding experience. People ask me, 'Why did you go to all that trouble if you're not making any money from it?' The answer, I suppose, is, 'I'm a writer.'"

A good one.

Sorcery at Caesars is entertaining history. Both fighters and their careers are nicely sketched: Leonard (the 1976 Olympic gold medalist and darling of America, who made $40,000 for his first pro fight) and Hagler (a talented amateur, who had turned pro three years earlier and earned fifty dollars for his first fight).

Hagler is sympathetically drawn. In a foreword to *Sorcery at Caesars,* Leigh Montville writes, "Marvin was the common man doing uncommon things. He began local and stayed local."

Conversely, it's clear that Marantz is not a fan of Leonard as a person. While acknowledging that there was "a touch of 007 in his suave and cold appraisal," the author opines, "Leonard was larger than life and sometimes smaller." Kenny Leonard (Ray's older brother) is quoted as saying,

"People look at Ray and say, 'Oh, he's a nice kid, little smile and every-thing.' But Ray got something inside of him, you know, it's terrible. It's a completely dark side."

Marantz does some interesting work in plumbing the depths of that dark side and the havoc that cocaine wreaked on Leonard's life in the mid-1980s. He also makes the case for believing that, at a crucial time in his career, Hagler succumbed to cocaine (although Marvin denies it).

Whatever the temptation, Mike Trainer (Leonard's longtime attorney) later observed, "Ray is always looking at the edge of the cliff, fascinated as to how close he can get to it." That fascination with life on the edge coupled with the lure of more glory and more dollars led Leonard to Hagler.

Marantz's writing flows nicely, and that's true of his description of the fight as well. Hagler was a 3-to-1 favorite. But he didn't bring his "A" game that night, while Leonard fought as well as he could.

Judge Lou Filippo scored the bout 115–113 for Hagler. Dave Moretti called it 115–113 in Leonard's favor. For the record, watching the fight on closed-circuit television, this writer had it 114–114. In other words, the decision could have gone either way. As it was, the third judge (Jo Jo Guerra, who was in la-la land) voted 118–110 for Leonard.

"Leonard," Marantz writes, "sold himself to two judges as a salesman sells a product, a con man sells a lie, or a magician sells an illusion. More important, he sold himself to Hagler, who gave him just enough respect and room to close the deal."

Or as Larry Merchant said years later, "Leonard stole it fair and square."

★   ★   ★

Four Kings by George Kimball recounts the epic nine battles con-tested among Sugar Ray Leonard, Marvin Hagler, Thomas Hearns, and Roberto Duran between 1980 and 1989.

It was a special time for boxing fans and more special for those who, like Kimball, experienced the drama firsthand from the inside.

These nine fights defined their participants' greatness.

Leonard-Hearns I and Hagler-Hearns are on the short list of "great-est fights of all time" with Leonard-Duran I close behind.

Leonard-Duran II was remarkable because of its "no mas" ending, while Hagler-Leonard, Hagler-Duran, and Duran-Hearns each had their own drama.

Leonard-Hearns II and Leonard-Duran III were anticlimactic. By then, the combatants were well past their prime.

Kimball writes with insight and humor. The bigger the fight, the better he tells it. He also offers a thought that's essential to anyone who wants to understand the sweet science.

"In the boxing ring," Kimball observes, "pain is not merely a possibility, but a certainty. The courage to persevere in the face of that pain distinguishes the boxer from the ordinary man."

Too often, fighters are predators in the ring and prey out of it.

Shelly Finkel's "Recruiting and Signing" Fund

Shelly Finkel is at odds with Lamont and Anthony Peterson, two fighters that he has co-managed since the inception of their professional careers. On April 30, 2008, the Petersons sent letters to Finkel terminating their relationship with him. They now claim that Finkel has defrauded them out of hundreds of thousands of dollars.

Over the years, Finkel has represented numerous champions, including Mike Tyson and the Klitschkos. He's boxing's version of Talleyrand, the French diplomat who served virtually every ruler from Louis XVI through the Reign of Terror, the rise and fall of Napoleon, and the Restoration.

Finkel's proponents say that he's a shrewd businessman who engineers deals in good faith that result in large sums of money being paid to his fighters.

Shelly's detractors have a different view. Don King (who has had his own issues with fighters) opines, "Anyone who tries to deal in good faith with Shelly Finkel winds up getting Finkeled. And that's not good. Finkeling is much worse than tinkeling. It's hard to explain to someone who has never been Finkeled what the experience is like. He does it with words, but words fail to describe it."

Everyone agrees that, as a manager, Finkel has a fiduciary obligation to his fighters. That's a different set of responsibilities from a promoter, whose job entails giving as little money as possible to fighters so he can keep as much money as possible for himself.

A decade ago, Lamont and Anthony Peterson were homeless, sleeping in abandoned automobiles on the streets of Washington, D.C. Then Barry Hunter (the owner of a local construction company) and his wife took them in. Hunter also taught the brothers how to box.

The Petersons are now recognized as having championship potential. Lamont is a twenty-four-year-old junior-welterweight with a 24–0 (11 KOs) record. Anthony, twenty-three, is a lightweight whose ledger stands at 26–0 with 19 knockouts.

The Petersons met Finkel in March 2003 at the U.S. National Amateur Championships. In July 2004, they signed boxer-manager contracts with him. Each fighter received a $21,000 signing bonus that was paid out over twelve months. At the request of the brothers, Finkel agreed to split his 30 percent managerial fee equally with Hunter, who became their co-manager.

At Finkel's urging, the Petersons signed bout agreements on a fight-by-fight basis with Prize Fight Promotions (a Tennessee company headed by Brian Young). Between 2004 and 2007, Prize Fight promoted approximately twenty fights for each of them.

Last month, the Petersons signed promotional contracts with Top Rank over the objection of Finkel, who was negotiating to sign them with Golden Boy. In response, on April 18, Finkel filed an arbitration proceeding against the brothers. Hunter was also named as a respondent in the proceeding.

Finkel's claim alleges that the Petersons and Hunter breached the provisions of the fighters' managerial agreements in that they retained Jeff Fried (a Washington, D.C., attorney) to negotiate a boxing promotion agreement with Top Rank on the Peterson's behalf without Finkel's consent; that no such promotional agreement can be entered into without Finkel's consent; and that the Petersons and Hunter have attempted to "freeze out" Finkel from the Petersons' boxing career in violation of his rights as a co-manager. It seeks $300,000 in damages, the award of attorneys fees, and injunctive relief.

Last week, Finkel declared, "These are two kids who didn't even make the Olympic team, and they're way ahead of the kids who beat them in the Olympic trials. I feel like I've done a phenomenal job with them. I always did what was best for them, and then they decided they can do without me."

"Why do you think they left you?" Finkel was asked.

"In my opinion, it's all about greed," he said.

On May 15, 2008, the Petersons filed an answer and counterclaim in the arbitration proceeding.

The Peterson's counterclaim alleges that, shortly after they signed with Finkel, Shelly suggested to Barry Hunter that the brothers have their professional bouts promoted by Prize Fight Promotions. As stated in the counterclaim, "Finkel described Prize Fight as a small promoter and represented to Anthony and Lamont (through Hunter) that it would be a good idea for the Petersons to initially fight 'under the radar' until they achieved great success, at which time an effort could be undertaken to put them together with a more prominent boxing promoter."

By late 2006, the Petersons were generating considerable interest in the boxing community. At that point, the counterclaim continues, "Hunter began to inquire of Finkel and Prize Fight Promotions as to when the Petersons were going to receive more lucrative fights. In response, Finkel told Hunter to be patient. But Prize Fight Promotions was more direct, and Hunter then learned something as to which [neither] he nor Anthony and Lamont had any knowledge: that Prize Fight had been promised by Finkel an exclusive promotional contract with the Petersons, that Finkel had received in excess of $400,000 in return for securing Prize Fight's exclusive rights, and that Prize Fight was upset because no such contract had been signed."

"In March 2007," according to the counterclaim, "Finkel denied [to Hunter] that he had received any monies in connection with promising to sign Anthony and Lamont with Prize Fight Promotions and claimed that the monies related to a totally separate deal having nothing to do with the Petersons. After Hunter told the Prize Fight Promotions principals that Finkel had denied receiving any such monies, they told him that Finkel had been lying and [Russ Young of Prize Fight] faxed to Hunter a letter that had been sent from Finkel to Prize Fight."

"Russ woke me up to the truth," Hunter says.

The letter, which is attached to the Petersons' counterclaim as Exhibit A, is dated October 15, 2004, written on Shelly Finkel Management stationery, addressed to Michael Lampley of Prize Fight promotions, and signed by Finkel.

In relevant part, the letter states, "Hi Michael, I want to follow up on your letter regarding the 2004 amateurs, a recap of our agreement, and where we are at present. Originally, we were supposed to be funded with $500,000 for the recruiting and signing of the best 2004 Olympians and amateurs. Instead, we ended up being financed for $425,000 of which

$25,000 went to [name unintelligible]. The status of the individual fighters is as follows: (1) Lamont and Anthony Peterson—They are going to be exclusively with Prizefight Promotions as we discussed. I believe that one or both of the brothers are going to put Prizefight Promotions on the map and, with a little luck, we will recoup all of your investment from them."

Six other fighters were listed in the letter. None of them signed with Prize Fight.

When the Petersons and Hunter learned about the letter, they weren't sure what it meant or what to do. Hunter says that he tried repeatedly to arrange for a conference call between himself, the Petersons, Finkel, and representatives of Prize Fight. The counterclaim alleges, "Finkel agreed but avoided causing the call to take place."

Then Finkel began urging the brothers to leave Prize Fight and sign a promotional contract with Golden Boy.

Finally, in spring 2008, the Petersons retained Jeff Fried (a Washington, D.C., attorney) to represent their interests. Fried recalls, "Anthony and Lamont came to me and said, 'All along, Shelly has been telling us we should be with Prize Fight. Now he's telling us, "Golden Boy, Golden Boy." And we don't understand about the $425,000. What should we do?'"

Fried and the Petersons decided that their approach should be, "Don't get even; get ahead. Let's decide who's the best promoter for this situation."

Thereafter, Fried sent identical proposals for the Petersons' services to Bob Arum at Top Rank and Richard Schaefer at Golden Boy. Arum telephoned the day he received the proposal and made a good offer. Schaefer took several days to respond. Then, he telephoned Fried and said, 'They can spar with Oscar; and Golden Boy will put them on the De La Hoya–Forbes undercard." But the offer that Schaefer ultimately made was much less appealing than Arum's. And as Fried later observed, "Lamont and Anthony want to be world champions, not sparring partners for Oscar De La Hoya."

In mid–April, the Petersons went to Fried's office for conference calls with Arum and Schaefer. "It was important to me that they speak directly to both promoters," Fried says. "I wanted them to hear directly from each guy what the offers were. After the conference calls, they told me that they absolutely wanted to go with Arum. The decision was totally theirs.

Lamont called Schaefer and told him that day. Richard was professional and gracious about it. Shelly responded in a different way."

"Lamont and Anthony didn't want to act against Finkel," Fried continues. "They wanted to move on. They're more comfortable in a gym than in a lawyer's office. But once Shelly filed for arbitration, they had no choice."

The counterclaim followed. It states that the Petersons signed their managerial contracts with Finkel without legal advice and without any review on their behalf by an attorney. It notes that, by virtue of his position as their manager, "Finkel incurred a fiduciary duty to act solely in their best interests and therefore owed them a duty of utmost fidelity, transparency, and honesty in all of his dealings with them."

It then claims, "Finkel egregiously violated his fiduciary duty . . . engaged in illegal and unconscionable conduct including but not limited to fraud, breach of fiduciary duty, and violation of the Muhammad Ali Act," and was terminated by the Petersons as their manager as a consequence of his "outrageous, disloyal, and illegal actions."

More specifically, the Petersons' arbitration filing alleges:

> • "Finkel entered into a secret agreement whereby he was paid approximately $400,000 in return for obtaining exclusive promotional rights to counterclaimants [for] Prize Fight Promotions without advising counterclaimants or their co-manager of his arrangement and, indeed, concealing it from them."
> • "Anthony and Lamont knew nothing about Finkel's arrangement, were not told about it until years after the management agreements were executed, and received no part of the consideration paid to Finkel. When eventually confronted with the facts regarding his breach of fiduciary duty and the Muhammad Ali Act, Finkel lied to the Petersons and claimed that the monies received by him were unrelated to the Petersons."
> • "Finkel insisted, against [the Petersons'] best interests and for his own purposes, on steering them to Golden Boy. In late 2007 and early 2008, when it became clear that counterclaimants' careers would be furthered by association with a prominent promoter, Finkel declined to seek out the best promotional arrangement for counterclaimants and, instead, endeavored to persuade counterclaimants to deal only with Finkel's favored promoter [Golden Boy], whose offer was inferior and who was touted by Finkel for Finkel's personal benefit and not in the best interests of counterclaimants."

When asked about the counterclaim, Finkel said that, in 2003, he entered into an agreement with a Tennessee investment group called AMP Entertainment. The signatories to that deal were Finkel and, on behalf of AMP, Mike Lampley (who is also an equity participant in Prize Fight) and third person named Don Mercer.

According to Finkel, "AMP agreed to fund me with up to $500,000 to scout and build relationships with kids who were hoping to be on the 2004 U.S. Olympic team. The $425,000 was reimbursement for my expenses. The deal was, if any of these kids made the team and signed with me when they turned pro, I would then go to promoters and tell them that AMP was interested in becoming involved. And if the promoter that the kids and I chose wanted AMP to be involved, AMP would put up all of the signing bonuses that the promoter paid to the fighter in exchange for AMP receiving fifty percent of the promotional profits. There was never a deal between me and Prize Fight. I had a deal with AMP. The $425,000 came from AMP. And if a future promoter didn't want AMP to be involved, then there was no further obligation to AMP."

Finkel said there is documentary evidence that supports his position, but declined to make the documents available to this writer.

Whatever deal might have existed between Finkel and AMP, counsel for the Petersons can be expected to make the following points with regard to the issues at hand:

> (1) The October 15, 2004, letter from Finkel to Lampley was addressed to Mike Lampley at Prize Fight, not AMP Entertainment.
>
> (2) Finkel said in an interview with this writer that the 2003 AMP agreement was limited to 2004 Olympians. The October 15, 2004, letter was written well after the 2004 Olympics, when it was clear that neither Peterson had made the 2004 U.S. Olympic team.
>
> (3) Finkel (as co-manager) paid $21,000 signing bonuses to Lamont and Anthony Peterson, but they never signed a longterm agreement with Prize Fight. Thus, even if the Petersons had been covered by the AMP agreement, there was no promoter's signing bonus for AMP to pay and AMP had no interest in the promotional profits from their fights.

The Petersons' case is reminiscent of litigation that flowed from a $1,925,000 "packaging fee" that Finkel received from Showtime in conjunction with his representation of Juan Diaz, Rocky Juarez, Jeff Lacy, and Francisco Bojado after the 2000 Olympics. That matter was quietly settled. This case might not go away so quietly, and the impact could be far-reaching.

During an April 4, 2007, teleconference call, Richard Schaefer introduced Rocky Juarez (who was fighting on the De La Hoya–Mayweather undercard) and told the world, "Before I turn it over to Rocky, I would like to mention as well Rocky's manager, Shelly Finkel. This is the first fighter Golden Boy is signing with Shelly. And I'm really happy with the relationship over the past months that I was able to develop with Shelly. It's a pleasure to work with Shelly. And I really appreciate the friendship and strategic alliance we have formed with Shelly."

When asked last week about his relationship with Golden Boy, Finkel said, "By my nature, I usually work with one promoter at a time. First it was Main Events. Then it was Gary Shaw. Right now, I'm bringing a group of young fighters to Golden Boy. But I've made no promise of exclusivity to anyone. Golden Boy has not reimbursed me for any expenses or paid one penny to me in conjunction with any of the fighters I represent except for my managerial fee, which is deducted from each fighter's purse and paid directly to me by Golden Boy. Each fighter is fully aware of what that fee is."

Meanwhile, Barry Hunter wants the boxing community to know, "I'm just happy that Lamont and Anthony are happy. They have a good promoter now, and I hope they get everything they deserve."

As for the Petersons themselves; Lamont says, "It's hard to put into words what I'm feeling. I feel betrayed; I feel used. We trusted Shelly. He was our manager. He was supposed to get the best opportunities for us, not for him. Shelly keeps saying, he loves us; he loves us. And look what he does. Now I know."

The 2008 presidential election was remarkable and gratifying.

More Important Than Boxing: 2008

In 1977, I left my job as a litigator for a Wall Street law firm to write. My first book served as the basis for a feature film starring Jack Lemmon and Sissy Spacek.

Missing told the true-life story of an American named Charles Horman, who was killed by the Chilean military in the aftermath of the 1973 coup that toppled Chilean president Salvador Allende. The book and film presented evidence that Horman was executed with the fore-knowledge of United States government officials because he'd stumbled upon evidence linking U.S. military personnel to implementation of the coup. One night, I asked Charles's mother what she thought was the most important message I could convey in the book. Her answer has always stayed with me:

"Charles's death," Elizabeth Horman told me, "taught me the lesson of political responsibility. I used to think that I could till the soil on my own little plot of land and let the rest of the world care for its own problems. What our country did in Vietnam, what happened to people overseas, was no concern of mine. I was wrong. I know now that each of us is obligated to fight for what is right and take responsibility for what our government does. If we don't, sooner or later, it will affect us all."

I've quoted Elizabeth Horman here because her words are the best and most heartfelt expression I know in support of a proposition that goes to the heart of life in a democracy: The rights and privileges we enjoy as citizens are accompanied by responsibilities.

As an American who feels that his country has been tarnished and badly damaged during the past eight years, I feel a responsibility to add my thoughts to the dialogue regarding the upcoming presidential election. Anyone who objects to the presence of politics on a boxing website need not read on.

In January 2005, I wrote, "Nothing is more appalling to those of us who oppose George Bush than the fact that millions of Americans voted for him in the belief that he somehow epitomizes good moral values. Moral values are about more than the lavish profession of a belief in Christ. We believe that there is no sense of decency or honor in the Bush administration and that it's morally rotten to the core."

John McCain's choice of Sarah Palin as his running mate has galvanized "the religious right" in support of his candidacy and put the issue of moral values back in the electoral spotlight. So let's talk about moral values.

America's Founding Fathers believed it was essential that the War of Independence against England be conducted with respect for human rights. The nation they'd founded was at risk and the British were engaging in atrocities against American civilians and soldiers. But George Washington, as commander-in-chief of the Continental Army, deemed it essential that the revolution remain faithful to its ideals. With regard to the detention of enemy combatants, he decreed, "Treat them with humanity and let them have no reason to complain of our copying the brutal example of the British Army in their treatment of our unfortunate brethren."

During the Civil War, Abraham Lincoln forbade any form of torture and put into place the first formal code of conduct for the humane treatment of prisoners of war. Dwight Eisenhower followed that example in World War II.

The Bush Administration has systematically undermined more than two centuries of American values in the conduct of war. The same people who designed and supported these excesses are in the vanguard of John McCain's presidential campaign.

John McCain's backers also take perverse pride in attacks on the environment. One of the applause lines that whipped this year's Republican National Convention into a frenzy was "Drill, baby, drill." There it was. Get some pipelines in that wilderness. Spill some oil on those beaches. We'll show those tree-huggers.

Preservation of the environment for future generations is a moral issue. The people who are telling us now that there's no need to worry about global warming are the same people who told us a month ago that the American economy was sound.

The Bush Administration and John McCain have consistently opposed greater regulation of financial institutions. They told us that multi-million-dollar Christmas bonuses on Wall Street and $140,000,000 executive severance packages were good for the economy. They stood by while the price of oil rose from $25.20 a barrel on 9/11 to over $100 a barrel and saw no problem in the multi-billion dollar profits of Exxon and other oil companies.

Now the economy is in chaos. And the same people who favored letting market forces dictate the flow of the economy want the American taxpayers to spend $700 *billion* to bail out big financial institutions.

The situation is reminiscent of the federal bailout necessitated by the savings and loan crisis that occurred during the administration of the first President Bush. Then, as now, a Republican president molded a political climate that enabled affluent transgressors to run wild. There was economic deregulation, a systematic weakening of enforcement provisions, and underfunding of the enforcers who were supposed to monitor behavior in white-collar sectors of the economy. "Liberal" ideologies were attacked, but supposedly conservative ideologies bordering in many instances on economic plunder were encouraged.

How much is $700 billion? Roughly $2,300 for every American man, woman, and child. Or calculated differently: if someone took a stack of hundred-dollar bills and lay them end to end, $700 billion would stretch to the moon and back and more than halfway back to the moon again. It would circle the Earth at the equator almost twenty-seven times. $700 billion dollars in hundred-dollar bills would weigh 7,709 tons.

Economic equity is a moral issue. Last year, the highest-earning 1 percent of Americans received almost one-quarter of all income in the United States. The top 10 percent received almost half. No logical-thinking person suggests that all people should be paid the same salary. But there should be some semblance of fairness in the system.

With all the economic problems we face today, John McCain is still defending the tax cuts for the rich that were enacted by the Republican-controlled Congress several years ago. And keep in mind; many of the people now pleading for the government to bail out the giants of Wall Street are the same people who, last year, opposed an increase in the minimum wage, which was then $5.15 an hour. These people have few values other than the accumulation of power and the service of wealth.

Caring for the elderly and poor is a moral issue. Where do the Bush Administration and John McCain stand on this issue? When the Republicans controlled Congress, they implemented changes in Medicare to preclude the federal government from using its buying power to negotiate lower prices from suppliers of medical equipment and prescription drugs. The result is that, last year, the federal government paid more than double the price that some consumers paid online and at retail pharmacies for items that range from power wheelchairs ($4,024 versus $1,452) to blood glucose strips ($36 versus $17 a box). Some suppliers of medical equipment and prescription drugs are profiting nicely from that prohibition. Meanwhile, John McCain has consistently opposed programs that would provide meaningful health insurance for tens of millions of Americans who are currently uninsured.

So much for "compassionate conservatism." Now let's get to the core "moral" issues that account for much of Sarah Palin's (and John McCain's) support. A lot of these issues revolve directly or indirectly around sex.

Last year, deputy secretary of state Randall L. Tobias resigned after acknowledging that he had been a customer of a Washington, D.C., escort service whose owner was charged by federal prosecutors with running a prostitution operation. Tobias (who is married) had previously directed the President's Emergency Fund for AIDS Relief. In that role, he emphasized abstinence and faithfulness to one sexual partner over condom use to prevent the spread of AIDS.

Republican senator David Vitter of Louisiana has been an outspoken defender of "family values." He has repeatedly attacked same-sex marriage as posing a threat to the sanctity of marriage (which he called "the most important social institution in human history"). Six weeks after Tobias's resignation, Vitter was confronted with a similar problem when it was revealed that he too had patronized an escort service operated by the so-called "D.C. Madam."

"This was a very serious sin," Vitter acknowledged. But he claimed to be off the hook, since he had "asked for and received forgiveness from God and my wife in confession and marriage counseling." The "family values senator" from Louisiana declined to discuss the matter further, saying, "Out of respect for my family, I will keep my discussion of the matter there; with God and them."

Less than a month after Vitter's confession, senator Larry Craig (Republican of Idaho) pled guilty to a charge of disorderly conduct after being arrested for soliciting sex from a plainclothes police officer in a men's bathroom at Minneapolis–St. Paul International Airport. While in Congress, Craig has vociferously opposed gay rights, voting against expanding a federal hate crimes law to cover offenses motivated by anti-gay bias and against a bill that would have outlawed employment discrimination based on sexual orientation.

Then there's Rudy Giuliani (the keynote speaker at this year's Republican National Convention), who had a much-publicized extra-marital affair with his former communications director, Cristyne Lategano. Then Giuliani embarked upon an even more public extra-marital affair with Judith Nathan before advising his wife by way of a television interview that he wanted a divorce.

And let's not forget Ted Haggard, president of the politically influential National Association of Evangelicals and pastor of the 14,000-member New Life Church in Colorado Springs. Haggard (one of the most powerful right-wing clergymen in America) was dismissed by the church oversight board after it was determined that he had "committed sexually immoral conduct."

More specifically, a gay escort named Michael Jones claimed to have had a three-year sexual relationship with Haggard. Initially, Haggard denied knowing Jones. Then he admitted receiving a massage from Jones in a Denver hotel room and buying methamphetamine from him, but claimed that he had never used the drugs and that they'd never had sex together. Taking Haggard at his word (which is a dubious proposition), why is a married evangelical clergyman who supports George Bush's political agenda receiving a massage from a male escort in a hotel room and buying illegal drugs from him?

Sexual misconduct isn't confined to the Republican Party. Bill Clinton, John Edwards, and Eliot Spitzer are proof of that. But the hypocrisy of the McCain–Palin campaign and their supporters on sexual issues is breathtaking.

Bristol Palin (Sarah Palin's unwed adolescent daughter) is pregnant. Television commentator Bill O'Reilly (the right-wing icon who, several years ago, paid a substantial sum to settle a sexual harassment claim lodged against him) says that Bristol's pregnancy should be off limits in the campaign and that "it's a personal matter." Of course, when Jamie Lynn Spears was pregnant, O'Reilly proclaimed, "The blame falls primarily on the parents of the girl, who obviously have little control over her."

It is hard to imagine what O'Reilly and his Republican brethren would have said and done if Chelsea Clinton had been pregnant at age sixteen. But rest assured; it would have been ugly.

Meanwhile, Bristol Palin's pregnancy shouldn't be an issue in this campaign. But Sarah Palin's crusade to ban teaching adolescents about any method of birth control other than abstinence should be.

If only Bristol had been taught about contraceptives in school. Whatever Sarah Palin taught her daughter at home, she and Mr. Palin fell short in educating Bristol in this area. There's a valid argument to be made that schools shouldn't give condoms to students. But schools should teach students what condoms do and what happens if you play sexual Russian roulette without one. In addition to getting pregnant, there are a lot of diseases that Bristol could have contracted; some of them deadly.

Of course, Governor Palin is a woman whose view of educating young people is that sex education is bad but creationism should be taught as science in our public schools.

Much of the support for the McCain-Palin ticket is grounded on religious faith. But just because someone believes that Jonah was swallowed by a whale doesn't mean that he or she has good moral values.

The simple acceptance of religious dogma or experiencing a moment of religious rapture doesn't make someone a good Christian. A good Christian, like any person of faith, is defined by his or her acts.

John McCain has acknowledged being unfaithful to his first wife after she was disfigured in a car accident. Then he left her to marry an heiress.

Much of the "religious right" seems to adhere to the view, "Jesus loves you and shares your hatred of homosexuals."

These people are lecturing us about moral values?

It would be nice to see John McCain, Sarah Palin, and their followers demonstrate good moral values rather than just pontificate about them. But real empathy and compassion are unwelcome in the McCain campaign.

My guess is that, if Jesus were walking among us today, he'd be opposed to discrimination on the basis of race, religion, and sexual orientation. He might well favor stem cell research as "pro-life." And whatever his position on those issues, I doubt that he'd be hunting caribou in Alaska with a high-powered rifle and telescopic sight. More likely, he'd be a community organizer seeking to improve the lot of the poor and downtrodden.

John McCain served this country well during the war in Vietnam. But during the past year, he has tarnished that service. The character of the campaign he has been running tells us a lot about his own character. There was a time when McCain was thought to stand for honor and principle. No more. Recent events have revealed him as the person he is, which is very different from the person he once was (or we thought him to be).

McCain could have used the 2008 presidential campaign to engender an honest dialogue about the future of America. Instead, he has allowed his political operatives to orchestrate an ugly national campaign based in significant measure on appeals to prejudice and deceit.

The choice of Sarah Palin as his running mate tells us all we need to know about John McCain's commitment to national security and the good of America. The choice was bizarre, almost frivolous. It tells us that his only "value" is winning the election and that he will put the nation at risk to achieve that goal.

Meanwhile, the conservative right has suddenly discovered that unregulated economic markets can lead to a worldwide economic disaster. Maybe that "meltdown" can be forestalled. But global warming can't be forestalled once the tipping point has passed. If terrorists acquire nuclear weapons, it will be virtually impossible to forestall their use.

Yet, on these crucial issues, McCain has no vision for the future. He simply parrots the Bush Administration; the same administration that invaded Iraq to "bring freedom to the Iraqi people" and has done nothing to halt the spread of nuclear weapons to North Korea and Iran. Indeed, for all its bluster, seven years after 9/11, the Bush Administration has failed to capture Osama bin Laden.

Let's be honest. If Barack Obama were white, he'd be leading by close to twenty points in the polls right now. The murky waters of bigotry are the real moral issue in this election. The question is whether or not America is ready to elect a black president; one with a strange-sounding name.

This election isn't about John McCain and Barack Obama. It's about America.

★   ★   ★

NOVEMBER 5, 2008: A NOTE ON THE
AMERICAN PRESIDENTIAL ELECTION

Anyone who visits this site and reads my articles knows that I had a strong emotional investment in this year's presidential election.

I came of age in the 1960s. John F. Kennedy was my boyhood hero. I lived through the civil rights movement, the war in Vietnam, and the sexual revolution. I experienced the Beatles, Muhammad Ali, and so many other markers of that era.

At the height of "The Sixties," the presidency of George W. Bush was unimaginable. None of us could have foreseen an administration that endorsed torture, advocated teaching "creationism" in the public schools, and repudiated the notion of a "Great Society" keyed to economic and social justice.

But there was another thought that was also unimaginable in the 1960s; that four decades later, the American people would elect an African American with the strange-sounding name "Barack Obama" as president of the United States. It just didn't seem possible.

Whatever the future brings, the American people have made a statement about our collective character. I woke up this morning feeling good about being an American.